D0661706

Academic Pipeline Programs

DIVERSIFYING PATHWAYS FROM THE BACHELOR'S TO THE PROFESSORIATE

Curtis D. Byrd and Rihana S. Mason

Jazmyn,
Each one, teach one!
Curtis Byrd &
Rihana Mason

**LEVER
PRESS**

Copyright © 2021 by Curtis D. Byrd and Rihana S. Mason

Lever Press (leverpress.org) is a publisher of pathbreaking scholarship. Supported by a consortium of liberal arts institutions focused on, and renowned for, excellence in both research and teaching, our press is grounded on three essential commitments: to be a digitally native press, to be a peer-reviewed, open access press that charges no fees to either authors or their institutions, and to be a press aligned with the ethos and mission of liberal arts colleges.

This work is licensed under the Creative Commons Attribution-NonCommercial 4.0 International License. To view a copy of this license, visit http://creativecommons.org/licenses/by-nc/4.0/ or send a letter to Creative Commons, PO Box 1866, Mountain View, CA 94042, USA.
The complete manuscript of this work was subjected to a partly closed ("single blind") review process. For more information, please see our Peer Review Commitments and Guidelines at https://www.leverpress.org/peerreview

DOI: https://doi.org/10.3998/mpub.12216775
Print ISBN: 978-1-64315-023-9
Open access ISBN: 978-1-64315-024-6

Published in the United States of America by Lever Press, in partnership with Amherst College Press and Michigan Publishing

Contents

Member Institution Acknowledgments   v

Foreword by Freeman A. Hrabowski III, PhD   vii

Introduction and Key Terms   I

Chapter I: Understanding Academic Pipeline Programs
and Their Origins   7

Chapter 2: Precollegiate Programs   33

Chapter 3: Collegiate Programs   67

Chapter 4: Doctoral/Graduate/Professional Programs   123

Chapter 5: Postdoctoral/Faculty Programs   179

Chapter 6: Closing Thoughts   213

Afterword by Ansley A. Abraham Jr., PhD   243

Appendix A   249

Appendix B   259

Appendix C   273

Bibliography   277

Acknowledgments   289

Member Institution Acknowledgments

Lever Press is a joint venture. This work was made possible by the generous support of Lever Press member libraries from the following institutions:

Adrian College
Agnes Scott College
Allegheny College
Amherst College
Bard College
Berea College
Bowdoin College
Carleton College
Claremont Graduate
   University
Claremont McKenna
   College
Clark Atlanta University
Coe College
College of Saint Benedict /
   Saint John's University

The College of Wooster
Denison University
DePauw University
Earlham College
Furman University
Grinnell College
Hamilton College
Harvey Mudd College
Haverford College
Hollins University
Keck Graduate Institute
Kenyon College
Knox College
Lafayette College Library
Lake Forest College
Macalester College

Middlebury College
Morehouse College
Oberlin College
Pitzer College
Pomona College
Rollins College
Santa Clara University
Scripps College
Sewanee: The University of
    the South
Skidmore College
Smith College
Spelman College
St. Lawrence University

St. Olaf College
Susquehanna University
Swarthmore College
Trinity University
Union College
University of Puget Sound
Ursinus College
Vassar College
Washington and Lee
    University
Whitman College
Willamette University
Williams College

FOREWORD

Freeman A. Hrabowski III, PhD

Academic Pipeline Programs serves as a valuable resource for K–12 educators, college and university administrators, faculty, students, and families interested in the wide range of academic programs—from precollege to higher education to careers. In particular, the authors emphasize and describe available initiatives for promoting underrepresented minority students through the education pipeline, a goal demanding focused attention in our increasingly diverse society.

This book opened our eyes to the depth of these initiatives and the myriad of ways they can benefit their participants. So often, when the public hears about minority programs, the reference is primarily to scholarships and other financial support. In reality, numerous programs offer many more benefits, from professionals who serve as mentors, champions and advocates to such academic support as tutoring and advising, networking opportunities, and professional development.

This book also provides broader context and rationale for these programs. Since World War II, the higher education enterprise has grown and evolved, taking on a central role in our society—a role that can reinforce societal divisions or enhance inclusion and social mobility depending on the way we manage it. The GI Bill of 1944, opposed by presidents at elite colleges at the time, created new opportunities for many and profoundly changed the way Americans viewed higher education. The landmark Supreme Court case of *Brown v. Board of Education* in 1954 began the process of dismantling segregation in higher education and widening opportunity. This process of broadening access continued with the civil rights movement, the Civil Rights Act (1964), the Voting Rights Act (1965), the Higher Education Act (1965), and the Higher Education Act Amendments (1972) that gave us Federal Pell Grants and Title IX.

Few realize how much growth we have seen in higher education. In 1940, just 5 percent of whites and 1 percent of Blacks had earned a college degree. With federal legislation in place, the percentage of Americans twenty-five or older who had earned a bachelor's degree increased to 10 percent in the mid-1960s when my campus, the University of Maryland, Baltimore County, was founded, 15 percent in the mid-1970s, 20 percent in the later 1980s, 25 percent in 2000, 30 percent around 2010, and 35 percent in 2015. This is progress indeed. Further, many more Americans of all backgrounds have attended college and earned bachelor's degrees. From 1965 to 2018, the percentage of non-Hispanic whites twenty-five or older with at least a bachelor's degree jumped from 10 percent to 39 percent. During that time, the percentage of Blacks in that age range with a bachelor's degree jumped from 4 percent to 25 percent. As of 2018, 56 percent of Asian Americans twenty-five and older have a bachelor's degree. For Hispanics and Native Americans, the attainment rate is 18 percent (US Census Bureau, 2020).

Fifty years ago, few families expected their children to attend college. In contrast, today, 94 percent of families say they want their children to go to college (Pew Research Center, 2012). Yet, the work is not complete. For example, while the bachelor's degree-attainment rate for Blacks has jumped by 21 percentage points from 4 percent to 25 percent from 1965–2015, the gap between whites and Blacks has actually widened from 6 to 14 percentage points. And our biggest challenge today is that low-income students still have just an 11 percent chance of completing a four-year degree by age twenty-four (Pell Institute, 2018).

While we have a general problem for retention, completion, and attainment, we also have a more specific and deeper problem of underrepresentation in science, technology, engineering, and mathematics (STEM) fields. In 2016, underrepresented minorities comprised 34.2 percent of undergraduates, 21.6 percent of those earning STEM bachelor's degrees, 13.2 percent of these awarded STEM master's degrees, and just 8.8 percent of doctoral awards in these fields (National Center for Education Statistics, 2018; National Science Foundation, "Field," 2019). Meanwhile, the percentage of the nation's science and engineering workforce that are underrepresented minorities was just 16.9 percent in 2017, compared to one-third of the nation's population (National Science Foundation, "Employment," 2019; US Census Bureau, n.d.).

Academic Pipeline Programs connects progress in degree programs to the lack of diversity in the professoriate. This is critical given the paucity of underrepresented minority faculty at most universities. While students on campuses nationwide have become increasingly diverse, the professoriate has remained primarily white. At four-year institutions, full-time faculty are 71 percent white, 11 percent Asian American, and about 10 percent underrepresented minority (Black, Hispanic, American Indian, Alaska Native, Native Hawaiian, or Pacific Islander). The rest identify as more than one race, have unknown race/ethnicity, or are international. At two-year institutions, demographics are 77 percent white, 4 percent Asian American, and about 15 percent underrepresented minority. Underrepresented minorities collectively represent about 11 percent of full-time faculty nationally at two- and four-year institutions, a low number when they comprise 32 percent of the US population, 28 percent of undergraduates at public four-year institutions, and 24 percent of undergraduates at private, nonprofit four-year colleges and universities. This is deep and pervasive underrepresentation (American Council on Education, n.d.; American Academy of Arts and Sciences, https://www.amacad.org /sites/default/files/academy/multimedia/pdfs/publications/resear chpapersmonographs/PRIMER-cfue/Primer-on-the-College-Stu dent-Journey.pdf).

At UMBC, we have approached the problem of underrepresentation in the professoriate in two ways. First, in the late 1980s, we initiated the Meyerhoff Scholars Program to prepare underrepresented minority undergraduates for doctoral programs and research careers in the natural sciences and engineering, based on a holistic, strengths-based approach that provides academic, social, and financial support. The National Institutes of Health has provided us a Better Utilizing Investments to Leverage Development (BUILD) Transportation Discretionary Grant for a program to extend the work of Meyerhoff to UMBC students in the natural sciences more broadly and the Howard Hughes Medical Institute has funded successful efforts to establish programs based on the Meyerhoff Scholars Program model at Pennsylvania State University and the University of North Carolina at Chapel Hill. Evaluation data from these two campuses have further demonstrated that Meyerhoff can be successfully replicated, and the Chan Zuckerberg Initiative has recently provided funding for replication efforts at the University of California, Berkeley, and the University of California, San Diego. Meanwhile, with an ADVANCE grant from the National Science Foundation, we pioneered initiatives to support hiring, retention, and advancement of women faculty in the sciences and engineering, initiatives we have now also extended to support underrepresented minority faculty. In addition, we have created a postdoctoral program as a recruitment vehicle and adapted a program developed by the University of Michigan in which majority faculty counsel departments on how to conduct inclusive searches and support new hires.

Perhaps the most distinctive aspect of *Academic Pipeline Programs* is the structural approach to describing the programs using the THRIVE Index (type, history, research, inclusion/identity, voice, expectations). Readers will appreciate the book's helpful suggestions for selecting programs and creating new ones. However, the ultimate assessment of these initiatives should be determined by the level of success of the participants. If an initiative is truly successful on one campus, the ultimate test is whether the program can be replicated in other places, such as the adaptation of the Meyerhoff program. Many people commented that the Meyerhoff program was a success at UMBC because the president was African American. Our Howard Hughes Medical Institute-funded replication has proven that institutions with leaders of all races can successfully implement these initiatives (Domingo et al., 2019b).

I hope readers will use this book as an inspiration to initiate programs and then work to sustain them over the long run—with the ultimate goal of replication. Inspiration, initiative, persistence, and grit will see these programs through to their much-needed success.

Freeman A. Hrabowski III
President
University of Maryland, Baltimore County

INTRODUCTION AND KEY TERMS

Academic Pipeline Programs: Diversifying Pathways from the Bachelors to the Professoriate is a comprehensive resource guide that illustrates academic pipeline programs from K–12 and beyond. Academic pipeline programs are diversity initiatives that support and propel underrepresented minority (URM) students along their educational journey by providing programming related to research, career, and life preparation. Academic pipeline programs are not the same as scholarship programs. In addition to funding, these programs provide a host of other benefits. Some of these benefits include research opportunities, preparation for advanced study, career and professional development, mentorship, and networking. The goal of these initiatives is to promote the advancement of URM students through various degree programs and diversify academic positions.

The primary goal of the book is to provide bread crumbs for URM students to complete the academic process and persist into careers. Moreover, this resource also describes numerous diversity initiatives with a variety of supporters of URMs in mind such as parents, high school counselors, college advisors, faculty, department chairs, college and university administrators, program directors, and employers. The book starts with an overview chapter that illustrates the increasing need and a historical basis for academic pipeline programs. We also center our discussion within the appreciative inquiry framework. The subsequent five chapters highlight hallmark programs within each step of the pipeline: pre-collegiate, collegiate, post-baccalaureate, graduate/professional, post-doctoral, and faculty. Each of the hallmark academic pipeline programs have been cataloged using the THRIVE Index (type, history, research, inclusion/identity, voice, and expectations) to provide a thorough description of each initiative. The THRIVE Index illustrates details such as each programs' historical background, activities, and benefits related to success in training toward the next steps in the academic process. The final chapter provides suggestions for choosing programs, creating new programs, and coordinating program activities. It also frames best practices of these initiatives.

We chose to spotlight academic programs based on their success and longevity. We then sent correspondence inquiring about interest in participating in this book. Based on each program's interest in being featured in our publication and commitment to completing the THRIVE Index, we selected the final set of highlighted initiatives. Contributors who completed the THRIVE Index and provided details of their programs are listed in appendix C (p. 275). In order to recognize more of the academic pipeline programs that exist, additional programs are included within the appendix. Further, throughout the text of the book, we spotlight several government and privately funded programs. Their websites can be found in appendix B (p. 261). The appendix is organized according to where a program falls within the pipeline structure, the location of the program, the disciplines that the program serves, and the institution/organization that supports the program. In order to keep the printed version affordable, appendix A (p. 251) is linked to a searchable geographic information system- mapped database of pipeline programs found at http://academicpipelinedatabase.net/.

Academic pipeline programs that are included in the database have condensed profiles. It is our intent to grow the database by requesting that more programs like the ones featured here complete the THRIVE Index tool. We will continue to partner with institutions to use the THRIVE Index tool on their campuses as well.

The following section lists key terms and acronyms used throughout the book. These terms and acronyms define significant concepts related to academic pipeline programs and the populations that they benefit. We understand that some terms may be defined differently by others or used in a different context. For the context of this book, the terms *underrepresented minority* (URM) and *underrepresented group* (URG) are used. Preference was given to URM in order to emphasize the fact that certain groups are smaller in number within academia and the workplace and many programs that are discussed have a historical context which is attributable to the term *URM*.

Key Terms

TERM	DEFINITIONS
academic pipeline programs	Diversity initiatives that support and propel underrepresented minority (URM) students along their educational journey by providing programming related to research, career, and life preparation.
Asian American, Native American, and Pacific Islander-serving institutions (AANAPISI)	Accredited, degree-granting institutions, where at least 10 percent of their enrollment comes from one of these groups.
Black, Indigenous, and persons of color (BIPOC)	A unifying term to represent all persons of color.
cultural capital	Dispositions, skill set, attitudes, and behaviors that foster academic attainment
Hispanic-serving institutions (HSI)	Accredited, degree-granting institutions with 25 percent or more total undergraduate Hispanic populations.
historically Black colleges and universities (HBCU)	Accredited, degree-granting institutions created for African Americans; established prior to the Civil Rights Act of 1964, most HBCUs were established in the southern United States following the Civil War (except two institutions).
lesbian, gay, bisexual, transgender, queer, intersex, asexual ally (LGBTQIA+)	Lesbian, gay, bisexual, transgender, queer, intersex, asexual, and other sexual and gender minorities.
liberal arts colleges (LACs)	Colleges with small enrollments that offer a broad range of fields and methods of inquiry in contrast to technical or vocational training.
low-income first generation (LIFG)	Students who are in the lowest socioeconomic quartile and whose parents who only hold a high school diploma or equivalent.

marginalized groups	Groups that do not hold positions of power or that have been historically underserved on the basis of age, dis(ability), first-generation status, gender, language use (e.g. bilingualism, bidialectalism), military/veteran status, foreign-birth status (e.g., undocumented immigrants, noncitizen of the United States), political ideology, race/ethnicity, religion, sexual orientation and socioeconomic status.
mentor	An influential individual with a higher ranking in the work environment who has advanced experience and knowledge so they can give you support, guidance, and advice for development.
minority-serving institution (MSI)	Schools that typically exceed 25–50 percent of the population with one of the historically underrepresented minority groups (African American, Asian American, Hispanic American, Native American/Native Alaskan, or Pacific Islander). The initial types of MSIs were established in the late 1900s (listed below), while in the 2000s, new legislation was created to include Asian American and Pacific Islander groups and predominately Black institutions (PBI), which didn't have the HBCU status based on the time frame of when they established (Center for Minority Serving Institutions, Timeline, 2014; Rutgers Graduate School of Education, 2021)
Near-peer mentoring	The age or status is similar between the protégé/mentee and the mentor
protégé/mentee	A person who is guided and supported by a mentor or coach.
sexual orientation	How a person characterizes their emotional and sexual attraction to others.
social capital	Networks of powerful people who provide inside information, invaluable coaching, and guidance in securing desirable positions and promotions and connections to succeed in the academy
Tiered peer mentoring	Combines mentors at multiple levels, including near peer and senior mentors together
THRIVE	An acronym that stands for the following characteristics: type, history, research, inclusion, identity, voice, and expectations

tribal colleges and universities (TCU)	Accredited, degree-granting institutions, funded under the Tribally Controlled Colleges and Universities Assisted Act of 1978 or Navajo Community College Act, and are controlled and operated by American Indian tribes.
underrepresented minority (URM)	A person who is underrepresented in various disciplines within the academy, comprised of the following racial backgrounds: African American, Hispanic American, Native American/Native, Alaskan/Pacific Islander.
veteran status	A person who has served in any branch of the armed forces

CHAPTER 1

UNDERSTANDING ACADEMIC PIPELINE PROGRAMS AND THEIR ORIGINS

It's hard to be what you can't see.
—Marian Wright Edelman, http://www.Childrensdefense.org/ch
ild-watch-columns/health/2015/its-hard-to-be-what-you-cant
-see/

Plotting a course through today's higher-education system and workplaces can be challenging for those who have not seen a pathway successfully navigated by someone else. All of us need assistance with our academic and career journeys. However, certain groups are less likely to receive this assistance without formalized programming and equitable systems in place. *Academic Pipeline Programs: Diversifying Pathways from the Bachelor's to the Professoriate* provides a spotlight on programs supporting diverse populations along their academic and career journeys. Diversity, equity, and inclusion (DEI) programming is critical given the underrepresentation of certain individuals in academia and the workplace. Particularly within the United States, underrepresentation in certain academic disciplines, coupled with the fact that 56 percent of college-bound persons are first generation (RTI International, 2019),[1] makes academic pipeline programs necessary. As a reader, one might find themselves fitting into one of several categories: (1) someone who wants to become more aware of academic pipeline programs and how to enroll, (2) someone mentoring those in the pipeline, or (3) someone who is in training to create, implement, or coordinate programs at an institution or organization.

Regardless of how a reader identifies, the rationale for the existence of academic pipeline programs at the beginning of this chapter will be useful. Later in the chapter, our newly developed index tool (THRIVE), is described to thoroughly understand each program, and this instrument is given context by the Appreciative Inquiry (AI) framework (Byrd, 2016; Cooperrider & Srivastva, 1987). For this chapter, we also use the seven dimensions of the THRIVE Index tool to provide an introductory review of academic pipeline programs and their components.

Unfortunately, in the twenty-first century, we still have many populations who live in marginalized worlds, without the same opportunities as their majority counterparts. High school and college students from low-income and first-generation (LIFG) families tend to graduate at lower rates than those from more affluent families. If one's background is LIFG and they identify as an underrepresented minority (URM) (e.g., African American, Hispanic American, Native American, Pacific Islander) or marginalized in the academy due to a host of factors (e.g., gender, gender expression, sexual orientation, dis[ability], age, language use, foreign-birth status, socioeconomic status, veteran status, etc.), then the likelihood of not succeeding in college or beyond increases (Perna, 2015).[2] The educational pipeline has many barriers for LIFG, URMs,

---

1. Websites are provided in appendix B for all hyperlinked programs and initiatives.

2. Although there are varying viewpoints on the term *minorities*, for this document, the word *minority* is used to provide context to underrepresentation in the

and other marginalized groups. These groups are often left out of conversations about procedures and policies in higher education or about financial opportunities that could support them obtaining a degree. Further, these students often are not aware of the nuances of academic research, expected behaviors, and cultural norms of higher education, as keys to opening the door to degree completion. Consistent monitoring, advisement, mastery of knowledge development, hands-on research experiences with faculty, and support networks provided by academic pipeline programs are all essential components of collegiate success for these underserved populations (Maton & Hrabowski, 2004).

Pipeline programs have successfully assisted LIFG and URM students in completing their academic journey via several core components. Academic pipeline programs offer a variety of services, such as test preparation; tutoring; specific skill training; college, graduate, and professional school or faculty preparation and exposure; research opportunities; enrichment programs and activities; mentoring; and supplemental instruction and summer training programs (Schultz et al., 2011). This book aids readers with finding academic pipeline programs and evaluating whether a program fits their needs. Even though our hallmark programs have been successful in their training efforts, some are experiencing growing pains.

The systems and policies of academic pipeline programs are being scrutinized to ensure that inequitable behaviors and practices are eradicated and that their structures are keeping in step with the rate of browning of the nation and numbers of LIFG students entering the academy. The academic pipeline programs mentioned in this book are not immune from this scrutiny. Given their historical underpinnings and funding sources, there is also

---

academy and the workplace. The term *underrepresented minority* is also still currently used by programs. We understand that other terms, like *underrepresented group* (URG) and *BIPOC* (Black, Indigenous, and people of color), have been more recently used to describe the populations we describe.

the ongoing need for academic pipeline programs to engage in self-evaluation and continuous improvement to remain true to their mission. These initiatives have been empowered through the engagement of alumni of pipeline programs challenging program policies and decision-making processes. For example, it has become more publicly apparent that some of our highlighted programs need transformation. Transformation has arisen from the of work Knowledge Is Power Program (KIPP) alumni who self-organized to rally for changes in program leadership. In fact, KIPP has also been more intentional about working with more diverse groups in institutions to transition students into college, such as working with many minority-serving institutions (e.g., historically Black colleges and Universities [HBCUs], Hispanic-serving institutions [HSIs]). The Ford Foundation Fellowship Program was another initiative recently challenged by its alumni to create better policies and practices related to fairness and equity, not only within its leadership but for the broader academy. Ultimately, as effective as these programs are in diversifying the academy, they will always need to be accountable to the populations they serve.

THRIVE INDEX

We created the THRIVE Index as a common framework to compare programs, highlighting their strengths and introducing a unique set of parameters to contextualize each program. The THRIVE Index provides an objective and comprehensive lens into each program, so one can determine if an initiative fits their need(s). Throughout the book, the THRIVE Index also serves as a tool for evaluating how academic pipeline programs promote the academic and social development of participants that is beneficial for program replication and sustainability. The THRIVE acronym stands for type, history, research, inclusion/identity, voice, and expectations (see figure 1.1). The THRIVE Index illustrates the value of each program, showcasing its longevity and usefulness to those navigating their academic and career journeys. The THRIVE Index also captures common-core features of academic pipeline programs (Schultz et al., 2011), which are demonstrated to impact underserved populations in the United States across seven dimensions.

THRIVE Index Defined

Type (T): where the pipeline program is structurally situated among its peers

History (H): what context, milestones, longevity, and educational outcomes have been achieved

Research (R): which research preparation program components are utilized by programs (roles, responsibilities, routines)

Inclusion/Identity (I): how the programs are used to create inclusion on campuses, programs and organizations as well as build identity among participants

Voice (V): how each program creates a positive environment for students and faculty to enhance their voice by overcoming barriers to enter the academy

Expectations (E): what participants receive and what program outcomes are available

The THRIVE Index went through a multistage validation process. A panel of expert reviewers (two academics with assessment-development experience and an academic pipeline program director) reviewed the items for readability and face validity. These experts offered feedback for the refinement of items. We retained twenty-two questions, which were given to the program directors of each of the hallmark programs featured in the book. Once we completed the analysis of the responses, we refined the THRIVE Index to include additional multiple-choice responses so that it would be possible to compare programs and look for similarities in best practices.

Type   History   Research   Inclusion/Identity   Voice   Expectation

Figure 1.1. The THRIVE logo.

We were able to investigate these initiatives and their organizations by framing our THRIVE Index tool questions using the Appreciative Inquiry (AI) intervention tool. AI is one of the methodologies of organizational development that advances new ideas for change by looking at the best of the collective to provide emerging interventions and recommendations (Bushe & Kassam, 2005). The THRIVE Index mirrors the AI cycle by allowing organizations the ability to imagine, empower, and illustrate the best version of themselves through their responses (Cooperrider et al., 1987). Our index tool reveals the positive possibilities of academic pipeline programs by showing their generative, strength-based programming for which AI is best known. The AI model situates and nicely frames our THRIVE Index by contextualizing each letter of our acronym through the AI 4-D model of discovery, dream, design, and destiny (see figure 1.2). Later, we will discuss THRIVE and the cycles of AI to create a rubric toward institutional change and inclusive excellence. The concept of inclusive excellence is based on lasting and successful change that fully integrates DEI into strategic planning, policies, systems, and curricula in order to create a complete cultural shift toward belongingness and community (Williams & Wade-Golden, 2013). Using each of the seven dimensions of THRIVE, we unpack the who, what, and why of academic pipeline programs for the remainder of the chapter.

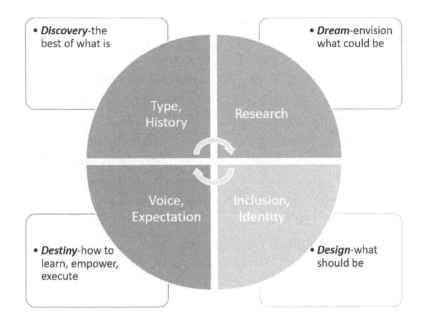

- *Discovery*-the best of what is

- *Dream*-envision what could be

Type, History

Research

Voice, Expectation

Inclusion, Identity

- *Destiny*-how to learn, empower, execute

- *Design*-what should be

Figure 1.2. AI framework mapped onto THRIVE dimensions.

Types of Pipeline Programs

The first dimension of THRIVE *T* refers to the type of program. Academic pipeline programs are packaged in many modes, frameworks, and styles. Typically, the common denominator between programs is the goal to support each person's advancement from one level of the academy to another. Although each pipeline program may vary in its scope or how it is administered, we have characterized the type of program based on several characteristics, including where a program is situated within an institutional structure, the institutions served, the types of students served, affiliated disciplines, and funding sources. Our research has allowed us to contextualize academic pipeline programs for the content of this book.

Types of academic pipeline programs can be sorted across several categories. The first category of programs serves only those at the host school or organization (e.g., course-based undergraduate research education [CURE], bridge programs, and enrichment programs, etc.). The second category of programs serves multiple sites nationally (e.g., government or privately funded initiatives). A subset of programs in this category are specific to institution type, such as minority serving institutions (i.e., HBCUs, HSIs, Tribal colleges and universities [TCUs], and Asian American, Native American, and Pacific Islander-serving institutions [AANAPISIs]) (Rutgers Graduate School of Education, 2014). By understanding the various types of programs, one will understand where the program is situated and be able to provide students with the ability to readily locate an initiative among others.

Further, determining the type of program will allow institutions the ability to apply for various awards that fit their needs. Examples of pipeline programs supported by governmental agencies include the National Science Foundation ADVANCE: Organizational Change for Gender Equity in STEM Academic Professions, the National Institutes of Health Research Initiative for Scientific Enhancement (NIH-RISE), the Health and Human Services Health Careers Opportunities Program, and the United States Department of Education Federal TRIO (TRIO) Programs. Examples of privately funded programs are the Mellon-Mays Undergraduate Fellowship Program and Alfred P. Sloan Research Fellowships.

The third category of programs are feeder programs between institution types (e.g., community colleges to four-year institutions, four-year institutions to doctoral-granting institutions, four-year institutions to professional schools). Additionally, there are pipeline programs independently serving broad audiences of underrepresented groups via specialized curricula (e.g., Science Education Alliance-Phage Hunters Advancing Genomics and Evolutionary Science [SEA-PHAGES]) or professional-development resources (e.g., the Annual Biomedical Research Conference for Minority Students [ABRCMS], the Society for Advancement of Chicanos/Hispanics and Native Americans in Science [SACNAS]).

Academic pipeline programs are also structurally arranged as interinstitutional partnerships to promote pathways to advancing academic study, scholarship, and research among diverse students. Partnerships allow students to transition from various undergraduate programs (two-year to four-year programs) and on to graduate and professional programs. Because small and mid-sized private colleges and universities enroll a higher proportion of LIFGs than public and private doctoral universities (Rine, 2015), interinstitutional partnerships are critical. Through interinstitutional partnerships (e.g., the University of California system; the Five College Consortium of Amherst College, Hampshire College, University of Massachusetts, Mount Holyoke College, and Smith College), students and faculty can gain access to additional resources and networks. Examples of academic pipeline programs also configured as consortia are the Louis Stokes Alliance for Minority Participation (LSAMP), the Leadership Alliance, and Alliances for Graduate Education and the Professoriate (AGEP).

HISTORY OF PIPELINE PROGRAMS

The second dimension of THRIVE, *H*, refers to the history of a program. For over fifty years, academic pipeline programs in the United States have been available to students at all levels of their academic career, including precollegiate, collegiate, graduate/professional, postdoctoral, and, most recently, faculty. The origins of programs focused on diverse groups date back the early 1900s. With an initial $1 million donation from John D. Rockefeller Sr. in 1903, the General Education Board (GEB) dedicated their mission to "promotion of education within the United States of America, without distinction of race, sex, or creed" (Fleming & Saslaw, 1992). The GEB examined the racial conditions of schools, evaluated and reformed medical colleges, implemented agricultural teaching demonstrations, and funded grants for conferences, fellowships, as well as black colleges, during the Great Depression. Before the GEB closed, it had a wide touch with educational programs, including rural elementary schools and colleges, as well as elite graduate institutions. John D. Rockefeller II continued his family's philanthropic legacy by partnering with the former president of Tuskegee University Frederick Douglass Patterson to form the United Negro College Fund (UNCF), an alliance to fund HBCUs.

Perhaps the oldest and now the largest precollegiate program known for assisting with academic persistence is the Boys & Girls Clubs of America (https://www.bgca.org/about-us/annual-report), formerly the Federated Boys Club. The Federated Boys Club was integrated as early as 1903, with reading rooms and vocational training accessible to black boys. Now the mission of the Boys & Girls Clubs of America is to inclusively serve young people to reach their full potential by implementing a variety of initiatives geared toward education and workforce readiness. Located in urban and rural areas, on military bases, and on native lands, Boys & Girls Clubs serve millions of youth annually through enrichment programming to prevent summer learning loss, enrich basic skills in middle school through tutoring, and prepare high schoolers for postsecondary education.

The Social Science Research Council (SSRC), founded in 1923, supports early scholars through fellowships, convenings, professional development, and mentorship. For more than ninety years, the SSRC has furthered the scholarship of those associated with the following disciplines: anthropology, economics, history, political science, psychology, sociology, and statistics. Ralph Bunche, a Nobel Peace Prize recipient, received a SSRC fellowship to complete his postdoctoral studies in anthropology. The SSRC encourages cross-disciplinary collaboration and innovation, as well as the promotion of unbiased voices to serves as policy makers worldwide. Some of their fellowships support recipients of other pipeline programs, like Mellon Mays (see chapter 3) and the Alfred P. Sloan Fellows (see chapter 4). During the same moment in the 1920s, Julius Rosenwald provided funding to start schools in black communities, funding for graduate-level university centers at HBCUs, funding for fellowships for African American artists, and grants for African American scientists (Beilke, 1997).

Another initiative among the first to provide programming and funding opportunities to support historically URMs, including HBCUs, was the Alfred P. Sloan Foundation. Specifically, the Sloan Foundation supported the Tuskegee Institute and UNCF, as others did in the early 1900s. In the 1950s and 1960s, the Sloan Foundation supported over twenty HBCUs, with an "institutions matter" motto. In the 1970s and 1980s, the Sloan Foundation took a more "money matters" approach, supporting URM students with fellowship programs going to medical school and into STEM disciplines. They financially supported other initiatives, such as the National Action Council for Minorities in Engineering (NACME) and the GEM Consortium, another program highlighted in this book. Suffice to say, the Sloan Foundation has been a pillar in the development of academic pipeline programs in the United States and is described in more detail later.

The next movement of pipeline initiatives happened in the 1960s. Many of the pipeline programs used by URMs today had their origins in the development of community colleges in 1960, based on the 1947 President's Commission on Higher Education (Gilbert & Heller, 2013). Community colleges were developed to assist with the preparation for and transition into four-year colleges, to provide affordable education, and to offer associate degrees or practical skills for employment (US Department of Homeland Security, 2012). The collegiate programming pathway continued with the creation of Title IV of the Higher Education Act of 1965. This legislation created student financial assistance in the form of Pell Grants, Gaining Early Awareness and Readiness for Undergraduate Programs (GEAR-UP), and TRIO Programs (Burke, 2014). These programs set the foundation for traditional pipeline programs, which support marginalized groups around the country. Programs such as the original TRIO Programs, Upward

Bound, Talent Search, and Student Support Services allow under-represented students to fluidly move from junior high to high school and then into college. Coupled with the opportunities of open access and admissions through community colleges and the grant aid of GEAR-UP and Pell Grants (Brock, 2010; Burke, 2014), many URM students began to thrive in their quest for a college education. Some of these programs and funding mechanisms are designed for students to directly apply to the federal government (e.g., Pell Grants), and some require institutions of higher education to apply for the grants to support these students. This book provides the fundamentals of the structure and purpose of these programs while also serving as a comprehensive resource guide to support parents, students, faculty, and administrators.

As institutions of higher learning are looking to align their schools with the vast numbers of diverse students entering the academy, academic pipeline programs can serve to support and enhance diversity, equity, and inclusion efforts. The US Census (2014) estimates ethnic minority populations, particularly African American and Hispanic American combined, will reach parity with the white majority population by 2044 (Colby & Ortman, 2015). Table 1.1 indicates that the numbers of URM students entering college, in general, are projected to nearly match the number of majority of students by 2022 and this trend continues into 2030 (National Center for Education Statistics, 2019). Schools that exceed 50 percent of the population with one of the historically underrepresented minority groups (Hispanic American, African American, or Native American) can qualify to have the distinction of an MSI and qualify for Title III funding under the Higher Education Act (US Department of Education, 2014). Many institutions in California and Texas have taken advantage of this support to financially and programmatically sustain their increasing Hispanic populations. All the above initiatives serve as a conduit to support underserved populations in their journey.

Many institutions around the country are equipping themselves

Table 1.1. Actual and projected numbers and percentages of college-bound, public high school graduates by race/ethnicity.

Ethnicity	2009–10 (Actual #)	2009–10 (Actual %)	2022–23 (# Projected)	2022–23 (% Projected)	2029–30 (# Projected)	2029–30 (% Projected)
White	1,871,980	60	1,619,670	49	1,475,140	45
Black	472,261	15	437,020	13	425,170	13
Hispanic	545,518	17	897,540	27	908,160	28
Asian/P. Islander	167,840	5	217,500	7	237,300	7
Native American A. Native	34,131	1	28,350	1	24,420	1
Two or more races	36,292	1	138,660	4	195,160	6
Totals	3,128,022	100	3,337,740	100	3,265,340	100

Source: National Center for Education Statistics, 2019.

with programs to support these projections. Example programs include extensions of the TRIO programs (developed in the 1970s, 1980s, and 1990s), such as Educational Opportunities Centers, the Ronald E. McNair Post-Baccalaureate Achievement Program, Upward Bound Math-Science, and Veterans Upward Bound. Further, there are a host of government-supported programs, such as the National Institutes of Health (NIH) and National Science Foundation (NSF) programs, which have been developed over the past two to three decades. More recently, there has been more attention given to the creation of programs to support individuals nearing the end of the pipeline (i.e., graduate students, postdocs, and faculty), assuring a comprehensive system of initiatives to support collegiate success among LIFG and URM individuals (see figure 1.3). Our current book brings awareness to these programs.

The history of academic pipeline programs highlighted in this book were gathered by asking specific questions detailing the creation of each initiative. We asked programs to reflect on the following: establishment year, the rationale for the creation of the program, significant milestones, namesake, number of students served, notable alumni, and level of the academic pipeline. We

A BRIEF HISTORY OF

PIPELINE PROGRAMS

Late 1800s-Early 1900s
Boys and Girls Clubs of America
General Education Board (GEB)
Rosenwald Schools and Fellowships
Social Science Research Council (SSRC)
United Negro College Fund (UNCF)

1950s
Sloan Foundation awarded its first minority focused grants

1960
TRIO Programs were formed with the Higher Education Act of 1965 including Upward Bound, Student Support Services and Educational Talent Search

1970s
More TRIO Programs: Equal Opportunity Centers, Veterans Upward Bound
American Psychological Association Minority Fellowship Program (APA-MFP)
Ford Fellowship Program (Ford Fellows)
MBA Consortium
National GEM Consortium (GEM)

1980s
More TRIO Programs: Ronald E. McNair Post Baccalaureate Program
California Predoctoral Sally Casanova Scholarship
FAMU Graduate Feeder Scholars Program (GFSP)
Howard Hughes Medical Institute (HHMI)
McKnight Doctoral Scholars Program
Mellon Mays Fellowship Program
UMBC Meyerhoff Scholars Program
Robert Wood Johnson Foundation
University of California (UC) President's Postdoctoral Fellowship Program

1990s
More TRIO Programs: Upward Bound/ Math Science
Alfred P. Sloan Minority Graduate Scholarship Program (SLOAN)
California Diversity Forum
Fisk-Vanderbilt Master's to PhD Bridge Program
Gates Millenial Scholars Program
Institute for the Recruitment of Teachers (IRT)
Knowledge is Power Program (KIPP)
Leadership Alliance
National Institutes of Health (NIH) Office of Minority Programs
National Science Foundation (NSF) PhD Project
Southern Regional Education Board (SREB) Doctoral Scholars Program

2000s
Amgen Program
Annual Biomedical Research Conference for Minority Students (ABCRMS)
College Advising Corps
Creating Connections Consortium (C3)
Institute for Broadening Participation (IBP)
Institute for Education Sciences (IES)
NASA- Harriett G. Jenkins Fellowship
National Center for Faculty Development and Diversity (NCFDD)
Rochester Institute of Technology Future Faculty Career Exploration Program (FFCEP)
Sisters of the Academy (SOTA)

Figure 1.3. A brief history of academic pipeline programs.

were intentional about gathering historical context at the level of detail that is included in each chapter. However, programs vary greatly on the historical records that are kept accessible for consumers. Adding *H* to as a part of the THRIVE Index tool promotes the transfer of culture and heritages of programs. The following section describes how research is an essential component of many pipeline programs, needed to prepare those navigating the academy.

RESEARCH PREPARATION

The *R* dimension of THRIVE represents research broadly including research preparation activities as well as roles, responsibilities, and routines that are related to entry into the academy. Much like the research environments that some liberal arts colleges create, pipeline programs promote research preparation by placing value on learning for learning's sake and allow students to discover their talents and callings. Research preparation comes in the form of precollegiate programs, which require participants to study the requirements of applying to college and find the appropriate fit based on their academic or career interests. Collegiate programs introduce beginning scholars to research methodologies and concepts, helping students develop academic skill sets that prepare them for advanced study, hash out advanced degree options, and better solidify career trajectories. Postbaccalaureate programs provide research and course preparation for medical schools, advanced professional degree programs and other graduate study, especially if applicant qualifications do not meet entrance criteria. Graduate and professional programs provide more purposeful research acumen by providing nuanced training on communicating one's expertise to multiple audiences and assisting students in gaining knowledge on discipline-specific cultural research dynamics (Tull, 2019). Within postdoctoral and faculty programs, various professional development opportunities include grantsmanship, publishing scholarly work, navigating the academic market, and preparation for the tenure process (Abraham, 2013).

We contextualize research preparation as programming and preparation for moving through the academic pipeline, as well as activities supporting career success. Research preparation is critical to the advancement of scholarship and advancing students and faculty in the academy, and we demonstrate how programs develop participants' skills, such as various methodologies, advanced writing, preparation for advanced coursework, and the actual completion of the research process. Without the critical component of developing participants research acumen, it would be difficult for these students to advance in the academic pipeline. Within the *R* there are also various roles, routines, and responsibilities associated with navigating the pipeline revealed in the events, social exchanges, and traditions.

INCLUSION AND IDENTITY DEVELOPMENT

Inclusion

The *I* dimension of THRIVE represents inclusion and identity. *I* illustrates how academic pipeline programs operate so that participants are included in a community of those they aspire to work with and a place to discover the intersection of their own identities. These programs often provide the support and safe spaces to allow URM students the opportunity to figure themselves out enough to not be "shook" by the inequalities they face in high school, on college campuses, or among colleagues in the academy. We are emphasizing programming that strengthens inclusionary practices for URMs. Initiatives that include a belongingness component have impacted career satisfaction (Brady et al., 2020).

In addition to providing an environment that welcomes URMs, academic pipeline programs incorporate instructional practices that bring their future academic and career selves to life. We adapted one of the University of Michigan's Center for Research on Learning and Teaching (CRLT) diversity and equity teaching resources for inclusive teaching to characterize *I*. The adaptation of their teaching principles provides a foundation to define inclusionary learning practices associated with academic pipeline programs:

1. Deliberately cultivate a learning/training/working environment where all are treated equitably, have equal access to learning, and feel welcome, valued, and supported in their learning/job (sense of belongingness).
2. Attend to social identities (described below under "Identity").
3. Seek to change the ways systemic inequities shape dynamics in teaching-learning spaces, affect individuals' experiences of those spaces, and influence program design.

Inclusion goes beyond focusing on diversity by instituting a culture of equity and social justice, respecting all backgrounds, and allowing intellectual creativity to focus on issues that are near to the lived experiences of URMs (Puritty et al., 2017).

Identity

Identity is multifaceted and relates to how people view themselves and others. Gee (2001) describes identity across four levels. Identity includes states (linked to nature), positions (linked to status within institutions), traits (linked to who others recognize us as), and experiences (linked to affinities shared among groups). Social-identity categories include several visible and invisible personal characteristics (Worthington, 2012), including age, dis(ability), first-generation status, gender, language use (e.g., bilingualism, bidialectalism), military/veteran status, foreign-birth status (e.g., undocumented immigrants, noncitizens of the United States), political ideology, race/ethnicity, religion, sexual orientation, and socioeconomic status.

Training in academic pipeline programs often emphasizes how the intersections of our social identities improve self-efficacy or the way that personal competence is viewed (Bandura & Schunk, 1981). For greater self-efficacy related to academic or career identity, it helps to see one's success despite the very demanding arena of academic institutions. Professional development activities present in academic pipeline programs promote retention in scientific careers due to the gains in self-efficacy and identity (Chemers et al., 2011). The approaches taken by academic pipeline programs to change participants' views of themselves are supported by social psychological research, which shows that certain training activities increase student achievement and career success (Krim et al., 2019; Williams, Ari, & Dortch, 2010; Williams, Ari, & Dortch, 2011; Yeager et al., 2019; Yeager & Walton, 2011), student retention (Murphy et al., 2020), and faculty hiring (Liu, Brown, & Sabat, 2019). The combined focus on inclusionary practices and creating a culture that embraces various identities and perspectives ultimately impacts the long-term engagement of URMs in the academy.

PROVIDING VOICE

V in the THRIVE Index represents voice. Academic pipeline programs open the door for URMs to "take a seat at the table" by allowing participants to bring their experiences and perspectives to the conversation. They allow individuals to enhance the expression of their academic *voice* and to define their own sense of purpose or belonging in the academy. McLeod (2011) suggests that voice is twofold. It includes expression from marginalized groups and listening from stakeholders in higher education. Voice can be used to promote equity and reform. When programming considers voice, participants are empowered to fulfill their career goals and make changes for other generations that follow. One of the most successful interventions related to voice is demonstrated through mentorship.

Mentorship

Many of these initiatives provide mentorship and networks to give voice to participants not well represented in their institutions. Mentors can come in many forms, from teachers and faculty to administrators and senior students. What is essential to these relationships is for the participant to grow and feel empowered as an individual, researcher, colleague, and scholar. Pipeline programs link those who lack academic role models with successful professionals in a very deliberate fashion. Many programs use mentorship to create and cultivate inclusive learning environments, foster research collaborations, and increase positive interactions among students, faculty, and administration (Nora & Crisp, 2007). Mentoring can be defined in a variety of ways, depending on the relationship between the protégé/mentee and the mentor.[3] According to Scandura and Williams (2004):

> A protégé is the person who is guided and supported by a mentor or coach. A *mentor* is an influential individual with a higher ranking in your work environment who has advanced experience and knowledge so he/she can give you support, guidance, and advice for your development. Your mentor can be from inside or outside your organization but is not your immediate supervisor. He/she is recognized as an expert in his/her field. Most of the mentor relations are long term and focus on general objectives of development. (p. 455)

The above definition portrays the numerous relationships that are common among most of the pipeline programs described

---

3. The terms *mentor* and *protégé* will be used interchangeably throughout this book.

throughout the book. This definition also portrays a mentee as an apprentice who receives knowledge in a hands-on way from someone who had knowledge about their level of the pipeline or who has already progressed further in the pipeline. Pipeline programs pair URM mentees with more seasoned peer, faculty, and/or administrator mentors in the context of a research or skill-related experience. The addition of mentoring increases the success of pipeline programs (Linn, Palmer, Berenger, Gerard, & Stone, 2015) and the ability of their participants to persist and navigate through the academy (Lunsford, Crisp, Dolan, & Wutherick, 2017; Toldson, 2019). Across pipeline programs, mentoring is either tailored to the individual protégé (e.g. near peer, peer, and senior mentors; Montgomery, Dodson, & Johnson, 2014) or a network of mentees and mentors (e.g. tiered mentoring; Rockquemore, 2013). The mentoring relationship seen in pipeline programs provides key attributes deemed as successful (Haggard, Doughtery, Turban, & Wilbanks, 2011): (1) a reciprocal exchange benefiting both the mentee and mentor, (2) developmental or aspirational benefits for the protégé, and (3) regular/consistent interactions over a period of time.

Academic pipeline programs are used to promote the exchange of social and cultural capital from the mentor to the mentee. Social capital refers to the sum of the actual or potential resources tied to a network of institutionalized relationships or memberships to a group (Bourdieu, 1977). URMs often lack in social capital or the networks of powerful people who provide inside information, invaluable coaching, and guidance in securing desirable positions, promotions, and connections to succeed in the academy (Bajaj, 2014; Byrd, 2016). Social capital usually allows for the attainment of other forms of capital like cultural capital. Cultural capital can be conceived of as institutionalized attitudes, behaviors, preferences, and goods that reflect the dominant culture (Lamont & Lareau, 1988). Cultural capital is unequally distributed and can be subject to scarcity (Lareau & Weininger, 2003). At all levels of the pipeline, protégés are individuals aspiring to obtain cultural capital (i.e., the disposition, skill set, attitudes, and behaviors fostering academic competence) from mentors who have reached a status in life beyond their current status (Farmer-Hinton & Adams, 2006; Yosso, 2005). Table 1.2 provides an overview of how certain social capital components (Coleman, 1988, 1990; Nishi, 2017) are fostered through the culture and structure of mentoring relationships within pipeline programs. The transmission of social and cultural capital is a necessary means for LIFG and URMs to successfully enter and become a part of the academy, connect to influential networks, and overcome the barriers their majority counterparts do not face (Byrd, 2016). The mentorship relationships developed in many pre-collegiate, collegiate, and graduate academic pipeline programs are used to advance students' academic careers and transferable skills used in acquiring future mentors.

Furthermore, the cultural and social capital and networks developed in a participant's academic journey helps them to overcome obstacles and provides the voice needed to become a self-motivated, confident, and successful career scholar. Voice brings a sense of belongingness in the academy that is fostered by allowing participants to convey their experiences and perspectives to the conversation This leads to collaborative discussions with everyone, and allows for constructive debates of issues while promoting diversity and inclusion (McLeod, 2011). Privileging voice may come from socialization in professional settings like interactions in workshops or conferences and/or from completing a project or published work within one's discipline of study. Participants in academic pipeline programs are given the chance to liberate their voice through a community of brave and safe spaces. Brave spaces (Arao & Clemons, 2013) allow for controversy with civility, respect, ownership of intentions and impact, and "no attack" zones. Safe spaces spark movements and activism. Activism has been demonstrated when alumni of pipeline programs challenge program policies and decision-making processes. The concept of voice allows for program development and growth among its participants.

Table 1.2. Components of social capital established within pipeline program mentoring structure.

Social Capital Components	Pipeline Program Mentoring Structure
Norms: standards of behaviors set for the relationship between protégé/mentees and mentors.	Protégé/mentee: mentor relationship structure varies by each pipeline program (e.g., regularly scheduled meetings and workshops, visible representation of diversity within the pipeline, social displays of scientific knowledge and practices).
Mores and Values: specific expectations to guide behavior in the context of the protégé in academic settings.	Protégés are shown academic customs, pitfalls, departmental politics, and taboos to avoid in order to succeed.
Networks: systems of social linkages to other members within the academy maintained through ties of the mentor's social network.	Protégés are allowed to attend functions with mentors (e.g., dinners, social events, retreats). Mentor and program directors provide access to academic resources and information needed for success (e.g., undergraduate, graduate, or postdoctoral training; standardized test preparation; writing and research workshops; tenure and promotion information).
Trust: community conducts their relations in good faith and no individual acts solely out of self-interest.	The protégé is recognized and valued by the mentor (e.g., coauthorship, graduate school/job references). Mentors are transparent about unspoken norms.

EXPECTATIONS OF THE PROGRAM

The final dimension in the THRIVE Index, *E*, characterizes academic pipeline programs by representing expectations for what participants or institutions will gain from these initiatives. This final component illustrates the evaluative components of programs, providing outcomes and results of programming. The purpose of this section is to see if programs are achieving their own goals and to see the comprehensive goal of diversity and inclusion in the academy. As with any assessment tool, it is essential to close the loop and learn about the outcomes of these academic pipeline programs.

Specific examples of the expectations of academic pipeline programs include external review, site visits, annual performance reports, and program surveys. They can include various key performance indicators (KPIs) that provide quantifiable measures of the successes of these initiatives. For participants, academic pipeline programs set the expectation of entering the academy through the pursuit of advanced study and higher learning. Expectations could drill down to simply completing a project, conducting research, developing intellectual property, publishing a scholarly work, earning a degree and moving to the next level of the pipeline, or finding employment. Essentially, the *E* of THRIVE provides a measure of what has worked over time and for whom and potential next steps for the evolution of programming.

As we dive into the programs and initiatives highlighted in the following chapters, we would like to provide readers with a few caveats. In these times, when structural and systemic racism is being brought to the forefront within society and organizations, we are aware that some of these programs may have had issues with inclusive and fair practices. While we understand that many of our programs have twenty to thirty years of tenure and have faced difficulties and challenges, our goal is to focus on the instrumental positive changes they have collectively brought to diversifying the academy.

BOOK ORGANIZATION

This publication highlights twenty-one well-established pipeline programs that support URM participants and prepare them from the beginning of college through to junior faculty positions and beyond. All highlighted programs have had a wealth of successful outcomes (e.g., graduation rates, retention rates, effective movement into next academic level). Moreover, the majority of the initiatives and programs in the book were established at least fifteen years ago. The following chapters will discuss each type of pipeline program along the academic journey (see figure 1.4). We provide an in-depth analysis of the programs in the following chapters using the THRIVE Index tool. Chapter 2 includes pre-collegiate programs: Knowledge Is Power Program (KIPP), College Advising Corps, United Negro College Fund Portfolio Project and Fund II Foundation STEM Scholars Program, and University of Maryland, Baltimore County (UMBC), high school to college, Meyerhoff Scholars Program. Chapter 3 highlights collegiate programs: Leadership Alliance, Mellon Mays Undergraduate Fellowship Program, Florida A&M University (FAMU) Graduate Feeder Scholars Program (GFSP), Institute for the Recruitment of Teachers, California Pre-Doctoral Program's Sally Casanova Scholarship, and Annual Biomedical Research Conference for Minority Students (ABRCMS).

Chapter 4 includes graduate programs: Southern Regional Educational Board (SREB)-State Doctoral Scholars Program, McKnight Doctoral Fellowship Program, Alfred P. Sloan Foundation Minority Graduate Scholarship Program, Ford Foundation Fellowship Program, National GEM Consortium, and Fisk-Vanderbilt Master's-to-PhD Bridge Program. Chapter 5 includes postdoctoral /faculty development programs: University of California (UC) President's Postdoctoral Fellowship Program, National Center for Faculty Development & Diversity (NCFDD) Faculty Success Program, Sisters of the Academy (SOTA) Institute, Rochester Institute of Technology (RIT) Future Faculty Career Exploration Program, and Creating Connections Consortium (C3). Chapters 2–5 also include several governmental- and foundation-funded pipeline programs to complete our snapshot of diversity initiatives advancing URM populations.

We end the book (chapter 6) with information that is helpful for using and developing academic pipeline programs. We provide suggestions on how to leverage programs at each level of the pipeline while highlighting themes that have made them successful based on the THRIVE Index. In addition, a model is introduced to aid institutions with coordinating pipeline programs across levels. Finally, using the THRIVE index, we document the majority of all the pipeline initiatives in the United States with an interactive appendix that is linked to a geographic information system (GIS). Because this book is offered as a paper and online open-access publication, the GIS aligns with the web format of Lever Press. Figure 1.4 provides an overview of the chapter structure of the book.

Chapter 1	Chapter 2	Chapter 3	Chapter 4	Chapter 5	Chapter 6	Interactive Appendix
Understanding Academic Pipeline Programs and Their Origins	Precollegiate	Collegiate	Doctoral/ Graduate/ Professional Programs	PostDoctoral/ Faculty	Closing Thoughts	
	Knowledge is Power Program (KIPP)	The Leadership Alliance	SREB State Doctoral Scholars Program	University of California (UC) President's Postdoctoral Fellowship Program		
	College Advising Corps	Mellon Mays Undergraduate Fellowship Program	Alfred P. Sloan Minority Graduate Scholarship Program	National Center for Faculty Development and Diversity (NCFDD)		
	United Negro College Fund (UNCF) –Portfolio Project –Fund II STEM Scholars Program	Florida A&M Graduate Feeder Scholars Program	Ford Foundation Fellowship Programs	Sisters of the Academy (SOTA)		
		Institute for the Recruitment of Teachers (IRT)	The National GEM Consortium	Rochester Institute of Technology (RIT) Future Faculty Career Exploration Program		
	University of Maryland Baltimore County (UMBC) Meyerhoff Scholars Program	California Predoctoral Sally Casanova Scholars	Fisk-Vanderbilt Master's to PhD Bridge Program			
		Annual Biomedical Research Conference for Minority Students (ABRCMS)		Creating Connections Consortium (C3)		

Figure 1.4. Chapter overview.

CHAPTER 2

PRECOLLEGIATE PROGRAMS

In chapter 2, we examine programs at the beginning of the academic pipeline. These initiatives build a foundation for underrepresented students to enter and persist in the pipeline (e.g., middle school, high school, college diploma). Academic pipeline programs for K–12 come in different forms, including in-school programs, after-school programs, out-of-school enrichment programs, summer camps, and residential bridge programs (Mason, 2020; Valla & Williams, 2012). Successful precollegiate pipeline programs are measured by their ability to (1) engage young people intellectually, socially, and emotionally; (2) respond to young people's interests, experiences, and cultural practices; and (3) connect discipline-specific learning within school, home, and other out-of-school settings (National Research Council, 2018). Programs highlighted in this chapter meet the standards above and support underrepresented minority (URM) students while they are beginning their advanced educational pursuits. In this section, we illustrate several of the hallmark programs (Knowledge Is Power Program [KIPP], College Advising Corps, the United Negro College Fund [UNCF] Portfolio Project and Fund II Foundation STEM Scholars Program, and the University of

Massachusetts, Baltimore County [UMBC], Meyerhoff Scholars Program) that have served thousands of students nationwide. KIPP represents a network of charter schools that are a type of educational ecosystem that focuses on success across all grade levels prior to college entry. This publicly funded network of college preparatory schools resembles Rosenwald-funded schools in their positioning in communities and their aim to reduce educational disparities (Carruthers & Wanamaker, 2013). College Advising Corps and the UNCF programs represent out-of-school enrichment partnerships and inclusive efforts, similar to the model exhibited by the Boys & Girls Clubs of America. The Meyerhoff Scholars Program is an example of a precollegiate summer bridge program that targets the transition from high school to the first year of college. Students are recruited from high school programs the summer before they enter college; therefore, the Meyerhoff Scholars Program was placed at the end of this chapter as it is a substantial initiative that bridges precollegiate students to college and beyond.

KNOWLEDGE IS POWER PROGRAM

Knowledge Is Power Program (KIPP) is a successful program that supports precollegiate students through the completion of their precollegiate career and beyond (Mathematica, 2015). A national network of more than two hundred college-preparatory charter schools, KIPP is the largest network, primarily serving African American and Hispanic students from low-income communities.

Type

Knowledge Is Power Program Academy

Place in the Pipeline	Precollegiate Students
Type of Students Served	Age, disability, first-generation, gender, language use (e.g., bilingualism, bidialectalism), foreign born (e.g., undocumented immigrants, noncitizen of the United States), political ideology, race/ethnicity, religion, sexual orientation, socioeconomic status (e.g., low-income)
Disciplines Served	N/A
Funding Source	Public federal, state, and local dollars, along with supplemental funding from charitable donations
Institutional Structure	Other/nonprofit
Length of Time in Program	Varies; preK–12
Geographic Location	Nationwide
Institutions Served	Two hundred and twenty-four schools; public charter schools with early childhood, elementary, middle, and high school programs
Program Accepts New Sites	Yes
Program Deadlines	Varies by school
Website	https://www.KIPP.org/

History

In 1994, KIPP was established as a middle school program, with the belief that helping children develop academic character would strengthen what they need for college. With these skills, children would have a better future for themselves and their communities. The KIPP approach stands apart from other programs by placing an emphasis on several factors (www.KIPP.org/our-approach). The factors in Kipp's approach include a belief that all students can learn and achieve; a focus on college graduation as the ultimate goal; an emphasis on rigorous academics while simultaneously developing character; a belief that visionary, empowered leaders are central to the development and operation of successful schools; and a belief that excellent teachers are critical to helping students succeed.

Alumni Success

At each level of the pipeline, from preschool to college, KIPPsters have improved academic outcomes. Preschool attendees in KIPP have higher early literacy and early math scores compared to non-KIPP attendees. Middle school KIPP academies are proven to have meaningful impacts on student achievement in math, reading, science, and social studies. Serving more than ninety thousand students, with more than eleven thousand alumni enrolled in colleges and universities nationwide (KIPP, 2017), KIPP has partnership agreements with over ninety colleges and universities that are committed to increasing college graduation rates for KIPP alumni. Alumni of KIPP academies complete college at a rate that exceeds the national average and at a rate that is three times higher than students with similar demographic characteristics who do not attend KIPP academies. Notable alumni include Rev. Calvon Jones (Morehouse College Alumnus and Yale Divinity School Student) and Jessica De Los Santos (cofounder of Savvy Bio and a student at Williams College).

Research Preparation

The KIPP approach provides personalized learning based on the needs, skills, and interests of students. The curriculum emphasizes high-quality, rigorous instruction, particularly for literacy and mathematics. Instructional design components include close and guided reading, literacy instruction for three to five hours per day, more than one hundred minutes of mathematics per day, and 90 percent participation in advanced-placement courses. In Lynn, Massachusetts, KIPP Academy Lynn has demonstrated increased reading and math scores, particularly for students who have limited English proficiency and are enrolled in special education (Angrist et al., 2011).

As an example of KIPP's commitment to preparation for college,

KIPP New Jersey Rise Academy has developed the Kits for Kids or Phoenix Architecture Program. This program teaches children about design thinking and social infrastructure. The program also partners with architects, who serve as mentors. It has been featured on the news for its potential lasting impact and for preparing students for STEM careers.

Students in KIPP academies are also provided with supplemental programming, including in-depth discussions about college and paying for tuition, and teachers and counselors assist with college planning. For example, KIPP counselors and school leaders in Atlanta, Georgia, received support to assist their students with raising their college entrance examination scores and selecting a college that matches their background and aspirations (McCray, 2018). In addition, KIPP academies provide networking events, career nights, mock interviews, and job shadowing opportunities.

Funding

As a financial incentive, KIPP schools use "K" dollars (Angrist et al., 2011). Students earn "K" dollars for reaching positive academic outcomes, like completing homework or passing exams. These "K" dollars can be exchanged for items from the school store.

Inclusion and Identity

Inclusion

Inclusion is modeled by KIPP through specialized pedagogical practices (e.g., multicultural teaching practices, use of preferred gender pronouns), structured dialogues and interactions (e.g., lab discussions, one-on-one sessions, virtual dialogues), orientation (e.g., reviewing norms, expectations, structures, goals, and/or protocols), the development of a sense of belongingness, and the creation of a safe space/climate/environment. The Kits for Kids program is inclusive by design, allowing any student who shows interest to be in the program. All students—whether general education, special education (physical or cognitive), and other—are allowed to enroll. While the program may appear to cater to high-performing students, no student was turned away if they showed interest and commitment.

Identity

Across the nation, KIPP academies are representative, enrolling many URMs, and some are even led by URMs. For example, the Kits for Kids program affirms different identities by being inclusive of all students who are interested in the program. The program was led by a college student team that was majority Latinx and women, it was facilitated by a campus program coordinator who is a white woman, and it was organized by a campus director of extended learning who is a Black man. Students who participated were biracial, Black, Nigerian, and Latinx.

The teaching and counselor training provided by KIPP sets the expectation that every KIPPster has unlimited potential. Teachers and counselors help students to navigate the social, academic, and financial challenges associated with pursuing a college degree or career. As a part of counseling, KIPP uses the College Match Strategies Framework. The College Match Strategies Framework includes steps that are critical for all students as they consider the appropriate college. All KIPP alumni get coaches and counselors who remain connected with students and help them through obstacles. Exploration of a student's passion, purpose, and priorities is integral to this framework. Five regional networks recently received microgrants to provide KIPP alumni who are on the verge of graduating with scholarships. These scholarships will allow them to persist through graduation despite financial emergencies. A digital tool is being developed to link students to college campuses that are appropriate for their financial needs and that will provide a community that is supportive of their diversity.

All of the programs at KIPP academies, particularly Kits for Kids, are 100 percent focused on self-efficacy. Students enrolled in the Kits for Kids program have the basic skills of math and science necessary to engage in the program, but none of them have competence in architecture. This gap allows students to be vulnerable with student leaders from the New Jersey Institute of Technology and to be willing to engage in learning a new skill set. By gaining a skill that many don't master, or even touch, until college, students are able to be leaders among their peers.

Voice

The KIPP model incorporates opportunities for students to exercise their voice during instruction and out of school activities. The KIPP model includes small-group instruction, which allows for personalized learning and dialogue with teachers. The curricula model is rigorous, personalized, and based on a student's learning needs. For example, at KIPP New Jersey Rise Academy, students exercise their voice by designing their own "classroom." All of students at KIPP New Jersey Rise Academy are able to use their experiences and perspectives when discussing what architecture, city planning, and design could, and should, look like. Out-of-school activities promote voice by bringing together a community of supporters during celebrations. Celebrations allow students, staff, and parents to recognize student accomplishments.

There is an effort by KIPP academies to hear and learn from alumni. A 2017 alumni survey (https://www.kipp.org/wp-content/uploads/2018/04/2017-Alumni-Survey-Results.pdf) was used to learn more about alumni experiences in college. Ultimately, the survey led to strengthened partnership agreements with colleges and universities so that alumni can be supported on college campuses and feel a sense of belonging. It was reported that KIPP alumni perceived a higher sense of belonging when they saw their peers at college and when they attended HBCUs. Recently, some

KIPP alumni have begun to use their voices to rally for changes to systems and leadership within certain KIPP sites.

Mentoring

Past participants serve as mentors (e.g., near-peer). Mentors provide regularly scheduled meetings with mentees and provide support with goal setting and career planning. Mentors provide mentees with access to academic resources (e.g., precollegiate training, standardized test preparation, writing workshops, and research workshops). Through a partnership with iMentor, a nonprofit organization, KIPPsters have the opportunity to apply for a one-on-one mentoring program. This partnership provides mentoring support while KIPP alumni are enrolled in college.

Expectations

The KIPP model is designed to help students persist through the K–12 pipeline, graduate from high school, and enter college. Students, teachers, and parents sign a "commitment pledge." Students are expected to arrive at school on time, complete their schoolwork, and work hard (Angrist et al., 2011). Through the combination of instruction and partnerships, students ultimately gain an education based in college preparation, which sets the course for whatever career pathway they choose. Through successful precollege preparation, KIPP aims for students to be successful in college and in their careers, and KIPPsters are expected to conduct research, develop their own ideas, and increase an academic skill area. Additionally, KIPP programs undergo several forms of evaluation, including external review and evaluations, site visits, and program surveys. The College Match Strategies Framework includes seven student behaviors and key performance indicators that are directed toward student persistence into college.

> **Precollegiate Governmental Academic Pipeline Programs**
>
> **Centers for Disease Control and Prevention**
> https://www.cdc.gov/
>
> **Office of Minority Health and Health Equity (OMHHE)** at the Centers for Disease Control and Prevention (CDC) sponsors strategic programming that prepares middle and high school students for careers in public health (https://www.cdc.gov/minorityhealth/).
>
> **CDC Museum Disease Detective Camp** is a fast-paced summer camp that encourages high school juniors and seniors to work in diverse public-health teams (https://www.cdc.gov/museum/camp/detective/index.htm).
>
> **National Aeronautics and Aerospace Administration**
> https://www.nasa.gov/
>
> **The MUREP (Minority University Research and Education Project)** K-12 Aerospace Academy builds knowledge and skills for high school students to pursue careers in STEM. Visit the website for current site locations (https://www.nasa.gov/stem/murep/MAA/index.html).

COLLEGE ADVISING CORPS

The mission of College Advising Corps (CAC) is to help transform individual lives, families, communities, and school systems. They believe every student deserves the opportunity to enter and complete postsecondary education. CAC is committed to increasing the enrollment of qualified low-income, first-generation, and underrepresented students in colleges. To do so, CAC places recent college graduates from partner universities with underserved high schools as full-time college advisors.

Type

College Advising Corps	
Place in the Pipeline	Precollegiate and collegiate students
Type of Students Served	URMs, low-income first-generation (LIFG)
Disciplines Served	N/A
Funding Source	Foundation
Institutional Structure	Other/high schools/colleges/universities
Length of Time in Program	Varies
Geographic Location	Nationwide
Institutions Served	Six hundred and seventy high schools
Program Accepts New Sites	No
Program Deadlines	Varies
Website	https://advisingcorps.org/

History

CAC began in Virginia in 2005 with funding from the Jack K. Cooke Foundation. Nicole Hurd, PhD (founder and CEO and the former dean and director of the Center for Undergraduate Excellence at the University of Virginia) began what was then called the College Guide program by placing fourteen recent University of Virginia (UVA) graduates in rural communities where rates for college attendance were below the state average. Due to its success, the program was expanded nationwide with funding from Lumina Foundation for Education. The Lumina Foundation invested $12 million over four years to expand the program nationally.

CAC assists participants with college applications and the college financial aid application process. The national organization supports students in sixteen states, including California, Georgia, Illinois, Kansas, Massachusetts, Michigan, Missouri, New York, North Carolina, Pennsylvania, South Carolina, Rhode Island, Texas, and Virginia. The national reach of this program in 2018–19 included 670 high schools. For example, the University of Georgia supports seventeen high schools, and Georgia State University

Advising Corps supports eight high schools. CAC is also partnered with KIPP.

Alumni Success

To date, CAC has served over 800,000 students. The approach of using near-peer advising has expanded economic opportunity for students of all backgrounds in urban and rural communities across the country. This approach has also prepared CAC advisors to lead change far into the future. In the first ten years of the program, CAC advisors have helped more than 372,000 students enroll in college. The goal is that, by 2025, CAC will more than double the impact of their first ten years and enroll one million students from low-income, first-generation, and underrepresented backgrounds in college.

Notable alumni of CAC include Clara Ramirez (first-generation graduate, Texas Christian University, and CAC adviser) and Lawrence Harris (graduate, University of Georgia, MA in higher education Administration, Graduate School of Education at Pennsylvania State University; director of the Athens Community Career Center).

Research Preparation

Through their tracking system, CAC has demonstrated several outcomes related to preparing high school students for college entry. Advisors assist high school students with their college applications, financial-aid forms, including the Free Application for Federal Student Aid (FAFSA) and scholarship applications. Overall, students who have met with a CAC advisor are more likely to aspire to go to college, participate in college-prep activities, apply to colleges, be accepted to college, and be committed to going to college in the fall. Figure 5 shows many of the program's outcomes as they relate to student research preparation using data that was collected over

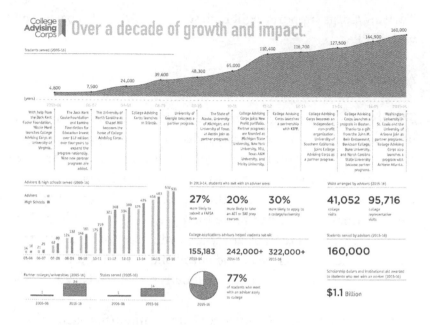

Figure 2.1. College Advising Corps outcomes over a ten-year period from 2005–16. *Source*: College Advising Corps.

a ten-year period between 2005–16 (see figure 2.1). Compared to students who do not partner with CAC advisors, students who participate are 20 percent more likely to take the SAT or ACT preparatory courses, 30 percent more likely to apply to a college or university, 27 percent more likely to submit a FAFSA, 26 percent more likely to apply for a scholarship, 24 percent more likely to apply to three or more colleges, and 24 percent more likely to be accepted to a college or university.

Inclusion and Identity

Inclusion

CAC is committed to creating an inclusive atmosphere for students, staff, and team members. Inclusive practices involving students in CAC are achieved through structured dialogues and interactions as well as orientations.

Identity

Various types of students are represented in CAC, including first-generation students, students from various racial and ethnic groups, students with varying gender identities and expressions and students with disabilities. CAC targets URMs but white students are also served. In addition, CAC embraces differences in identities within their staff or team, and CAC encourages staff to invest the knowledge that varying experiences and social identities bring toward the support of students. They commit time and resources to make sure that their leadership is diverse and takes part in cultural competency training.

Voice

Advisors serve as a bridge between students, teachers, and parents. They become anchors in their communities and help students express their college-related aspirations. Advisors share their stories, which, in turn, motivates parents and students to continue down the collegiate pathway. Some CAC alumni even become college advisers.

Mentoring

CAC uses a near-peer mentor approach. Mentors are peers of program participants (e.g., near peer, tiered peer, etc.). The near-peer approach places recent college graduates as mentors in high schools. Advisors meet with high school students, either one on one or through small groups. Advisors draw upon their own experiences with mentors and counselors to guide high school students toward a college that is the best fit for their background.

Expectations

The ultimate goal of CAC is to impact underserved communities and to prepare advisors to become agents of change. Success can be measured along several dimensions that are all rooted at the individual level. The success of CAC may translate into students attending college open-house events, visiting a college campus, learning how to apply to college, completing one or more college applications by their due date, completing financial-aid forms, and committing to going to the college to which they have been accepted. The ultimate goal of CAC is to enroll one million students in higher-education programs by 2025.

CAC conducts external review and evaluation, annual performance reports, site visits, and program surveys. It is challenging to gauge the program's full impact because their national presence spans thirty chapters and across seven hundred high schools. Key performance indicators include the number of one-on-one meetings, the number of SAT/ACT registrations, the number (more than one or more than three) of college applications completed, the number of FAFSAs assisted, the number of FAFSAs completed, and the number of family engagements completed.

Precollegiate Governmental Academic Pipeline Programs

National Institutes of Health

https://www.nih.gov/research-training/training-opportunities

The National Institutes of Health (NIH) grants a variety of programs to institutions nationwide to support education at the precollegiate level and hosts students at their campus.

Summer Internships in Biomedical Research for High School Students (HS-SIP) gives high school students the opportunity to spend a summer working at NIH with a scientist engaged in biomedical research. Students are exposed to distinguished lectures, career and professional development workshops, and college-readiness activities. Participants also create a research poster (https://www.train ing.nih.gov/programs/hs-sip).

National Science Foundation
https://www.nsf.gov/

Research Assistantships for High School Students (RAHSS) seeks to broaden participation during precollege years. As part of a new or renewal proposal, NSF provides funding to support the training of high school students who are under-represented minorities, persons with disabilities, or gender minorities (https://www.nsf.gov/funding/pgm_summ.jsp?pi ms_id=500035).

Pathways to Science is a web resource that provides a listing of K–12 teaching resources and a listing of summer programs for middle and high school students that are either free of cost or that offer scholarships for tuition (https://www.pathwaysto science.org/k12.aspx).

UNITED NEGRO COLLEGE FUND

The United Negro College Fund (UNCF) has a long history of partnering with philanthropists and HBCUs to prepare high school
and college students. In 1944, John D. Rockefeller Jr. led a coalition of bankers and business executives to support the aspiration
of Frederick Douglas Patterson, the former president of Tuskegee Institute (today University), to start the UNCF. The mission
of UNCF "is to build a robust and nationally-recognized pipeline
of under-represented students who, because of UNCF support,
become highly-qualified college graduates and to ensure that our
network of member institutions is a respected model of best practice in moving students to and through college" (https://www.un
cf.org/our-mission). Since its founding, UNCF has expanded its
mission to ensure African American students are college ready.

The UNCF sponsors the Empower Me Tour (EMT). A free, col-
lege- and career-readiness roadshow, EMT shares information,
tools, and resources with students and parents to help them make
college decisions. The tour also offers high school students and
their families a full day of college-readiness workshops and panel
discussions. Panel discussants include guest educators, entrepreneurs, and business executives who share their educational journeys. High school students also meet admission counselors from
UNCF-member HBCUs. These HBCUs, in turn, offer on-site college admissions and institutional scholarship awards to students
who come prepared with letters of recommendation, transcripts,
and ACT/SAT scores. During the 2016–7 tour, nearly $3.8 million
in scholarships were awarded and more than eight hundred students were offered on-site college admissions to UNCF-member
institutions. The tour has made stops in Atlanta, Chicago, and
Minneapolis. Other programs sponsored by UNCF include the
Portfolio Project and Fund II Stem Scholars Program, which fund
the precollegiate journey.

Type

UNCF Portfolio Project	
Place in the Pipeline	Precollegiate students (high school juniors and seniors)
Type of Students Served	URMs, LIFG
Disciplines Served	N/A
Funding Source	Funding from charitable donations
Institutional Structure	Other/nonprofit
Length of Time in Program	Eleven weeks
Geographic Location	Seattle, Washington; Marysville, Washington; Tacoma, Washington; and Portland, Oregon
Institutions Served	Local colleges and universities; HBCUs
Program Accepts New Sites	N/A
Program Deadlines	August 1
Website	https://scholarships.uncf.org/Program/Details/809da477-9a1d-4d2d-b643-09b0ae7e347a

History

The Portfolio Project was developed in 2006 to assist students in their junior and senior year of high school apply to colleges and scholarships. The Portfolio Project is a partnership between UNCF and the Seattle Rotary Foundation, College Access Now, YMCA Multicultural Achievers Program, YMCA Minority Achievers Program, and Leisure Hour Jr. Golf Program. The Portfolio Project is in its thirteenth year of operation.

Alumni Success

The Portfolio Project has several successful outcomes (garfieldptsa. org) Approximately 548 students and 166 mentors have participated in the program. The Portfolio Project has an 82 percent student completion rate. A large number of participants (70 percent) have received scholarship support. Notable alumni are Dae Durisko (student, Seattle University; founder, Seattle University Sustainability

Coalition) and Dureti Jamal (student, Boston University; graduate, Young Executives of Color, University of Washington).

Research Preparation

The Portfolio Project provides an eleven-week introductory boot camp to prepare underrepresented students for the college and scholarship application process. The Portfolio Project advises high school juniors and seniors on how to make appropriate college choices and exposes students in the Pacific Northwest to scholarship opportunities, local colleges and universities, and HBCUs. Students also learn about college entrance requirements. Students are made aware of the CommonApp (https://www.commonapp .org/) to assist with college applications.

Workshops and Professional Development

The Portfolio Project provides an environment for students to create a portfolio of the documents needed to gain entrance into college, including their application, FAFSA, and scholarship applications. The Portfolio Project also includes access to SAT/ACT preparatory resources from the Princeton Review. One of the workshop sessions is devoted to a college fair.

Funding

The Portfolio Project scholarship ranges from $500 to $3,000. Transportation assistance is available for students who qualify for free or reduced lunch.

Inclusion and Identity

Inclusion

Students are shown how to network and interact with college recruiters. Through networking events, students are given insight into the expectations of what is needed for them to succeed in colleges. Students are also exposed to a variety of Portfolio Project site locations. Because events are hosted at the sites of community partners, students are provided with exposure to a setting outside of their comfort zone. This helps them foster a sense of belongingness.

Identity

Students are prepared to present the best representation of themselves. This preparation leads up to the college fair. They are asked to bring their whole selves to the sessions. Tackling the challenge of building their portfolio helps them identify aspects of themselves that will be a benefit toward their college experience. They also receive motivation to pursue their career goals from both students and recruiters who share similar characteristics like themselves.

Voice

As part of the programming, students learn social skills that help them prepare for the culture of college beyond academics. Each One Teach One is an example of an annual event where program graduates get celebrated for their achievements. This event is one of many where a village of supporters can hear about students' accomplishments.

Mentoring

The mission of the Portfolio Project is to increase the number of URM and low-income college and scholarship applicants. The UNCF provides mentors and guest speakers who assist with essay writing and social-skills development activities. Volunteer mentors support students in ensuring that they gather all of their college-entrance data, manage their college and scholarship applications, and package their qualifications into a portfolio.

Expectations

Ultimately, the UNCF Portfolio Project strives to ensure that students create a portfolio that will support their efforts in getting accepted into college and receiving the necessary financial assistance to become successful college graduates. An example of a key performance indicator is the number of students who are accepted into college.

Type

The Fund II Foundation UNCF STEM Scholars Program	
Place in the Pipeline	Precollegiate students
Type of Students Served	African American students graduating high school
Disciplines Served	STEM
Funding Source	Public federal, state, and local dollars, along with supplemental funding from charitable donations
Institutional Structure	Other/nonprofit
Length of Time in Program	Varies
Geographic Location	Nationwide
Institutions Served	Sixty-nine institutions (eleven HBCUs)
Program Accepts New Sites	N/A
Program Deadlines	Application due March 3
Website	https://www.uncf.org/programs/fund-ii-uncf-stem-scholars

History

The inaugural class of Fund II Foundation Scholars was accepted in 2016. The Fund II Foundation was designed to identify five hundred African American high school students who are pursuing careers in STEM disciplines. The Fund II Foundation was established, as part of the Cradle to Greatness framework, to train talented high school students who have been underserved.

The Fund II Foundation Scholars program was developed by Robert F. Smith (founder, chairman, and CEO of Vista Equity Partners) and UNCF president and CEO Michael L. Lomax, PhD, to address the lack of diversity in the tech industry. Smith is now the president of the Fund II Foundation. The purpose of the Fund II Foundation's partnership is to create a robust pipeline of African American students who are well prepared for careers in the tech industry to become the next generation of innovators and entrepreneurs. The first cohort of one hundred students represents twenty-nine states and seventy-one colleges and universities. Of these institutions, seven are HBCUs (including UNCF-member institutions Morehouse College, Spelman College, Tuskegee University, Wilberforce University, and Xavier University of Louisiana), and seven are Ivy League institutions. The second cohort included eighteen STEM scholars attending ten HBCUs. The third cohort included thirty-six scholars attending twelve HBCUs, seven of which are UNCF-supported HBCUs (Claflin University, Clark Atlanta University, Fisk University, Morehouse College, Spelman College, Oakwood University, and Xavier University of Louisiana.)

Alumni Success

The inaugural class included a *Forbes* "30 Under 30" winner and a budding international researcher. Alumni include Augusta Uwamanzu-Nna (finalist, 2016 Intel Science Talent Search; student, Harvard University). Uwamanzu-Nna was included in the "energy" category for *Forbes* "30 Under 30" list and won the talent search for discovering that adding an ingredient to cement slurries helps keep offshore oil wells from leaking. Another notable alumnus is Kaila Helm (graduate, Newburgh Free Academy in Newburgh, New York; student, University of Pennsylvania). Helm traveled to Ghana to study at the Kumasi Center for Collaborative Research in Tropical Medicine. The third cohort of one hundred STEM scholars is comprised of fifty men and fifty women, with an average grade-point average (GPA) of 3.8 (Market Insider, 2018).

Research Preparation

Fund II Foundation Scholars receive scholarships, internships, mentoring, and other tools to help them reach their goals. The program is committed to fostering the development of entrepreneurship through high-impact and research-driven internships. Participants in the Fund II Foundation UNCF STEM Scholars Program will be prepared to have careers in the technology industry and to become the next generation of innovators. Scholars have access to online academic and STEM-specific wraparound support services.

Workshops and Professional Development

The inaugural class of scholars met for a leadership summit on July 29–31, 2016, in Atlanta. The leadership summit provided an opportunity for students to plan their academic and career goals. Guest speakers included notable African American experts within the STEM fields, including Ebony McGee, PhD, assistant professor of diversity and urban schooling at Vanderbilt University, and Karl Pendergrass, PhD, a UNCF/Merck postdoctoral fellow and director of medical affairs for the cardiovascular and metabolic disease team at Merck. Linda Wilson, Fund II Foundation executive director, also welcomed the scholars at the summit. Students learned about their entrepreneurial potential by participating in an ideation challenge focused on building an app from scratch.

Funding

Each scholar receives a total award package of up to $25,000, which includes scholarships and a stipend for STEM internships over five years. During their freshman and sophomore years of college, scholars receive a stipend of $2,500, which then increases to $5,000 during their junior and senior years. There is an additional $5,000 stipend for a STEM internship.

Inclusion and Identity

Inclusion

Fund II Foundation UNCF STEM Scholars become a part of the community. A weekend-long orientation is used as a platform to welcome students into a lifelong network of scholars. Cohorts are formed to promote their academic and career successes. Partnerships are made through networking with alumni. Research and tech partnerships also expand the ability of scholars to enter into the science and engineering workforce and be motivated to form their own tech startups.

Identity

Fund II Foundation Scholars are exposed to workshops during orientation and the leadership summit. Scholar identity is affirmed in several ways. Scholars are welcomed into a community through an orientation. During the orientation, they introduce themselves to all of the scholars in their cohort and get introduced to persons who help them build aspects of themselves. Alumni and speaker presentations allow the scholars to see that it is possible for them to be successful in STEM fields. During orientation, scholars also share their perspectives about their disciplines, their career goals, and their experiences from their school settings. During the orientation and leadership summit, scholars discuss topics like imposter syndrome and the life stories of other URMs.

Voice

Fund II Foundation UNCF STEM Scholars are welcomed into conversations during the orientation, leadership summit, and networking events. Scholars are empowered to share their stories at these events. Scholar alumni (e.g., near peers) return to share their experiences and progress with new cohort members. Alumni are encouraged to help support new scholars in their career journey.

Expectations

This initiative was designed to solve the need for more talented African American scholars to pursue areas of STEM and innovation. Students are funded to complete their undergraduate education and to complete STEM research projects or internships. The ultimate goal is to train undergraduates to enter the workforce and become leaders in the age of ongoing automation and digitization of traditional manufacturing.

Precollegiate Governmental Academic Pipeline Programs

US Department of Agriculture

https://www.usda.gov/

The US Department of Agriculture (USDA) is a long-standing partner with nationwide precollegiate programs.

Jr. Minorities in Agriculture, Natural Resources, and Related Sciences (MANNRS) Pre College Initiative Program promotes diversity in precollegiate students' academic, professional, and leadership skills. The program is designed to spark interest in science, technology, engineering, agricultural, and mathematics fields (STEAM) for children enrolled in grades 7–12. Students who are pursuing college degrees in agriculture, natural resources, and environmental sciences are eligible. The USDA provides hands-on sessions at the high school symposium and conference (https://www.manrrs.org/jr-manrrs-membership).

US Department of Education

https://www.ed.gov/

The US Department of Education (USDE) offers funding for precollegiate programs to public and private institutions nationwide.

Gaining Early Awareness and Readiness for Undergraduate Programs (Gear Up) provides funding at the state level to provide services at middle and high schools in highly impoverished areas. Early-intervention services and scholarship support are also provided (https://www2.ed.gov/programs/gearup/index.html).

Talent Search Program identifies and assists youth who have the potential to succeed in college. The goal of Talent Search is to increase high school graduation rates and college enrollment rates. The program offers academic, career, and financial counseling (https://www2.ed.gov/progr ams/triotalent/index.html).

Upward Bound supports high school students so that they are prepared to enter college. Academic preparation includes mathematics, laboratory science, English composition, English literature, and foreign languages. Programming also includes cultural activities, tutoring, counseling, mentoring, and financial and economic literacy (https://ww w2.ed.gov/programs/trioupbound/index.html).

Upward Bound Math-Science helps students develop their math and science skills in preparation to pursue postsecondary degrees and careers in math and science. Programs include academic instruction, cultural events, tutoring, mentoring, access to information related to postsecondary education opportunities, preparation for college entrance exams, and college financial-aid information (https://www2 .ed.gov/programs/triomathsci/index.html).

MEYERHOFF SCHOLARS PROGRAM

The Meyerhoff Scholars program has been recognized by the National Science Foundation and the *New York Times* as a national model for training students who are interested in pursuing doctorate degrees. Scores of representatives from federal agencies, campuses, and corporations across the country have visited UMBC's campus to learn more about the program's success. The College Board's National Task Force on Minority High Achievement praised the Meyerhoff Scholars Program as an example that could provide broader educational lessons.

Type

Meyerhoff Scholars Program	
Place in the Pipeline	Precollegiate/collegiate students
Type of Students Served	URMs, LIFG
Disciplines Served	Computer and information sciences, engineering, life sciences, mathematics, physical sciences
Funding Source	State funds, private donors, agencies, foundations, corporations, and individual donors (e.g., National Science Foundation, NASA, IBM, AT&T, and Sloan, Lilly, and Abel Foundations)
Institutional Structure	Other/nonprofit
Length of Time in Program	Four years of scholarships and programming
Geographic Location	Northeast
Institutions Served	University of Maryland, Baltimore County; predominantly white institutions (PWIs) and minority-serving institutions (MSIs)
Program Accepts New Sites	No
Program Deadlines	December 1
Website	https://meyerhoff.umbc.edu/

History

The University of Maryland, Baltimore County (UMBC), Meyerhoff Scholars Program was established in 1989 to provide financial assistance, mentoring, advising, and research experience to African American male undergraduate students committed to obtaining PhD degrees in math, science, and engineering. Women were admitted into the program in 1990, and, in 1996, the program was opened to people of all backgrounds who are committed to increasing representation of URMs in science and engineering. The program is now open to all high-achieving high school seniors who are interested in pursuing a PhD or MD/PhD in STEM, as well as those who are interested in the advancement of URMs in the sciences and related fields. The program is named in honor of its cofounder Robert Meyerhoff.

The nomination-based application process is open to prospective undergraduate students of all backgrounds who plan to pursue doctoral study in science or engineering and are interested in the advancement of URMs in those fields. The program's success is built on the premise that, among like-minded students who work closely together, positive energy is contagious. By assembling high-achieving students in a tight-knit learning community, the program enables students to inspire one another to do more and better.

Alumni Success

The Meyerhoff Scholars Program has been at the forefront of efforts to increase diversity among future leaders in science, engineering, and related fields. The UMBC Meyerhoff Scholars Program has served more than 1,400 students, with over eleven hundred alumni across the nation, including over three hundred students enrolled in graduate and professional programs. Notable alumni include Jerome Adams, MD (twentieth surgeon general of the United States), Naomi Mburu (Rhodes Scholar, 2018), Kyla McMullen, PhD (first black woman to earn a PhD in computer science, University of Michigan), Kizzmekia Corbell, PhD (scientific lead, NIH project to develop a coronavirus vaccine), and Kafui Dzirasa, MD, PhD (associate professor of Neurobiology, Duke University).

Research Preparation

Meyerhoff Scholars receive a variety of resources to assist them with research preparation. These resources include merit scholarship, monthly academic advising, peer mentoring, research experience, standardized test preparation, study groups, specialized coursework, and professional development workshops. While summer research internships are required, sustained academic-year experiences are highly encouraged.

The model for the Meyerhoff Scholars Program attributes the following thirteen key components to the success of their students (adapted from https://meyerhoff.umbc.edu/13-key-components):

- administrative involvement and public support
- faculty involvement
- family involvement
- financial aid
- mentoring
- personal advising and counseling
- program community
- program values
- recruitment
- study groups
- summer bridge
- summer research internships
- tutoring

The exhaustive nature of these components combines buy in at all levels (e.g., institutional and parental), financial incentives, multiple career-focused skill-building opportunities (e.g., summer research internships, summer bridge, etc.), and a layered support system (e.g., faculty involvement, personal advising and counselors, study groups, tutors, etc.).

Funding

Meyerhoff Scholars receive four-year scholarships or a merit award. In-state student awards range from $5,000 to $15,000 per year. Out-of-state awards range from $10,000 to $22,000 per year. Scholarships assist with covering tuition, mandatory fees, and other expenses. Financial support is contingent upon scholars maintaining a B average in STEM majors.

Inclusion and Identity

Inclusion

A variety of Meyerhoff's programming elements are related to inclusionary practices, including having scholars network with UMBC's administration, deans, faculty, and staff to get a better understanding of the culture and expectations of college. Inclusionary practices also include connecting scholars early on with principals and leaders across the campus who are experts in diversity, equity, and inclusion, such as the Women's Center, the Office of Equity and Inclusion, and the director of inclusive excellence in the Office of Student Affairs. Scholars also participate in a specialized diversity and inclusion workshop.

Identity

The Meyerhoff Scholars Program starts with a strengths-based approach that affirms that students have competencies and abilities. From there, they assess where students are and work to help them grow and develop as they work toward their goals and objectives. A cohort model surrounds students with a critical mass of URM STEM students with similar goals and aspirations. Academic identity is also promoted through academic and professional advising and coaching, workshops, sessions with mentors, speaker series with URM STEM professionals, and parent engagement to help demystify STEM practices, expectations, and pathways.

Voice

The program office serves as a space for students to share information, voice their concerns, gather, study, and relax. Meyerhoff Scholars are exposed to a humanities course called Race, Science, and Society. Students are empowered, through personal support and encouragement, to persist toward their goals. Families are involved through special events and through the Parents Association. The Parents Association provides a platform for mutual support and for fundraising.

Mentoring

The Meyerhoff Scholars Program provides a robust community for highly motivated and diverse STEM students with similar goals and aspirations. Each scholar is paired with a mentor (near-peer), who is recruited from a pool of Baltimore-Washington area professionals in science, engineering, and health. Juniors and seniors mentor freshmen and sophomores under the direction of program staff. During laboratory research experiences, faculty serve as mentors. Scholars have the opportunity to be mentored by campus, local, national, and international faculty members. Faculty form interpersonal relationships with scholars, provide help and encouragement, and raise academic expectations for students. Program alumni serve as mentors and coaches. They are role models and examples of success in STEM graduate programs and careers. Alumni also serve as workshop speakers.

Expectations

The goal of the program is to increase diversity among future leaders in science, engineering, and related fields. Scholars are required to maintain a 3.0 GPA, apply to graduate schools, and pursue a graduate degree. Program participants are required to construct short-term and long-term goals with program staff and to revisit their plans. The Meyerhoff experience is intended to create an environment that positively reinforces achievement.

Ken Maton, PhD, (UMBC) leads a team of researchers who evaluate and conduct research on the program. The tools used to evaluate the program include surveys of current scholars and alumni as well as a review of the transcripts of current scholars and alumni. Key performance indicators of the Meyerhoff Scholars

Program include high retention rates, designating students as a STEM major, a cumulative and semester GPA above 3.0, substantive research experience by the start of the junior year, completion of an undergraduate STEM degree, and acceptance into a graduate, professional, or postbaccalaureate program.

Precollegiate Governmental Academic Pipeline Programs

US Department of Agriculture
https://www.usda.gov/

Summer internship programs are open to high school students, including those who are homeschooled. Summer activities include an internship program, résumé writing seminar, mock interview, etiquette and ethics seminars, career exploration day, and field day activities. Programs are open to students with disabilities and veterans. College and graduate students are also eligible. Internships can be completed in the fall or year-round (https://www.dm.usda.gov/employ/student/index.htm).

US Department of Energy
https://www.energy.gov/

The US Department of Energy's Office of Energy Efficiency & Renewable Energy (EERE) sponsors a variety of education and workforce activities for middle and high school students, including hands-on learning and internship opportunities. There is also a special STEM program for girls (https://www.energy.gov/eere/office-energy-efficiency-renewable-energy).

SUMMARY

Precollegiate programs prepare students to enter community colleges or four-year colleges and universities. The services and environments created by precollegiate academic pipeline programs have been demonstrated to increase pass rates in gatekeeper courses (Gonzalez Quiroz & Garza, 2018), increase collegiate grade-point averages and graduation rates (DesJardins & McCall, 2014; Maton, Hrabowski, & Schmitt, 2000), increase self-efficacy (Strayhorn, 2011) and foster the pursuit and attainment of STEM (Kitchen, Sadler, & Sonnert, 2018; Palmer, Maramba, & Dancy, 2011) and non-STEM careers (Strayhorn, 2011). Commonalities among the programs include application assistance, college advising, research-oriented summer experiences, and social and financial support. Each program has a track record of increasing the number of URM students who become successful high school graduates, college applicants, and, ultimately, college graduates. The success of each initiative has either spawned partnerships or the creation of other programs that have tried to replicate the effective components. College Advising Corps partners with KIPP in order to expand their reach to URM students. Programs like the Meyerhoff Scholars Program have prepared its trainees to become STEM entrepreneurs, chief scientific officers, and even a US surgeon general (Domingo & Sathy, 2019). Other institutions who use the Meyerhoff Scholars Program as a model are discussed in chapter 6. These types of institutional partnerships also appear as features of some of the collegiate programs discussed in chapter 3.

Precollegiate Program Commonalities Using the THRIVE Index

Program	Type	History	Research	Inclusion/Identity	Voice	Expectations
Knowledge Is Power Program (KIPP) **College Advising Corps** **United Negro College Fund Portfolio Project and Fund II Foundation STEM Scholars Program** **UMBC Meyerhoff Scholars Program**	Pre-collegiate	all programs or sponsoring organizations have been in existence for greater than ten years	core academic skill training college/career pathway preparation academic advising College/industry partnerships	networking professional development (e.g., workshops related to self or academic identity) orientation	alumni are used in programming mentoring (e.g. near peer, one on one)	high school completion college admission/enrollment college completion

CHAPTER 3

COLLEGIATE PROGRAMS

In this chapter, we examine programs at the collegiate level of the academic pipeline. These initiatives move students toward their *calling*. A calling is either a guiding force, a sense of personal fit or well-being, and a non self-centered set of priorities (Hunter, Dik, & Banning, 2010). In keeping with this definition, academic pipeline programs at the collegiate level provide:

- access to academic and research-related training, which spark intellectual curiosity in a student's prospective career discipline,
- awareness of what is expected to succeed in college and graduate/professional school,
- mentors who serve as models for the next level of the pipeline, and
- affiliation with a community that supports a student's ability to complete the baccalaureate degree and achieve an identity as a professional within academia.

In this section, we illustrate several programs committed to guiding undergraduate students through their academic journey (the Leadership Alliance, the Mellon Mays Undergraduate Fellowship Program, Florida A&M University's Graduate Feeder Scholars Program, the Institute for Recruitment of Teachers, the California Pre-Doctoral Program's Sally Casanova Scholarship, and the Annual Biomedical Research Conference for Minority Students). Pipeline programs sponsored by governmental agencies are also included in this chapter. The governmental programs range from summer only to yearlong or multiyear experiences. Examples of community college bridge programs and course-based undergraduate research experiences are discussed in the summary section.

THE LEADERSHIP ALLIANCE

The Leadership Alliance is a well-established program that has supported the research and professional development of underrepresented minorities (URM) undergraduates for many years. The Leadership Alliance has evolved to include over thirty institutions involved in undergraduate research and now offers programming for graduate students.

Type

The Leadership Alliance	
Place in the Pipeline	Undergraduate students, graduate students, early-career professionals
Type of Students Served	URMs, gender minorities, low-income first-generation (LIFG)
Disciplines Served	Computer and information sciences, engineering, humanities, life sciences, mathematics, neuroscience, physical sciences, social sciences
Funding Source	National Institutes of Health, the National Science Foundation, and foundation grants
Institutional Structure	members: predominantly white institutions (PWIs), historically Black colleges and universities (HBCUs), Hispanic-serving institutions (HSIs), minority-serving institutions (MSIs)
Length of Time in Program	Ten weeks during summer
Geographic Location	Providence, Rhode Island
Institutions Served	Thirty-five-member nationwide consortium (PWI and HBCU)
Program Accepts New Sites	Yes
Program Deadlines	February 1
Website	https://www.theleadershipalliance.org/

History

Established in 1992, the Leadership Alliance is a national consortium currently comprised of more than thirty leading research and teaching institutions. The consortium represents a successful collaboration among historically Black colleges and universities (HBCUs), Hispanic-serving institutions (HSIs), Asian American, Native American, and Pacific Islander-serving institutions (AANAPISI), minority-serving institutions (MSIs), Ivy League institutions, Carnegie-classified Research 1 institutions, and private industries. The Leadership Alliance's mission is to develop underrepresented students into outstanding leaders and role models in academia, business, and the public sector. For a quarter century, the Leadership Alliance has developed and implemented evidenced-based initiatives at critical transition points along the academic pathway to identify, train, and mentor the next generation of researchers and scholars in all academic disciplines.

Alumni Success

The most critical measure of the success of the Leadership Alliance is the training progression and career outcomes of its alumni. More than half (55 percent) of undergraduates who have participated in the national Summer Research Early Identification Program (SR-EIP) have matriculated into graduate programs. Successful matriculation led ultimately to 582 Leadership Alliance alumni obtaining their doctorate degrees (PhD, MD/PhD, or JD/PhD) since the program was established. Notable alumni include Wallace Derricotte PhD (assistant professor, Morehouse College) and Checo Rorie, PhD (associate professor, North Carolina A&T State University).

Research Preparation

The Leadership Alliance is committed to the idea of recruiting, mentoring, and training talented URM students at critical transitions along the academic pathway. The work of this initiative has significantly contributed to the emergence of the next generation of leaders in the research workforce. Drawing upon a nationwide partnership with nearly thirty years of expertise in training and mentoring, the Leadership Alliance has established and continuously innovates upon evidence-based programs. These programs begin at the undergraduate level with SR-EIP. The SR-EIP provides hands-on, cutting-edge summer research experiences, which are designed to produce research-focused, highly qualified scholars who are competitive for graduate training programs across the academy. The Leadership Alliance recently introduced a new initiative called the First-Year Research Experience (FYRE). This program is designed to increase the participation of first-year URM students from MSIs in the SR-EIP. The culminating event of the summer research experience is the Leadership Alliance National Symposium (LANS), a national networking conference providing an important venue for approximately four hundred undergraduates to present results on research conducted in their SR-EIP placement. Also, LANS offers skill-building, networking, and professional development opportunities tailored to the training needs of undergraduates, graduate students, and doctoral scholars (Leadership Alliance alumni who have completed a PhD or MD/PhD degree).

To address strategies for successful research development and support, the Leadership Alliance partners with experts from the Council on Undergraduate Research (CUR) to conduct training sessions on "developing grantsmanship skills." Representatives from various professional societies and federally funded programs are invited to participate in meet-and-greet sessions, which provide opportunities for advanced scholars to network and develop professional connections to assist in their career advancement. Networking activities are designed to span the entire symposium experience, which offers both discipline-specific and broad-based networking opportunities.

Academic Year Workshop Program

To engage students during their first academic year, prior to any potential summer research experience, the Leadership Alliance developed two academic-year workshops (called What Is Research? and Collaborative Learning) that position students to build critical skills for use in classroom and research settings. The What Is Research? workshop seeks to introduce students to research careers and promote further exploration of these careers by participants. Participants discuss the underlying motivations for conducting research, such as discovery and problem solving, as well as the myriad contexts in which research takes place. Participants have the opportunity to learn more about approaches to research and to put some of those principles into practice through interactive research activities. Participants also receive information on how to apply for paid summer research opportunities at universities across the country.

The next workshop is called Collaborative Learning, which is an opportunity for students to explore the peer-learning process and consider how to form a successful study or research group. Studies show that working in groups improves students' performance in class and on tests, as well as in research contexts, and this workshop illustrates this process. Collaborative Learning teaches students how to form and maintain collaborative learning groups. This workshop covers the steps to establish a group and includes time for practicing some learning techniques. By the end of the workshop, students should have all of the tools they need to start collaborative learning groups.

Summer Research Early Identification Program

SR-EIP is a fully paid summer internship providing undergraduates with training and mentoring in the principles underlying the conduct of research. The program prepares students to pursue competitive applications to PhD or MD/PhD programs. The program offers faculty-mentored research experiences in the life and physical sciences, social and behavioral sciences, and the humanities at more than twenty research institutions across the country. For participants, SR-EIP is a gateway to ongoing resources, mentoring, and professional networks to support them along their chosen career path. Students work for eight to ten weeks under the guidance of a research mentor, thereby gaining theoretical knowledge and practical training in academic research and scientific experimentation. Students participate in research seminars and professional development activities throughout the program, culminating in the LANS, at which all participants make oral or poster presentations on their summer research project. All students receive a living stipend. Host institutions cover the cost of travel and housing. Applications are competitive and students can apply to up to three research sites through one common application. To participate in SR-EIP, a student must meet several criteria: (1) full-time enrollment in an accredited public or private college or university in the United States or its territories, as recognized by the US Department of Education, with good academic standing (>3.0 GPA); (2) completion of at least two semesters of undergraduate education, with at least one semester remaining, by the start of the summer program; and (3) demonstration of a committed interest to pursue graduate study toward a PhD or MD/PhD Those who are documented US citizens, noncitizen nationals, or permanent residents in possession of an alien registration receipt card (I-551), or another legal document of such status, at the time of application are eligible to participate.

Leadership Alliance National Symposium

All undergraduate participants in the SR-EIP come together with graduate students, postdocs, and doctoral scholars from various research career sectors for the LANS. The symposium is a national networking and professional development event for Leadership Alliance stakeholders at all career stages. The Leadership Alliance continues to innovate and implement programming that (1) builds effective research communication skills, (2) provides tailored professional development responsive to the academic or career needs of each participant, and (3) engages all participants in structured networking and mentoring activities among peers and national role models. The "orientation/networking" session provides an overview of the symposium, and moderators discuss expectations for symposium participants. Undergraduates receive a conference tool before arriving to help them highlight their goals and organize the information and contacts they may obtain during the conference.

To facilitate networking among participants and assist them in maintaining long-term contacts, the Leadership Alliance gives business cards to each undergraduate and graduate student participant. The undergraduate orientation provides mentorship to students on how to navigate a professional conference, as the majority of LANS undergraduates have not previously participated in a national conference. For example, among the 2014 LANS participants, only 18 percent had participated in the Annual Biomedical Research Conference for Minority Students (ABRCMS) and only 4 percent had participated in the Society for Advancement of Chicanos/Hispanics and Native Americans in Science (SACNAS). Networking activities with business cards are planned for participants and LANS coaches. To help rising sophomores navigate the conference, the Leadership Alliance designates doctoral scholars as LANS coaches.

Career Development Workshop for Graduate Students and Postdoctoral Fellows

A successful two-day workshop was created specifically for graduate students and postdoctoral fellows. Postsurvey qualitative data show that, while career development activities existed at participants' institutions, the career development workshop served as a safe space for participants to engage in conversations about research careers outside of academia and develop a new professional network. This new mentoring activity allowed for a recruiting expansion of graduate students and postdoctoral fellows who have not previously participated in a Leadership Alliance program. It includes three core components:

- TLA Talks (TED-style talks) from professionals who represent a variety of career sectors.
- Interactive sessions on career exploration and planning.
- Speed networking to round out workshop activities.

Informal, storytelling sessions are an effective strategy to share diverse professional journeys and insight into varied career options. Using a round-robin format, representatives from academia, as well as public and private sectors, introduce themselves, and participants have time to meet and discuss career opportunities. Before the workshop, the Alliance Executive Office also posts job opportunities to TLA Connect.

Poster and Oral Presentations

One of the goals of the Leadership Alliance is to engage a substantial portion (70 percent) of undergraduate participants in oral presentations, while the remaining participants present posters. All rising sophomores are required to do a poster presentation, unless instructed by their faculty mentor to deliver an oral presentation. The presentation experience at LANS is conducted in a supportive environment and fosters the development of critical communication skills. Students receive constructive feedback from graduate students, who review their posters or moderate their oral presentations. At the research site, all undergraduates will receive a conference guide and presentation guidelines, developed by Leadership Alliance members, to help them navigate the meeting and to provide instruction in effective communication strategies.

Professional Development Sessions

Based on feedback from students and program coordinators on the challenges of successfully applying to graduate school, a mock interview session was introduced and continues to be refined. The graduate school application process is addressed through discipline-specific panels chaired by graduate admissions deans from Leadership Alliance institutions and is complemented by the Leadership Alliance's "Tips on Preparing for and Applying to Graduate School."

Multiple panelists are doctoral scholars from diverse cultural, academic, and career backgrounds in first-career appointments. Featuring these scholars creates a career-affirming atmosphere and networking opportunity for undergraduates. Doctoral scholars discuss their research, share their professional journeys, and reflect on their strategies for success in their careers and life. These events further serve as professional development opportunities for the Leadership Alliance's advanced scholars to present and be recognized on a national level.

The program offers enhanced programming for undergraduates and has added a new session called "Applying to Postbaccalaureate Programs." Increasingly, students are taking time off after completing their undergraduate degree. For many, this additional time is used to help strengthen their applications to graduate programs. Students have the opportunity to engage with a panel of administrators who have completed postbaccalaureate programs to inform students of their postgraduate options. Panelists are now employed in either academia or the industry.

Funding

Students receive a stipend, as well as travel and housing expenses, from the sponsoring research institution. Stipend amounts vary by institution. A grant from the Mellon Foundation provides funding for the stipends for scholars studying in the humanities and social sciences.

Inclusion and Identity

Inclusion

The Leadership Alliance promotes inclusionary practices through its resource guides (such as its "Guide to Mentoring Undergraduates in Summer Research"), professional development sessions at LANS (such as "Can We Talk: Conversations around Race in the Academy"), and continual revision of its inclusionary practices based on the disparate knowledge of Leadership Alliance members. At biannual business meetings, members review everything from application language to best practices in inclusionary housing.

Identity

The Leadership Alliance uses longitudinal pre-/post-data collected from student surveys, and social cognitive career theory (SCCT) is applied as a conceptual framework to examine how research engagement, skill development, and mentorship aspects of a summer research program affect students' commitment to pursue a research career. Self-reported knowledge of research skills, time engaged in research activity, and understanding of and attitudes toward pursuing graduate study were measured in relation to the classification of students' home undergraduate institution, level of students' preexisting research experience, and students' demographic factors. The results of the program provide evidence of specific programmatic components that are beneficial for URM students from varying academic and cultural backgrounds, and the results describe important aspects of summer research programs contributing to students' ability to persist in science careers.

Fostering participants' self-efficacy is a priority of Leadership Alliance programming. Mentors structure research experiences to challenge participants, which results in the growth of their research skills. Longitudinal and peer mentoring ensure that participants always have an opportunity to draw upon necessary insights and best practices for navigating any challenges. Participants routinely report feeling like they can thrive in their research careers after their research experiences.

The Leadership Alliance's collective programs affirm and celebrate all identities through its support of diverse scholars throughout their academic and professional pathway. The Leadership

Alliance believes that a continuum of mentoring leads to a solid legacy of scholars. Leadership Alliance doctoral scholars are the legacy of dedicated partners who have successfully mentored students throughout their academic and career pathways. These students will become the mentors of tomorrow, who will, in turn, guide the next generation. This continuum crosses disciplinary and generational boundaries and, as a consequence, affirms students' identity as scientists and scholars.

In evaluations of the Leadership Alliance, students were prompted to evaluate their confidence surrounding a potential career as a scholar and researcher in both the presurveys and postsurveys. Students were given five prompts and asked their level of agreement with each of the following sentiments:

- I have the ability to have a successful career as a researcher.
- I possess the motivation/persistence required for a career in a research-oriented field.
- I have a strong interest in pursuing a career as a researcher.
- My desire to become a researcher is strong enough to help me overcome barriers I might encounter in pursuit of this career.
- I am confident that I can understand research procedures.
- I am prepared for more demanding research.

When we looked at results, we found significant improvement in each of the prompts between presurvey and postsurvey, which indicates the program improved students' confidence in their research abilities and preparedness for a career in research. The post-survey "strongly agree" results are similar across each of the prompts.

Leveraging the National Symposium, which convenes a diverse mosaic of undergraduates, graduate students, postdoctoral fellows, faculty, and administrators from across the country, the Leadership Alliance is able to orchestrate strategic conversations on (1) strengthening collaborations between academia and industry to develop a diverse workforce, (2) building student confidence and success in STEM through increased self-efficacy and exposure to mastery experiences, (3) increasing discussions around implicit bias and stereotype threat, and (4) leveraging national mentoring programs to expose students to role models and share mentoring experiences.

Coaching Groups

For junior faculty, the Leadership Alliance has collaborated with Dr. Rick McGee and the National Research Mentoring Network (NRMN) to sponsor an NIH Grant Writers Coaching Group. The Grant Writers Coaching Groups are rigorous programs that strive to provide investigators with tailored support that aligns with their current stage of professional development. The model employed for faculty from MSIs involves very direct, specific feedback on multiple iterations of a proposal over three to six months. Participants receive feedback as each part of the proposal is written, starting from an extended session on crafting the "specific aims" page and then progressing through each section of the proposal. Participants can work on most types of NIH proposals (e.g., F32, K99/R00, diversity supplements, other K– and R– mechanisms). Grant writing coaches, who are carefully selected and trained by senior faculty members, provide feedback at each coaching group meeting. Participants are expected to actively write proposals such that sections can be reviewed on a biweekly basis. Coaching groups may provide some guidance on the scientific basis of the proposals, but they are ideally designed to complement input and feedback from colleagues and mentors working in the respective field. Faculty from MSIs are invited to complete the coaching group application, which collects information to help identify coaching expertise. The faculty participants and coaches first meet at the LANS for a two-day meeting, which includes an orientation to the activity, networking with participants and coaches, and small-group working sessions on proposal materials. Coaching groups continue to meet virtually for up to six months. Also, LANS provides an opportunity to continue conversations and networking opportunities among faculty and administrator participants. For example, LANS includes a workshop on implicit bias, which is informed by the *Fair Play* video simulation that allows students to experience academia through the perspective of a Black graduate student.

Voice

The Leadership Alliance is intentional about celebrating and privileging the voices of its community. They have developed a "speaker series" that showcases the expertise of doctoral scholars, as well as postdoctoral fellows and faculty from Leadership Alliance partner institutions, by providing opportunities to speak about their research, career promoting, or topics related to professional development. A list of alumni and their contact information is organized by region (e.g., Northeast, Mid-Atlantic, South), which is a cost-effective approach to organizing seminars that will reach a broader audience. The Leadership Alliance promotes the expertise of faculty from MSIs through conversations with faculty at PWIs, as well as through the exchange of perspectives on concrete strategies for achieving institutional transformation and establishing research or programmatic collaborations.

Given the ongoing debate on the means and processes to achieve a diverse and competitive twenty-first-century workforce, the Leadership Alliance organizes public briefings with leaders in academia, as well as with the public and private sectors. These discussions involve looking at trends to diversify academic institutions at all levels and devising strategies to meet these evolutionary changes. As the landscape of higher education is ever changing, the impact of presidents from diverse institutions, who lend their collective expertise, is critical to the task of examining today's challenges and producing a diverse cadre of professionals to enrich the US workforce.

The aggregation of institutions in regions across the United

States affords the opportunity to engage in collaborative discussions at the regional level. Convening educators who work in conjunction with leaders in the public and private sectors has contributed to efforts to build a solid foundation for sustainable collaborations and to innovate on and expand programming and exposure to role models and mentors in all career sectors. These collaborations support the intellectual growth of faculty and foster opportunities for student-research presentations that will inform a new narrative that unites diverse perspectives and capitalizes on innovative research and scholarship.

Longitudinal Mentoring

LANS has always included activities for graduate students and post-doctoral fellows who are alumni of the SR-EIP and have matriculated into or completed doctorate degrees. While sessions have been designed specifically for their professional development, the activities are often limited in time and scope. Each year, the Leadership Alliance invites alumni to LANS to serve as mentors and role models for undergraduate and graduate student participants. Moreover, the leading role of these scholars is to serve as near-peer mentors. The provided activities are designed to support emerging and early-career PhDs, equipping them with the advanced skills necessary for their professional development as researchers and promoting interdisciplinary networking and intergenerational mentoring. Graduate students and postdoctoral scholars, in their roles as moderators and poster reviewers, are tasked with providing feedback to the undergraduate student presenters using a brief comment form. The goal of this skill-building activity is to enhance their confidence with managing research communication sessions, in both formal and informal interactions, and to reinforce participants' ability to mentor undergraduates effectively. Alliance coordinators, skilled in leadership development, will lead the training session for moderators. Moderator assignments are related to their broad, disciplinary expertise, and the guide "Tips for Moderating a Symposium Session" is distributed before the conference. Workshops for graduate students and doctoral scholars target grant writing, engaging professional societies, and balancing work and life.

Expectations

The overall goal of the Leadership Alliance is to diversify the workforce. To this end, the program supports members of the collegiate, graduate, postdoctoral, and junior-faculty pipeline to succeed in their academic endeavors. Participation in the Leadership Alliance enhances the experience and empowerment of underrepresented groups by leveraging the expertise and infrastructure of the Leadership Alliance consortium. New partnerships with NIH-funded programs were created to develop innovative approaches that (1) improve knowledge development and skill building through scalable and exportable workshops that are designed to introduce first-year undergraduates to the culture and benefits of research; (2) enhance the unique tiered-mentoring structure at LANS to engage the full spectrum of URM scholars, from rising sophomores to junior faculty and early-career professionals; (3) expand efforts to incorporate new career development mentoring for graduate students and postdoctoral fellows by leveraging the expertise of the Beginning Educator Support Team (BEST) Consortium; (4) create new opportunities for faculty from MSIs to develop grant-writing skills; and (5) sustain tracking and monitoring practices to ensure a continuity of mentoring and networking on a national level.

Nearly half (46 percent) of our doctoral scholars work in higher education. Of these, one in every three is either tenured or on the tenure track. More than a quarter (27 percent) have gone into the private sector or industry. Eight percent have entered the public sector. The remaining 19 percent are in other career sectors, such as nonprofits and NGOs. Students who participate in the Leadership Alliance SR-EIP matriculate to graduate school at a high rate

(55 percent). Across the consortium, more than one in every six participants (16.9 percent) enters a graduate program at their summer research site. Currently, the Leadership Alliance is tracking roughly seven hundred former participants in the SR-EIP who are now pursuing PhDs. Each of the Leadership Alliance's programs is rigorously analyzed during the design phase by internal and external evaluators to ensure clear, measurable outcomes.

Collegiate Governmental Academic Pipeline Programs

Centers for Disease Control and Prevention
https://www.cdc.gov/

The Office of Minority Health & Health Equity (OMHHE) at the Centers for Disease Control and Prevention (CDC) sponsors strategic programming, which focuses on professional growth experience through research placements, internships, and fellowship programs. These programs span precollegiate, collegiate, and graduate levels. These programs have been supporting students for more than two decades (Duffus et al., 2014) (https://www.cdc.gov/healthequity/about/index.html).

CDC Undergraduate Public Health Scholars (CUPS) Program supports undergraduate and graduate students who are considering public health careers to benefit a more diverse, better-trained public health workforce (https://www.cdc.gov/healthequity/features/cups/index.html).

Maternal Child Health Careers/Research Initiatives for Student Enhancement-Undergraduate Program (MCHC/RISE-UP) at the Kennedy Krieger Institute is a ten-week summer program that supports rising collegiate students at the junior and senior levels. Recent graduates are also eligible. Students have access to a national network of institutions, including the Kennedy Krieger

---

Institute; the Johns Hopkins University School of Medicine, Nursing, and Public Health; the University of South Dakota Sanford School of Medicine's Center for Disabilities; and the University of California, Davis, MIND Institute in order to learn more about research, clinical, and community practice in public health (https://www.ke nnedykrieger.org/training/programs/center-for-diversity -in-public-health-leadership-training/mchc-rise-up).

Kennedy Krieger Institute's Maternal Child Health-Leadership Education, Advocacy, and Research Network (MCH-LEARN) is a nine-week summer program for undergraduate freshmen and sophomore students. The program includes monthly meetings throughout the academic year. The goal of the program is to increase the number of historically disadvantaged and underrepresented students who enter graduate school in maternal-child health fields (https://www.kennedykrieger.org/sit es/default/files/library/documents/training/13457_MCH -LEARN%20Fact%20Sheet%20Updates%202017_IA _0.pdf).

Dr. James A. Ferguson Emerging Infectious Diseases Research Initiatives for Student Enhancement (RISE) Fellowship Program (Ferguson Fellows) is a ten-week summer program that pairs collegiate students with mentors at the CDC; the Johns Hopkins University School of Medicine, Nursing, and Public Health; the Maryland Department of Health and Mental Hygiene; and the Baltimore City Health Department (https://www .kennedykrieger.org/training/programs/center-for-divers ity-in-public-health-leadership-training/ferguson-rise).

Morehouse College's Project Imhotep is an eleven-week summer program that serves collegiate students at the junior and senior levels as well as postbaccalaureate students by providing discipline specific knowledge related to biostatistics, epidemiology, and occupational safety (https://www.morehouse.edu/academics/centers-and-institutes/public-health-sciences-institute/project-imhotep/).

Morehouse College's Public Health Leaders Fellowship Program (MCPHLFP) is a ten-week summer program for URM collegiate students preparing for leadership roles in the field of public health. Students receive mentorship, practice with statistical software, and complete a research project (https://www.umass.edu/sphhs/2020-public-health-leaders-fellowship-program).

Columbia University Medical Center's Summer Public Health Scholars Program (SPHSP) is a ten-week summer program for juniors and seniors, as well as postbaccalaureate degree students, who are undecided about their career goals. The program includes seminars, lectures, exposure to public-health leaders, opportunities to design an oral presentation and paper, and visits to the CDC (https://www.ps.columbia.edu/education/academic-programs/additional-educational-opportunities/summer-youth-programs/college-post-baccalaureate/summer-public-health-scholars-program-sphsp).

University of Michigan School of Public Health Future Public Health Leaders Program (FPHLP) is a ten-week mentored summer program for collegiate students at the sophomore, junior and senior levels who are undecided about their careers. Postbaccalaureate students are also eligible. Participants receive mentored leadership and career training. They also increase their knowledge, motivation, and commitment to health equity (https://sph.umich.edu/fphlp/).

University of California, Los Angeles, Public Health Scholars Training Program is an eight-week summer program that provides undergraduates with mentored training to explore the various fields of public health through hands-on training, group activities, leadership and professional development activities (https://ph.ucla .edu/prospective-students/ucla-public-health-scholars-tr aining-program).

Public Health Leadership and Learning Undergraduate Student Success (PLLUSS) Program provides a summer research experience for sophomores and juniors to increase interest in public-health research and practice in health equity. Participants are encouraged to produce peer-reviewed articles and attend a national public-health conference (http://www.ugrese arch.umd.edu/documents/PLLUSSProgram.pdf).

Association of State Public Health Nutritionists (ASPHN) Health Equity Internship Program serves undergraduate and graduate students from MSIs and offers the opportunity for students to apply their academic and problem-solving skills to real-life work experiences while serving public-health programs (https://asphn.org/health-equity-internship-program/).

Hispanic Association of Colleges and Universities (HACU) National Internship Program (HNIP) serves students enrolled in undergraduate, graduate, and professional programs https://www.hacu.net/hacu/HNIP.asp).

MELLON MAYS UNDERGRADUATE FELLOWSHIP PROGRAM

The Mellon Mays Undergraduate Fellowship (MMUF) Program is the signature program of the Andrew W. Mellon Foundation. The program is well established and has supported the research and professional development of URM undergraduates for thirty years.

The Mellon Foundation produced a documentary to honor their commitment to diversity and inclusion in the academy, which can be viewed at https://www.youtube.com/watch?v=Ho1kXOAdGVU &feature=youtu.be.

Type

Mellon Mays Undergraduate Fellowship Program	
Place in the Pipeline	Undergraduate students
Type of Students Served	URMs, gender minorities, LIFG
Disciplines Served	Humanities, social sciences
Funding Source	Andrew W. Mellon Foundation
Institutional Structure	PWIs and MSIs
Length of Time in Program	Varies
Geographic Location	Nationwide
Program Accepts New Sites	No
Program Deadlines	Varies
Institutions Served	Forty-eight institutions; three consortia
Website	www.mmuf.org

History

The MMUF Program is the centerpiece of the Andrew W. Mellon Foundation's initiative to increase diversity in the faculty ranks of institutions of higher learning. Established in 1988 by William G. Bowen, then president of the Mellon Foundation, and Henry Drewry, a Mellon program associate, the MMUF Program began with an initial cohort of eight member institutions. Since then, the program has grown to include forty-eight member schools and three consortia, including three South African universities and a consortium of HBCUs within the membership of the United Negro College Fund (UNCF). In 2003, the program received its current name to symbolically connect the program's mission to the achievements of Benjamin Mays, PhD.

Alumni Success

As of 2019, over 5,000 students have been selected as fellows, nearly nine hundred of whom have earned PhDs and over four hundred of whom are now tenured faculty members. Another seven hundred and fifty fellows are currently enrolled in PhD programs. Notable alumni include Jessica Walker (literature, sciences, and arts [LSA]) collegiate fellow, assistant professor, University of Michigan), Jericho Brown (winner of the Pulitzer Prize in Poetry), and Kyra Gaunt (ethnomusicologist, assistant professor, State University of New York at Albany).

Research Preparation

The MMUF Program is designed to give undergraduate fellows intensive and ongoing research experience, beginning at an earlier point in their careers than is typical for most college undergraduates. Fellows are typically selected in their sophomore year based upon their academic ability and their aspiration to pursue a doctorate degree. During their undergraduate years, MMUF fellows are expected to conduct individual research projects under the guidance of faculty mentors, culminating in final thesis papers or presentations during their senior years. Fellows present their research, exchange ideas, and discuss academic life and graduate school preparation.

Workshops

Structured programs include workshops on topics like taking the Graduate Record Examinations (GRE), writing and research, public speaking, effectively working with mentors, presenting at conferences, publishing, and securing graduate school funding.

Conference Presentations

The foundation strongly encourages participation in MMUF's regional conferences for undergraduate fellows. The regional MMUF undergraduate conferences, which in most cases take place annually, bring together MMUF fellows and coordinators from member institutions (https://www.mmuf.org/about/member-ins titutions) in the same geographic region. The conferences allow fellows to present their research, critique the research of other fellows, make connections in the program outside their institutions, and gain an early sense of the academic conference experience. There are seven regional conferences, with some of the more significant regions conducting mini conferences, which split the list of participating schools according to geographic proximity and alternate with the larger all-region events.

Funding

The fellowship provides stipends for research activities, structured programming, support for summer research, and repayment of undergraduate loans up to $10,000.

Postbaccalaureate Training

The MMUF program also includes postcollegiate programming that complements and sustains the undergraduate initiative and supports fellows as they enter and complete graduate school. Through grants to the Social Science Research Council (SSRC) (https://www.ssrc.org/fellowships/view/mellon-mays-predoctoral -research-grants/) and the Woodrow Wilson National Fellowship Foundation (https://woodrow.org/fellowships/mellon/), two non-profit organizations with proven track records in training graduate students and academics, the Mellon Foundation provides PhD-bound MMUF fellows with a targeted array of graduate initiatives, including conferences, writing seminars, and grants designed to support fellows at critical junctures in graduate school. MMUF's support continues into fellows' postdoctoral careers, with two events designed for MMUF PhDs, the SSRC's PhD retreat and Woodrow Wilson Junior Faculty Career Enhancement Fellowship Program.

Inclusion and Identity

Inclusion

Cohort development, in the form of occasions for students to share their aspirations and scholarship with wider academic communities, is a key factor in MMUF's success. The cohort model builds a sense of community among fellows on campus. The support of like-minded peers enhances the growth of scholars. Also, there are institutional reunions for MMUF alumni, which keep fellows connected, motivated, and on track. The program's success is a synergy of commitment and effort among students, faculty, mentors, and coordinators, all of whom work together to change and diversify teaching and scholarship in higher education.

Identity

The MMUF program trains fellows in academic research methods and writing practices and provides activities designed to enhance fellows' socialization into the conventions and expectations of academic culture. As required, fellows meet together regularly with campus coordinators, faculty mentors, and each other. Scheduled forums, colloquia, and social opportunities give students and mentors abundant opportunities for discussion and collaboration. These events incorporate activities to help fellows understand the culture and environment of academia and to provide them with opportunities to develop their intellectual and social skills. This training helps fellows develop skills that will allow them to persist and thrive in graduate school and in faculty careers. Program activities address the specific needs of students from underrepresented groups who are navigating predominantly white institutions. Many fellows also touch upon identity issues in their academic research.

Voice

Fellows in the MMUF Program have the opportunity to disseminate their research through publication in an undergraduate journal. Every year since 1995, the Harvard University MMUF program has published the *MMUF Undergraduate Journal*, a collection of scholarly articles by undergraduate fellows from member institutions. The aim of this rigorously edited journal is not only to serve as a showcase for fellows' research and scholarship but to provide undergraduates with an early glimpse into the processes and expectations of scholarly publishing.

Mentoring

Even though program structures vary from institution to institution, they follow a common set of guidelines. Campus programs are built around the interrelated ideas of scholarly research, faculty mentoring, cohort effect, and community-support networks. The program makes extensive use of faculty and other mentors (e.g., near peer, tiered peer), many of whom are themselves from underrepresented groups and can share their own experiences, challenges, and best practices in establishing themselves as scholars. Mentors provide support with academic or discipline-specific knowledge through direct teaching of academic customs, pitfalls, departmental politics, and taboos. Mentors also provide psychological and emotional support.

Expectations

The objective of the MMUF is to address the problem of under-representation in the academy at the level of college and university faculties. The goal of the MMUF is to increase the number of students from underrepresented minority groups who pursue PhDs and to support the pursuit of PhDs by students who may not come from traditional URM groups but nonetheless demonstrate a commitment toward the goals of the MMUF. These goals require that MMUF fellows earn acceptance to graduate school, earn a degree, obtain employment (industry or other sector), and move to the next level of the pipeline (e.g., college to graduate school, graduate school to postdoctoral research, graduate school to faculty). Fellows are expected to accomplish several academic goals, including completing courses, increasing academic skill area(s), conducting research, persisting through their current degree program(s), and completing a capstone or thesis project. Fellows are also expected to enhance their professional development by developing intellectual property, publishing scholarly work as defined by an academic discipline, presenting at a conference or symposium, mentoring program alumni, and persisting in research (e.g., applying to other research programs, completing other mentored research experiences).

Fellows and coordinators with MMUF report to the program annually on their progress, providing data on program outcomes. The program regularly uses this data to compute statistics (e.g., the percentage of fellows continuing into PhD programs) for each member campus and asks underperforming institutions to submit plans for improvement.

Collegiate Governmental Academic Pipeline Programs

Health and Human Services
https://www.hhs.gov/

The US Department of Health and Human Services sponsors programming through their Bureau of Health Workforce (BHW) to improve the health of URM communities and to prepare a workforce committed to serving underserved populations. Several programs are targeted toward developing an educational pipeline for URMs in health professions. The National Health Careers Opportunity Program (HCOP) Academies serves precollegiate, collegiate, postbaccalaureate, and graduate students.

Health Careers Opportunity Program (HCOP) assists students from disadvantaged backgrounds with entering a health profession by offering a variety of programming (https://www.hrsa.gov/grants/find-funding/hrsa-18-007).

Indian Health Service

American Indians Into Psychology Program (Indians Into Psychology Doctoral Education) is a five-year program designed to recruit and train students into the discipline of Clinical Psychology. The program is targeted toward collegiate and graduate students who identify as Native American and Alaska Natives (https://www.ihs.gov/dhps/dhpsgrants/america nindianpsychologyprogram/).

FLORIDA A&M UNIVERSITY GRADUATE FEEDER SCHOLARS PROGRAM

The Florida A&M University (FAMU) Graduate Feeder Scholars Program (GFSP) is a well-established program that has supported the research and professional development of URM undergraduate students to advance into graduate studies for many years. It is a national partnership agreement with more than forty universities. The consortium develops a cadre of students who are committed to pursuing master's and doctorate degrees. The overall goal of the GFSP is to ensure that students at FAMU who are inducted into the GFSP have the opportunity to earn a graduate degree in their field of choice, fully funded. Therefore, this program prepares scholars for all aspects of graduate education prior to applying for their program of choice.

Type

Florida A&M University Graduate Feeder Scholars Program	
Place in the Pipeline	Collegiate–Graduate
Type of Students Served	URMs, gender minorities, LIFG
Disciplines Served	Not discipline specific
Funding Source	Florida A&M University
Institutional Structure	PWIs and MSIs
Length of Time in Program	Varies
Geographic Location	Southeast
Program Accepts New Sites	Yes
Program Deadlines	Varies
Program Benefits	Stipend, tuition waiver
Institutions Served	Serves students at FAMU but is a feeder to forty-one-member consortia
Website	http://www.famu.edu/index.cfm?graduatestudies&GraduateFeederScholarsProgram

History

Two years into his young administration, Frederick S. Humphries, PhD, the eighth president of FAMU, worked tirelessly to reestablish the brand of the university. His goal was to attract the nation's top young scholars of color (both student and faculty). To achieve this goal, he first needed to create programs at the university to entice these scholars to choose FAMU over some of the nation's most prestigious colleges. Therefore, in 1987, Humphries elevated the Division of Graduate Studies, created in 1957, to the School of Graduate Studies and Research (SGSR) and Continuing Education. His objective was to enhance graduate offerings at the university while also attracting top researchers in the nation to the university. Humphries also gave Charles U. Smith, PhD, the newly appointed dean of SGSR and Continuing Education, the charge to establish partnerships with universities with graduate programs that FAMU did not offer. These partnerships aimed to create a pipeline of opportunity for African American scholars who began their academic pursuit at FAMU. This aim would fully support Humphries's recruiting mission by providing scholars of color an opportunity to have their entire education fully funded—from the bachelor's to doctorate degree. He also wanted to contribute to the academy by facilitating the training of the next generation of professors and researchers who were URMs. Thus, the FAMU Graduate Feeder Scholars Program was created.

Since its inception, the GFSP has developed partnerships with over forty research universities throughout the nation, creating graduate and post-graduate opportunities for FAMU students for nearly a generation. In July 2015, David H. Jackson Jr., PhD, a former GFSP fellow, was appointed as the associate provost of graduate education and dean for the school of SGSR and Continuing Education. His priority was to reinvigorate GFSP by making it relevant for the twenty-first-century college student. Therefore, in the fall of 2017, he appointed Reginald K. Ellis, PhD, as his assistant dean and liaison for GFSP. Since 2015, more than four hundred fifty students have been inducted into the program, with a number of them receiving the FAMU Feeder Fellowship at a partner institution.

Alumni Success

Most recently, Taylor Darks (FAMU class of '19), a former women's basketball player, earned the FAMU Feeder Fellowship to attend Florida State University to pursue a doctorate in sociology. Likewise, Khayah Peters (FAMU class of '18) earned the FAMU Feeder Fellowship at the University of Central Florida to pursue a doctorate in physical therapy. Dean Jackson is proud of these scholars' accomplishments and even more excited about the potential success of each GFSP scholar. Since its inception, GFSP has served nearly 3,500 students. Notable alumni include Chanta Haywood, PhD (vice president for institutional advancement and research, vice president for external affairs, and executive director, Fort Valley State University), David H. Jackson Jr. (professor of history, political science, public administration, geography, and African American studies, FAMU), Darius J. Young, PhD (associate professor of history, FAMU), and Taylor Darks, PhD (author, activist, athlete).

Research Preparation

This program creates opportunities for undergraduate and graduate students to gain admission into and funding for graduate programs FAMU does not offer.

Workshops

The program includes a curriculum-based workshop series, and students are required to attend five workshops. Three of the workshops require students to submit a writing assignment that has been revised based on feedback from the workshop. The three assignment-based workshops are called "Statement of Purpose," "Research Writing Sample," and "CV/Résumé." In partnership with the university's career center and the Quality Enhancement Plan,

GFSP ensures experts are leading these workshops. Dean Jackson's vision for the program includes professional development workshops to ensure that students are prepared for the application process at research-intensive universities and are prepared to succeed in the program of their choice after admission. Each workshop ends with a program evaluation, which is reported directly to the Office of University Assessment. The program uses these reports to create better programing for Graduate Feeder Scholars.

Funding

Students are awarded a stipend of $7,250. Scholars also receive a tuition waiver up to twelve credit hours as well as a health insurance subsidy. These financial incentives are available during fall and spring semesters only.

Inclusion and Identity

Inclusion

Conferences are held annually for scholars. During conferences, several workshops are dedicated to helping scholars understand how they fit into the larger academic culture. An example of a topic that is included in the workshops is the transition from HBCUs to PWIs. Alumni serve as speakers during annual conferences.

Identity

The GFSP provides an opportunity for graduate professors at traditional universities to interact with URM students at an HBCU throughout their matriculation. Many partner schools have campus visitation programs that fund the cost of travel, lodging, and meals so students can tour the campus while meeting with faculty, staff, and students. The facilitators of the workshop series are faculty members who have experienced the graduate school process themselves. Many questions about the graduate school experience are answered in these settings.

Voice

GFSP includes language that requires each partner institution to have an on-campus liaison. The liaison works directly with scholars to address any issue that arises once they have been accepted into the program. Before being inducted into GFSP, many students are unaware of the graduate admissions application process. The program not only prepares them for the graduate application process but it also prepares them for the expectations of graduate school.

Mentoring

There is a strong near-peer mentorship component to the program. Program representatives at each institution may serve as mentors or advisors. Staff, including deans, also serve as mentors for the program. Alumni serve as workshop speakers. Mentoring is an additional way to enhance the voice of GFSP participants.

Expectations

The goal of this program is to provide greater opportunity for students at FAMU to continue their education beyond undergraduate studies. The expectation is that scholars will present at a conference or symposium, publish a scholarly work as defined by their academic discipline, increase an academic skill area(s), earn acceptance to graduate school, earn a degree, and move to the next level of the pipeline. As previously stated, GFSP has serviced nearly thirty five hundred students since 1987. Moreover, legions of scholars have gone onto graduate study and are now serving as mentors in their particular field of study.

Collegiate Governmental Academic Pipeline Programs

National Institutes of Health
https://www.nih.gov/

Several branches of the National Institutes of Health (NIH) offer extramural research training opportunities. We highlight examples of NIH initiatives provided through various branches. This section highlights the opportunities for community college, undergraduate, and postbaccalaureate students. These initiatives are for both institutions and students.

Bridges to the Baccalaureate Research Training Program (T34) provides support to institutions to help students making the transition from two-year community colleges to four-year baccalaureate programs. Awards are made to domestic private and public educational institutions. Partnerships or consortiums must include at least two colleges or universities (https://www.nigms.nih.gov/Research/Mechanisms/Pages/BridgesBaccalaureate.aspx).

Research Training Initiative for Student Enhancement (RISE) Program supports research-active institutions in training a diverse pool of students to complete PhDs in biomedical fields (https://www.nigms.nih.gov/Training/RISE).

Maximizing Access to Research Careers (MARC) Undergraduate Student Training in Academic Research (U-STAR) is an undergraduate training program for institutions with a research-intensive environment. The goal of the MARC program is to train a diverse group of undergraduates to complete their baccalaureate degrees and transition to higher degrees (PhD, MD/PhD) in biomedical research. See Hall, Miklos, Oh, & Gaillard (2016) for outcomes of the MARC U-STAR program (https://www.nigms.nih.gov/training/marc/pages/FAQs.aspx#a1).

Minority Health and Health Disparities Research Training Program (MHRT) provides support to domestic institutions to provide domestic and international training opportunities for undergraduate, postbaccalaureate, and graduate students, as well as to residents and fellows (https://www.nimhd.nih.gov/programs/extramural/domestic-international-research-training.html).

Postbaccalaureate Research Education Program (PREP) supports those from underrepresented or disadvantaged backgrounds who recently received a baccalaureate degree to pursue a research doctorate in biomedical sciences. Grants are made to research-intensive institutions (https://www.nigms.nih.gov/training/PREP/Pages/default.aspx).

National Institute of Diabetes and Digestive Kidney Diseases (NIDDK) Diversity Summer Research Training Program (DSRTP) provides undergraduate students from underrepresented areas with a mentored research experience in one of two labs (Bethesda, Maryland, or Phoenix, Arizona) for ten weeks. Participants present their research to the NIH community (https://www.niddk.nih.gov/research-funding/research-programs/diversity-programs/research-training-opportunities-students/diversity-summer-research-training-program-dsrtp).

National Institute on Drug Abuse (NIDA) Recruitment & Training Program for Under-Represented Populations (RTURP) offers students enrolled in high school, college, graduate school, or medical school a paid, mentored research position for eight to ten weeks (https://irp.drugabuse.gov/organization/diversity/recruitment-under-represented-populations/).

See figure 2 in Valentine, Lund, & Gammie (2016) for an illustration of NIH programs across the full pipeline spectrum and Gazley et al. (2014) for a review of the programs.

INSTITUTE FOR THE RECRUITMENT OF TEACHERS

The Institute for Recruitment of Teachers (IRT) was launched in order to reduce the underrepresentation of minority groups (e.g., African American, Latinx, and Native American) who entered into teaching, administrative, and counseling professions. The institute comprises a consortium of forty-three colleges and universities and partners with other organizations, such as the Leadership Alliance, the Mellon Mays Undergraduate Fellowship Program, the Ronald E. McNair Post-Baccalaureate Achievement Program, the Gates Millennium Scholars Program, Bonner Scholar Program, and the Woodrow Wilson-Rockefeller Brothers Fund Fellowship for Aspiring Teachers of Color.

Type

Institute for Recruitment of Teachers	
Place in the Pipeline	Undergraduate students
Type of Students Served	URMs, gender minorities, LIFG
Disciplines Served	Education, humanities, social sciences, mathematics, computer science
Funding Source	Phillips Academy; individual donors
Institutional Structure	PWIs and MSIs
Length of Time in Program	One year
Geographic Location	Nationwide
Program Accepts New Sites	Yes
Program Deadlines	March 1
Institutions Served	Forty-three member consortia
Website	www.andover.edu

History

The IRT was founded in 1990 by Kelly Wise, dean of faculty at Phillips Academy and later the executive director of IRT, with a mission to "deepen the pool of talented URMs entering the teaching profession in our country." The institute was designed to increase the number of African American, Latinx, and Native American students pursuing advanced degrees in teaching, counseling, and administrative careers at both the K12 and university levels. In 2004, IRT reaffirmed its commitment to eradicating racial disparities at all levels of education. The institute also made a commitment to select outstanding college students and recent graduates from all backgrounds, including Asian and white students, who are committed to these ideals. Over 2,401 students have been served since the inception of the program.

Alumni Success

It is important to underscore the extraordinary record of the program. Since IRT's inception in 1990, nearly every IRT applicant has been admitted to at least one graduate school, and most have been admitted to four or more. Approximately 90 percent of these students have received full tuition waivers and partial-to-full fellowship funding for up to six years of graduate study. The Institute has produced a significant number of alumni at both the master's and PhD levels. Approximately nine hundred alumni have completed their terminal master's degrees, and over 340 PhDs have been awarded to IRT scholars. Alumni serve as faculty and administrators nationwide, including twenty-seven tenured faculty and ninety-one tenure-track faculty. To date, more than forty IRT alumni are leading programs, departments, and institutions, as associate directors, directors, deans, principals, superintendents, and even campus presidents. Notable alumni include Lisa Woolfolk, PhD (associate professor of English, University of Virginia), Brandy Monk-Payton, PhD (assistant professor of communication and media studies, Fordham University), and Chera D. Reid, PhD (director of strategic learning, research, and evaluation, Kresge Foundation).

Research Preparation

Workshops

The Institute offers two programs: the Summer Workshop and the Associate Program. The Summer Workshop is for college juniors and seniors who intend to pursue graduate study. Each year, twenty-five to thirty interns are selected by IRT to participate in an intense, four-week summer workshop at Phillips Academy before or after their senior year of undergraduate study. The workshop typically runs in July. Included in the workshop are lectures, seminar discussions, small-group meetings, writing conferences, films, debates, practice teaching sessions, and presentations by nationally known educators, scholars, poets, and artists. Embedded within the workshop is a graduate-level curriculum comprising critical, cultural, and educational theory.

Students prepare for the GRE and work on their statements of purpose. All IRT scholars receive ten to twelve application fee waivers to apply to schools within the consortium. All IRT scholars also receive a discount on their GRE test. Interns in the program are provided free GRE preparation, and all IRT scholars receive a discount for GRE course preparation. Interns are also provided with personalized and interactive advising with editing statements of purpose, résumés, and writing samples.

The institute supports students throughout the graduate-school application process. At the end of the third week in July, the IRT hosts its annual Recruiters' Weekend, which is attended by more than sixty academic deans and graduate admissions representatives from consortium institutions who are eager to speak with potential candidates about their graduate programs. There is a chance for students to develop teaching and facilitation skills.

Geared toward rising seniors, recent college graduates, students with master's degrees, and working professionals, the Associate Program is a yearlong program that prepares students to pursue graduate education. Approximately ninety students enroll in the Associate Program.

Funding and Support

Participants receive a $1,200 stipend, travel expenses, and room and board.

Inclusion and Identity

Inclusion

In an effort to ensure an inclusive and safe space, IRT utilizes the campus of Phillips Academy to their advantage. Interns have access to the resources of the campus. In addition, IRT is lucky to work with Catherine Wong, PhD, from Boston College, who is chair of the consortium. The consortium is a group of graduate schools and universities that recruit IRT scholars. Every year, consortium representatives come to the Summer Workshop to recruit IRT scholars and to meet with other representatives. The meeting provides an opportunity for collaboration and brainstorming between institutions.

Identity

The advising process for IRT participants allows them to gain insight and awareness of graduate school expectations and culture. Interns also attend "chalk talks," which are opportunities for faculty to discuss their experiences with graduate school and navigating the professorate.

Voice

The institute believes teacher diversity contributes to inclusive classroom environments. Interns use the Summer Workshop curriculum to their advantage. The curriculum and facilitation by IRT faculty enable students to enter a classroom space unlike any other. Interns also receive constant feedback and support from faculty prior to applying to graduate school. Associates receive individual counseling from July through April, which focuses on the application process, essay writing, and admissions and matriculation decisions. The institute's approach is to demystify the process for all students, while still encouraging their voice and choice in programs.

Mentoring and Counseling

In addition to the Summer Workshop curriculum, the strategic plan for IRT includes activities to sustain professional development and a mentoring network of intellectuals, educators, advocates, and partners. The institute offers extensive counseling as individuals navigate their graduate education. Students receive individual counseling related to their interests. Scholars participate in one-on-one advising with IRT staff and a trusted group of advisors. Advisors coach students on finding the best fit for their graduate school program, focusing on each student's identity and research interests. Alumni testimonials suggest that this support system gave them a greater sense of self-confidence.

Alumni impact various academic disciplines. They pursue careers as educators (e.g., teachers, principals, superintendents) as well as serve as counselors and school psychologists. They become role models in these settings. Alumni meet during the IRT alumni weekend to get additional professional development to support and to discuss their careers with Summer Workshop attendees.

Expectations

The goal of IRT is to diversify the teaching workforce. Scholars are expected to commit to a career in education and to graduate from graduate school. Exposing participants to IRT's rigorous training and support helps students committed to teaching with a social justice perspective complete their graduate school applications and persist through their graduate programs. The outcomes for IRT include the number of advanced degrees pursued by alumni, the types of influential positions held by alumni, and progress toward tenure for alumni who are on the tenure track. Outcomes are documented in an annual report.

Collegiate Governmental Academic Pipeline Programs

National Aeronautics and Aerospace Administration
https://www.nasa.gov/

The Minority University Research and Education Project (MURAP) invests in institutions to recruit and retain URM students, including girls, women, and persons with disabilities, into STEM fields. Awards are granted to HBCUs, MSIs, Asian American, Native American, Pacific Islander-serving institutions (AANAPISIs), and tribal colleges and universities (TCUs).

NASA Community College Aerospace Scholars offers an opportunity to visit NASA. The program also includes an online course to help with the transition between a two-year and four-year degree. Online STEM-related workshops are also offered during the year (https://www.nasa.gov/stem-ed-resources/nasa-community-college-aerospace-scholars.html).

Minority University Research and Education Project (MUREP) is designed to financially support underserved undergraduates, including girls, women, and persons with disabilities through a variety of initiatives at MSIs, HBCUs, AANAPISIs, HSIs, and TCUs. Competitive grants allow institutions to support mentored research, academics, and technological capacity (https://www.nasa.gov/stem/murep/home/index.html).

National Science Foundation
https://www.nsf.gov/

The National Science Foundation (NSF) provides several funding opportunities that link URM students to research training experiences with faculty across the United States. These funding opportunities are sponsored through NSF's Broadening Participation in Research in STEM and HBCU Excellence in Research Programs.

Broadening Participation in Engineering (BPE) is NSF's effort to increase the pool of STEM innovators nationwide. Since 2013, grant awards have been linked to expanding access to STEM education, addressing the career needs of STEM professionals and addressing STEM students' identity and motivation (https://www .nsf.gov/funding/pgm_summ.jsp?pims_id=505632).

Historically Black Colleges and Universities-Undergraduate Program (HBCU-UP) was established by NSF in 2000 as a way to diversify the STEM workforce. The program provides awards to develop, implement, and study models and approaches that improve the preparation and success of URMs in STEM graduate programs and the workforce (https://hbcu-up.org/).

Louis Stokes Alliance for Minority Participation (LSAMP) is a grant program to develop strategies to increase the quality and quantity of URM students who complete baccalaureate degrees in STEM and who continue on to graduate studies in these fields. The program has over forty-five alliances and over four hundred participating institutions. It was established in 1991 in honor of congressman Louis Stokes (https://www.nsf.gov/fundi ng/pgm_summ.jsp?pims_id=13646).

> **Significant Opportunities in Atmospheric Research and Science (SOARS)** is an undergraduate-to-graduate bridge program that broadens participation in the atmospheric and related sciences (meteorology, chemistry, physics, engineering, mathematics, ecology, and the social sciences) (https://soars.ucar.edu/).

CALIFORNIA PRE-DOCTORAL PROGRAM'S SALLY CASANOVA SCHOLARSHIP

The California Pre-Doctoral Program's Sally Casanova Scholarship was created to grow the number of prospective California State University (CSU) faculty. The scholarship assists CSU students who have experienced economic and educational disadvantages. The program prepares students to succeed in doctoral programs and prepares them for teaching and research careers at the college or university level.

Type

California Pre-Doctoral Program's Sally Casanova Scholarship	
Place in the Pipeline	Collegiate
Type of Students Served	URMs, gender minorities, LIFG
Disciplines Served	Business management, communication, computer and information sciences, education, engineering, humanities, life sciences, mathematics, neuroscience, physical sciences, social sciences
Funding Source	CSU Office of the Chancellor and California Lottery Funds
Institutional Structure	N/A
Length of Time in Program	Annual
Geographic Location	California
Program Accepts New Sites	No
Program Deadlines	Applications are available in early December. The deadline is late February.
Institutions Served	CSU system
Website	https://www2.calstate.edu/csu-system/faculty-staff/predoc

History

The California Pre-Doctoral Program was designed in 1989 to increase diversity within the pool of university faculty by supporting the doctoral aspirations of students in the California State University system. Each year, the California Pre-Doctoral Program awards funds to a limited number of juniors, seniors, and graduate students enrolled in the CSU system. These funds are designated to enable current students to explore doctoral study, and the funds prepare students to succeed in doctoral programs in their chosen field of study. Students who are selected for this prestigious award are designated Sally Casanova Scholars as a tribute to Sally Casanova, PhD.

Alumni Success

The program is now in its thirtieth year and has served 2,254 students. Notable alumni include Stephanie Evans (director for the Institute of Women's, Gender, and Sexuality Studies, Georgia State University), Trevor Auldridge (Americorps, W. E. B. Du Bois Institute at Harvard, University of California, Santa Barbara, doctoral student), and Anibal Serrano (*Small Wars Journal*, El Centro Fellow).

Research Participation

The program prepares both undergraduate and graduate students through three primary mechanisms: mentoring, research-related activities, and campus visits. Students are paired with a faculty member in their respective discipline. There are also opportunities to participate in a fully funded, collaborative research experience. Campus visits to doctoral-granting institutions allow students to prepare for doctoral-level research and preview the roles and expectations of faculty members on CSU campuses.

Those scholars who are not admitted into a doctoral program are provided with an opportunity to participate in a fully funded, eight-week summer research experience at any doctoral-granting institution in the United States at the end of their scholarship year.

Workshops

Students have access to professional development workshops held during the California Forum for Diversity in Graduate Education. Topics are related to graduate admissions and tips for succeeding in graduate school.

Funding

Funding from this program can be used for presenting research at professional conferences and symposia. Additional financial support is available for GRE preparation courses and exams, graduate school application fees and materials, and membership to professional organizations and journal subscriptions.

Inclusion and Identity

Inclusion

The program is nondiscriminatory in mission and in practice, both in the system-wide office and on each campus. Scholars work inclusively with faculty mentors in their respective discipline who help guide their personal and academic journeys through the academy. Scholars are recognized and supported at all levels. They are provided with opportunities and resources designed to enhance their academic journey. Scholars are also invited to a predoctoral dinner and reception the Friday before the forum.

Identity

Through multiple networking opportunities and events, held both CSU system wide and in conjunction with the California Forum for

Diversity in Graduate Education, the scholars are invited to educational sessions supporting their self-identity and self-efficacy. In their testimonials, many scholars say that the Sally Casanova Scholarship helped with their personal growth and increased their confidence as a scholar.

Voice

The title of Sally Casanova Scholar brings with it a sense of prestige and elite recognition for scholars. Scholars face barriers, such as imposter syndrome and feelings of ineptness, during their academic journey. Workshops, training, and mentoring are provided to help prepare scholars for discussions with faculty and recruiters from doctoral-granting institutions. These diverse scholars have the opportunity each year to participate in the California Forum for Diversity in Graduate Education and are introduced to recruiters from doctoral-granting institutions across the nation. They are provided with an exclusive evening event where they present their research topics and have one-on-one meetings with recruiters. As highly sought-after CSU students, these scholars are provided with fee waivers and cost-free visits to the campuses that are actively recruiting them.

Mentoring

In addition to workshops and training, one-on-one mentoring is provided. Each scholar works inclusively with a faculty mentor in their respective discipline who helps guide their personal and academic journey through the academy. Mentors assist with choosing a doctoral program or institution and guide scholars to understand the life of a graduate student and the expectations of faculty members (teaching, research, and service). In addition, the faculty mentor assists in the dissemination of research and exposure to prospective faculty as doctoral-level mentors. Counseling and retention practices are provided at the campus level by faculty mentors and campus coordinators for the Pre-Doctoral Program. Occasionally, the director will provide support to students who reach out and ask.

Expectations

The goal of the program is to increase the diversity of the pool of newly minted PhDs from which CSU draws its faculty. While not required, the participants are strongly encouraged to pursue their doctorate degree. Each year, around 40 percent of the scholars are accepted into fully funded PhD programs. The program is designed for students interested in obtaining a research doctorate. International students or students interested in obtaining a professional degree (e.g., law, medicine, dentistry, pharmacy) or an MBA degree, for example, are not eligible. The ultimate goal is to experience the roles and expectations of CSU faculty members.

Collegiate Governmental Academic Pipeline Programs

US Department of Agriculture
https://www.usda.gov/

The US Department of Agriculture (USDA) is a long-standing partner with nationwide collegiate programs.

Minorities in Agriculture, Natural Resources and Related Sciences (MANRRS) promotes diversity in college students' academic, professional, and leadership skills. Students can participate in an internship program and annual conference (https://info.manrrs.org/summer blminternship).

US Department of Education
https://www.ed.gov/
TRIO Programs

The Department of Education grants a variety of programs to public and private institutions nationwide to support education at the collegiate level and the transition to graduate programs. Programs originated in the 1960s with the signing of the Educational Opportunity Act. More programming was funded into the 1990s. See McElroy & Arnesto (1998) for a review of the programs.

- **The Student Support Services (SSS) Program** provides college students with opportunities for academic development, assistance with basic college requirements, and motivation toward the successful completion of their postsecondary education. Programs have the flexibility to offer academic tutoring programs and counseling programs for parents and students. The goal of SSS is to increase college retention and graduation rates (https://www2.ed.gov/programs/triostudsupp/index.html).

- **The Ronald E. McNair Post-Baccalaureate Achievement Program** prepares college students for doctoral studies by involving them in mentoring, research, academic enrichment activities, and conferences and workshops (https://www2.ed.gov/programs/triomcnair/index.html).

- **Veterans Upward Bound** assists veterans with the development of academic and other necessary skills to obtain a postsecondary education. Programs provide mentoring, tutoring, counseling, and academic instruction in core content areas. Nationwide, the program supports community colleges and public and private universities and agencies (https://www2.ed.gov/programs/triovub/index.html).

US Department of Commerce
https://www.commerce.gov/

National Oceanic and Atmospheric Administration (NOAA) Educational Partnership Program with Minority Serving Institutions (EPP/MSI) Undergraduate Scholarship Program supports rising juniors enrolled at MSIs studying a STEM discipline related to NOAA's mission. Students can receive funding for two years to conduct research at a NOAA facility. United States nationals are eligible to apply. Students receive funding to support an eleven-week summer internship, including a housing allowance. Other activities include conference travel and research presentation (https://www.noaa.gov/office-education/epp-msi/undergraduate-scholarship).

US Department of Energy
https://www.energy.gov/

Environmental Management Minority Serving Institutions Partnership Program (MSIPP) offer ten-week STEM internships at the Department of Energy (DOE) national laboratories for college and graduate students attending accredited minority-serving institutions. Other activities include lab tours, professional development workshops, seminars, lectures, and social activities (https://www.anl.gov/education/minority-serving-institutions-partnership-program).

ANNUAL BIOMEDICAL RESEARCH CONFERENCE FOR MINORITY STUDENTS

The Annual Biomedical Research Conference for Minority Students (ABCRMS) is a conference that provides professional development opportunities for students from community colleges and four-year colleges and universities as well as postbaccalaureate students, graduate students, and their faculty mentors. The conference is one of the largest professional conferences for URM students who look to pursue advanced training in the biomedical and behavioral sciences, including STEM.

Type

Annual Biomedical Research Conference for Minority Students	
Place in the Pipeline	Precollegiate, Collegiate, PostBaccalaureate, Graduate
Type of Students Served	URMs, gender minorities, LIFG
Disciplines Served	Engineering, life sciences, mathematics, neuroscience, physical sciences, public health, social and behavioral sciences
Funding Source	National Institutes of Health
Institutional Structure	Not restricted
Length of Time in Program	Annual
Geographic Location	Nationwide
Program Accepts New Sites	No
Program Deadlines	Friday after Labor Day for abstracts; third week of August for travel awards
Institutions Served	Nationwide
Website	http://www.abrcms.org/

History

ABCRMS was established in 2001. In order to move STEM fields forward, it is crucial to increase the diversity of people working in these fields, which means the inclusion of URMs, veterans, and people with disabilities. Social and behavioral sciences and public health were added as an additional area of emphasis, as the need for URM professionals in these areas has grown. The first conference was hosted by the American Society for Microbiology (ASM) in 2001, and it was founded to encourage URM, first-generation, veteran, and disabled students to pursue higher education in STEM. Today, ABRCMS is one of the largest professional conferences for underrepresented students, and it provides program directors and faculty with the tools they need to help their students succeed.

Alumni Success

The first ABRCMS in 2001 drew approximately 1,800 participants, while, in 2018, ABRCMS brought together approximately 4,700 attendees. Since 2001, ABRCMS has served approximately 36,000 students. Notable alumni include Victor Ocasio Ramirez, PhD (postdoctoral fellow, Duke University) and Shelsa Marcel (Gilliam Fellowship winner, bioinformatics and computational biology graduate student, University of North Carolina). There are several types of programs to prepare attendees for graduate study, including professional development sessions, a graduate school recruitment fair, and virtual workshops and sessions, which are housed on the conference website (http://www.abrcms.org/).

Research Preparation

The conference was developed to provide URM students in STEM fields with opportunities to demonstrate scientific knowledge, learn about research in the biomedical and behavioral sciences, develop professional skills, and access professional networks. The conference delivers these opportunities by (1) encouraging undergraduates to pursue advanced training and careers in the biomedical and behavioral sciences and (2) providing faculty mentors, advisors, and program leaders with resources for facilitating student success.

Highlights from the four-day conference include:

- Poster and oral presentations by undergraduate and postbaccalaureate students
- Scientific and professional development sessions

- Over 400 exhibit booths
- Networking and mentoring opportunities
- Plenary speakers
- Conference programming tracks for undergraduates, graduates, and postdoctoral scientists, as well as nonstudents
- An awards banquet

During the conference, students are exposed to notable speakers who are pioneers in their fields or who have been engaged in groundbreaking efforts to support science, innovation, or societal change. These speakers include Neil deGrasse Tyson, PhD (Hayden Planetarium, New York, New York), Mae Jemison, PhD (the first African American woman astronaut), the Honorable Ambassador Andrew Young (a former congressman and notable civil rights leader), and the family of Henrietta Lacks (an African American woman whose cancer cells led to important medical breakthroughs).

Webinars

In 2018, ABRCMS established ABRCMS Online. The goal of ABRCMS Online is to expand programming to a broader audience, especially to those who may not be able to afford to attend the in-person conference.

Funding and Support

The conference offers travel awards for first-time student presenters. Presenters can receive full or partial travel awards. These awards cover some combination of housing, registration, and airfare costs. Faculty mentors can also apply for Judge Travel Awards. Award deadlines are usually before the abstract deadlines.

Inclusion and Identity

Inclusion

The conference is very inclusive and considered a leader in promoting and ensuring diversity in STEM. The environment at ABRCMS promotes diversity and inclusion in all programming and offerings, and, during the meeting, the environment is structured to empower attendees, including students and faculty mentors. The conference infuses inclusivity into their programming by offering designated spaces (e.g., prayer and meditation spaces for different religious faiths, lactation rooms, etc.) and diverse menus (e.g., vegan, nut free) that demonstrate that all are welcome at the conference.

Identity

The conference is unique because the number of URM students, speakers, faculty mentors, and exhibitors in attendance exceeds the number of URM scientists who are typically represented on most campuses (Casad, Chang, & Pribbenow, 2016). The attendance at ABRCMS has exceeded five thousand in recent years. Frequently attending and winning awards at ABRCMS promotes one's ability to identify as a scientist and is related to self-efficacy. There is a positive relationship between the frequency of ABRCRMS attendance and both research self-confidence and science self-efficacy (Casad et al., 2016). Greater research self-efficacy was, in turn, related to students' intentions to pursue graduate school.

Voice

Mentoring

The conference promotes informal mentoring. Students and mentors find each other during ABRCMS and establish informal mentoring relationships. The seating during the dining sessions is conducive to networking through informal conversations. Testimonials from attendees suggest that talking to new people helps build future collaborative relationships. Returning ABRCMS attendees have demonstrated a greater sense of belonging in science fields compared to first-time attendees (Casad et al., 2016). The active learning atmosphere of ABCRMS also creates a higher sense of belonging for URM students than non-URM students (Casad et al., 2016).

Expectations

The program continues to stay fresh and up to date, so participants gain new information each year. Students are encouraged to set short-term and long-term goals, and sessions are organized to teach them how to master goal setting. Participation in programmed ABRCMS events enhances students' ability to disseminate their research through research presentations. Students also develop a network through contact with faculty, peers, and program speakers.

Collegiate Academic Pipeline Programs

Robert Wood Johnson Foundation
https://www.rwjf.org/

Summer Health Professions Education Program supports rising freshmen or sophomores pursuing a health career. Students receive a stipend ($600) and participate in small-group clinical rotations as well as assistance with the admissions process to a professional school (https://www.shpep.org/). A free online version of the program is available.

SUMMARY

All of the programs discussed prepare students to obtain their baccalaureate degree and to enter graduate or professional school. Undergraduate research experiences have been demonstrated to contribute to URM students' understanding of the research process, awareness of what college and graduate school is like, and increased confidence in pursuing their vocational aspirations (Carpi, Ronan, Falconer, & Lents, 2017; Russell, Hancock, & McCollough, 2007). The presence of other commonalities, like participation in research experiences, receipt of faculty mentor support, and connection to a cohort of peers who have similar characteristics, all help in college retention and graduation (Palmer, Maramba, & Dancy, 2011; Perna et al, 2009; Rincon, 2018). Each program provides topical workshops or seminars related to academic identity or self-identity. Some programs utilize alumni for these workshops, whether as facilitators or notable speakers, and alumni are used as role models. Students are exposed to the culture of graduate school and are assisted with relating to this culture by their mentors. Students are empowered through research presentation and publication opportunities. All of these components combined have led to successful outcomes (e.g., college retention, college graduation, graduate school admission, terminal degrees granted).

There are additional experiential learning opportunities provided to undergraduate students that give a foundation for student success in college and graduate school. These opportunities include community college bridge programs and course-based undergraduate research experiences (CUREs). Bridge programs that link community colleges to four-year institutions are starting points for many URM students, including Hispanic students (Clewell et al., 2005). Bridge programs at community colleges include specialized coursework, career development services, and transition services. Summer bridge programs also typically involve activities like workshops and seminars, career counseling, and social activities, and they tend to offer students an opportunity to experience college life by staying in college residence halls (Clewell et al., 2005).

An example of a national CURE curriculum is the Science Education Alliance-Phage Hunters Advancing Genomics and Evolutionary Science (SEA-PHAGES; https://seaphages.org/) program sponsored by the University of Pittsburgh and the Howard Hughes Medical Institute (HHMI). This two-semester, discovery-based undergraduate research course covers topics related to microbiology, genome annotation, and bioinformatics and has served a diverse group of over 4,800 students at 73 institutions. Students engage in personalized research projects, and SEA-PHAGES has demonstrated increased student learning, interest in the sciences, and retention in the biological sciences (Jordan et al., 2014).

We have highlighted only some of the larger academic pipeline programs at the collegiate level. Due to the fact that opportunities differ by status (e.g., freshman, sophomore, junior, senior), it is possible to take advantage of multiple opportunities. Chapter 6 includes a discussion of how to leverage these programs as a student and how to identify funding opportunities that can be used to build training programs within an institution. The next chapter highlights programs that support individuals at the graduate and professional level of the pipeline.

Collegiate Program Commonalities Using the THRIVE Index

Program	Type	History	Research	Inclusion-Identity	Voice	Expectations
Leadership Alliance Mellon Mays Undergraduate Fellowship Program (MMUF) Florida A&M University Graduate Feeder Scholars Program (GFSP) Institute for Recruitment of Teachers California Pre-Doctoral Program's Sally Casanova Scholarship Annual Biomedical Research Conference for Minority Students (ABRCMS)	collegiate	all programs or sponsoring organizations have been in existence for twenty years or longer.	professional development (e.g., GRE preparation, research methods) develop research aptitude and acumen (e.g., research project, research presentation) funding (e.g., stipend, travel)	workshops (e.g., self-identity, academic identity) exposure to graduate school culture and expectations	mentoring (e.g., peer mentoring, one-on-one research experience with faculty) publication opportunities	college retention graduate school admission and enrollment acquisition of doctorate degrees (PhD, MD/PhD, JD/PhD)

CHAPTER 4

DOCTORAL/GRADUATE/ PROFESSIONAL PROGRAMS

In chapter 4, we examine programs toward the end of the academic pipeline These initiatives create spaces for underrepresented students as they pursue graduate degrees (e.g., master's, doctorate degrees) and professional degrees (e.g., MBA, MD, PharmD). The programs highlighted in this chapter are primarily graduate degree programs that support URM students while they pursue advanced degrees and assist them with preparation for postdoctoral and faculty posts. Professional degree programs are highlighted in the appendix. Further, we have included examples of governmental graduate programs, based on several agencies.

Overall, specialized training programs enhance the likelihood of doctorate degree completion and advancement into faculty and administrative posts. Further, these programs provide the socialization, faculty mentorship, professional involvement, professional development, and environmental support that allow URM graduate students to persist and succeed in the academic world (Blockett, Felder, Parrish, & Collier, 2016). In this section, we will illustrate some hallmark underrepresented minority (URM) doctoral programs (the Southern Regional Education Board's State Doctoral Scholars Program, the Alfred P. Sloan Foundation Minority Graduate Scholarship Program, the McKnight Doctoral Fellowship Program, the Ford Foundation Fellowship Program, the National GEM Consortium, and the Fisk-Vanderbilt Master's-to-PhD Bridge Program) that produce diverse PhDs who have gone on to become some of the top scholars in the nation.

SOUTHERN REGIONAL EDUCATION BOARD'S STATE DOCTORAL SCHOLARS PROGRAM

One of the stalwart programs that supports URM doctoral students through their PhD program is the Southern Regional Education Board's (SREB) State Doctoral Scholars Program (DSP). The program has been around for over twenty-five years and assists in increasing URM students within the pipeline into the professoriate and industry.

Type

SREB State Doctoral Scholars Program	
Place in the Pipeline	Doctoral students
Type of Students Served	URMs
Disciplines Served	All majors
Funding Source	Other funding
Institutional Structure	SREB, a nonprofit organization
Length of Time in Program	Length of doctoral program (or dissertation cycle)
Geographic Location	Sixteen states, primarily in the southeastern United States (but not limited to this region)
Institutions Served	Fifty-seven (https://www.sreb.org/states)
Program Accepts New Sites	Yes
Program Deadlines	January 1 through March 31
Website	https://www.sreb.org/doctoral-scholars-program

History

Established in 1993 to address the dearth of URM faculty on college and university campuses, SREB has produced more than 940 graduates, with 122 graduates earning tenure. The program has served 1,664 students as of spring 2019. The program has impressive outcomes, including:

- High retention and graduation rates (nearly 90 percent).
- High faculty employment rate (75 percent employed in higher education as faculty, administrators, or postdoctoral researchers).
- High employee rate in SREB states (nearly 70 percent).
- Reduced time to degree (scholars entering the program with a bachelor's degree graduate on average in 5.1 years, and scholars entering with a master's degree graduate on average in 4.8 years).
- Impact in many fields of study (37 percent in STEM, 28 percent in social and behavioral sciences, 15 percent in humanities, and 20 percent in other fields of study).

Alumni Success

A significant component of the success of any pipeline program is the outcomes of its alumni. Of all the graduates of the SREB State DSP, 836 are employed—81 percent in education and 91 percent in higher education. Further, 122 graduates of the program are tenured faculty members. Notable alumni include Annice Yarber-Allen, PhD (interim dean of the College of Letters and Sciences, Columbus State University), Rana Johnson, PhD (associate vice president for Inclusive Excellence and Strategic Initiatives, Indiana State University), Kent Smith, PhD (professor, anatomy and cell biology, Oklahoma State University, Center for Health

Sciences), Robert Osgood, PhD (associate professor, Department of Biomedical Sciences, Rochester Institute of Technology), and Janice Underwood, PhD (first chief diversity, equity, and inclusion officer, Commonwealth of Virginia).

Research Preparation

The program provides professional development, mentorship, community building, networking, and financial support, and SREB addresses areas that have been shown to be barriers for URM students who are seeking to earn a PhD and become faculty members.

Workshops and Professional Development

The annual Institute on Teaching and Mentoring provides workshops, recruitment, and networking opportunities to enhance professional development and provides PhD scholars with effective tools to be successful as faculty in postsecondary institutions. At the institute, there are multiple sessions dedicated to the practice of "good" mentorship, and the institute prepares participants to overcome the barriers and obstacles that are not faced by majority peers. At the annual meeting, experts deliver key program services and interventions in their field as well as on specific topics through focused, concurrent sessions.

Funding

The DSP provides a full financial package with support in conjunction with institutional resources. Scholars receive a three- to five-year package that covers tuition, fees, stipends, and expenses associated with attending the annual institute. Further, scholars are eligible for the Dissertation Award, which is a one-year package that supports students who have completed all of their coursework and comprehensive exams and are preparing to defend their dissertation.

Inclusion and Identity

Inclusion

The DSP provides scaffolding (programming) in a "safe" space, which allows participants to thrive in an environment where they are not the only person of color pursuing an advanced degree. The program is unique in providing professional development opportunities for faculty mentors, and DSP offers specialized curricula and workshops (e.g., training for participants, directors, and faculty on imposter syndrome, implicit bias, microaggressions), orientations (e.g., reviewing norms, expectations, structures, goals, protocols), personalized counseling services, development of an academic sense of belongingness (e.g., meetings with doctoral scholars and peer researchers, exchanges at academic conferences), and the creation of a safe space. The DSP sponsors a four-day meeting that engages all program participants, and SREB has an online platform that allows program participants to identify and communicate with one another.

Identity

The program is acutely aware of the centrality of race and ethnicity when assisting participants with the development of their academic identity. Program participants are admitted to the program with faculty mentors who assist them with gaining the coping and self-affirming skills necessary to succeed in their doctoral program and pursue faculty positions. As participants matriculate through their graduate programs, they attend an annual professional development conference, where they are provided with shared online experiences during the process of searching for positions and where they are celebrated as they end their doctoral programs and enter into the academy. This program highlights and speaks volumes about each participant's intellect, determination, and thirst for personal achievement.

Voice

Mentoring

The institute, sponsored by the DSP, is the largest annual gathering of URM PhD scholars in the nation. Because graduate education hinges on mentorship, organizers of the program encourage informal and formal networking at the institute. Staff provide direct counseling and advocacy for scholars. Further, all program services are designed to improve retention, graduation, and faculty employment. Program outcomes confirm the success of the program's structures and services.

The annual meeting provides all program participants with access to over fifty breakout sessions, which are designed for scholar interaction. These breakout sessions provide opportunities for various collaborations, which affirm each scholar's ideas and contributions to the academy. They also have an active social media presence that encourages participation and interaction.

Expectations

The program's goal is to increase faculty diversity by increasing the number of URM students who earn a PhD and seek academic careers. The goal of the institute is to provide a safe environment for doctoral scholars to share insights and survival tips for success in graduate work. They also build community among themselves and with faculty representatives, which enriches their mentoring, research, and teaching strategies.

Overall, the program has served 1,767 minority doctoral scholars and graduated 1,016 PhDs. Key indicators and metrics to understand the success of the DSP are the following: PhDs earned, time to degree, fields of study, type of employment, and state of employment.

Graduate Governmental Academic Pipeline Programs

US Department of Health and Human Services
https://www.hhs.gov/

The US Department of Health and Human Services sponsors programming through their Bureau of Health Workforce (BHW) to improve the health of URM communities and to prepare a workforce committed to serving underserved populations. Several programs are targeted toward the development of an educational pipeline for URM students to matriculate into graduate-level health professions programs and to complete graduate-level programs in the health professions or allied health professions programs (e.g., postbaccalaureate programs).

HBCU Behavioral Health Ambassador Program (BHAP) trains graduate students with the knowledge of how to bring awareness of careers in behavioral health to college students on HBCU campuses. Mentoring, mini-conference attendance, and a stipend are provided. (https://www.myhbcucares.org/behavioral-health-ambassador-program/).

HRSA Area Health Education Centers are designed to enhance education and training networks within communities and academic institutions in order to increase diversity among health professionals, broaden the distribution of the health workforce, and improve health-care delivery in rural and underserved communities. Public and private accredited schools of allopathic and osteopathic medicine are eligible (https://www.hrsa.gov/grants/find-funding?status=All&bureau=640).

HRSA Graduate Psychology Education Program (GPE) is designed for doctoral-level psychologists interested in providing mental and behavioral health care in settings that provide services to underserved and/or rural populations. The program is open to APA-accredited schools in all fifty states and territories, including Tribal Colleges and Universities (TCUs) (https://www.hrsa.gov/grants/find-funding/hrsa-19-002).

HRSA Public Health Training Centers (PHTC) funds public health and other programs providing graduate or specialized training in public health. Through cooperative agreements, training at these centers includes technical, scientific, managerial, and leadership competencies. This program funds regional Public Health Training Centers and the Preventive Medicine Residency with Integrative Health Care Training Program (https://www.hrsa.gov/library/training-centers).

ALFRED P. SLOAN MINORITY GRADUATE SCHOLARSHIP PROGRAM

The Alfred P. Sloan Minority Graduate Scholarship Program (SMGSP) has consistently assisted URM students in their pursuit of doctorate degrees and beyond. Working with a variety of institutions in providing sponsorship, mentorship, and professional development opportunities to ethnic minorities around the United States, the SMGSP is one of the first fellowship programs to support URM students and institutions in the country.

Type

Alfred P. Sloan Minority Graduate Scholarship Program	
Place in the Pipeline	Doctoral students
Type of Students Served	URMs
Disciplines Served	Engineering, life sciences, mathematics, physical sciences
Funding Source	Alfred P. Sloan Foundation (private foundation)
Institutional Structure	Nonprofit organization
Length of Time in Program	Other, annually, life of doctoral program
Geographic Location	Specific institutions
Institutions Served	Eight institutions served
Program Accepts New Sites	No
Program Deadlines	Depends on institution attending
Website	www.sloanphds.org

History

The Alfred P. Sloan Foundation is most widely known for its support of basic research projects and programming to improve public understanding about science, technology, engineering, mathematics, and economics. Its founder, Alfred P. Sloan, also provided funds that helped establish institutional entities, including the Sloan School of Management at the Massachusetts Institute of Technology and the Sloan Kettering Institute, now the Memorial Sloan Kettering Cancer Center in New York City. Less well known is the foundation's six-decade history of support for historically underrepresented minorities and women in a variety of scientific and technical fields. This support has been central to the foundation's mission and follows historical developments related to the civil rights movement, school integration, and federal support for URMs seeking baccalaureate, professional, and graduate degrees (Joskow, 2016).

The foundation's diversity efforts have two major thrusts:

1. *The Education and Professional Advancement for Underrepresented Groups.*[1] Grants under this program have been specifically aimed at increasing the diversity of higher education and the scientific and research workforce in STEM fields. In 2019, the program was renamed the Program for Diversity, Equity & Inclusion in STEM Higher Education.
2. *Public Understanding of Science, Technology & Economics.* Grants under this program highlight the contributions of women and URM scholars and promote the work of women and URM authors, directors, screenwriters, and playwrights.

All of the foundation's programs support the diversity of the scientific and research workforce, regardless of fields of interest. Sloan's grant-making processes have been enhanced to ensure that grantees, regardless of the nature of their particular project, are mindful of diversity and structure their grant-funded work in ways that promote the inclusion of women and URMs.

The Alfred P. Sloan Foundation's first minority-focused grants were made in the 1950s, when issues of educational equity and racial injustice in education were at the forefront of popular consciousness. The initial grants were focused on strengthening educational institutions that primarily educated Black students and aimed to strengthen the educational and administrative resources of historically Black colleges and universities (HBCUs). Among its contributions was a $1 million grant to the Tuskegee Institute to help it build and equip its engineering school, expanding the educational offerings available to students.[2] The foundation made regular contributions to the annual fundraising drive of the United Negro College

---

1. The Foundation uses the term *underrepresented groups* to denote four populations historically and currently underrepresented in STEM fields: African Americans/Blacks, Hispanics/Latinx, Native Americans and Alaska Natives, and women of all ethnicities.

2. Dollar figures used here reflect computations made in 2016 to reflect then-current dollar values for awards made earlier.

Fund (UNCF), including a $4 million donation in 1963. It launched a matching gift program to help HBCUs build their endowments and fundraising infrastructure and continued its support of this program through the 1960s. By the late 1960s, the foundation selected a different model for expanding URM education and advancing diversity: direct support of URM students themselves. The foundation's new strategy focused on empowering minority students to take advantage of educational opportunities that were, in principle, increasingly open to them. From 1960 to 1980, the foundation launched four major fellowship programs, first providing fellowships for Black students entering medical school, an area that, at the time, showed very little representation of Black students. The second major fellowship program focused on expanding URM enrollment in graduate programs in business management. In 1974, the foundation launched a third program aimed at expanding URM enrollment in undergraduate engineering schools, and in 1980, it announced a fourth fellowship initiative focused on increasing URM enrollment in graduate public management and administration programs.

What began as an effort to build and equip the engineering school at the Tuskegee Institute has matured into the Sloan Foundation's most enduring effort to boost minority enrollment in engineering programs. Led by Percy A. Pierre, PhD, then Sloan program director and dean of the College of Engineering, Architecture, and Computer Sciences at Howard University, the Minorities in Engineering program resulted in the development of several institutions that continue to advance minority inclusion in engineering today, such as the National Action Council for Minorities in Engineering, Inc. (NACME) and the National GEM Consortium (Pierre, 2015). Pierre recognized that few African Americans were graduating from high school with knowledge of or interest in engineering, which led to fewer undergraduate degrees granted to URMs, fewer URM enrollments in graduate programs, fewer master's and doctorate degrees granted, and fewer URM engineers in industry, research, and academia.

So began a new strategic focus of the foundation to develop the URM PhD (MPHD) Program that would increase the number of degrees granted in STEM fields to students of color by incentivizing students to join PhD programs that were more successful than average in graduating URM PhDs. This program, begun in 1995, continued the foundation's tradition of providing direct support to students, but this support was restricted to students in STEM graduate programs where a dedicated faculty champion had demonstrated an effective ability to mentor URM doctoral students through to completion of their PhDs. Although designed to support Black, Latinx, and American Indian/Alaska Native (AI/AN) students, the MPHD program attracted relatively few AI/AN students. With such low numbers, it was nearly impossible to achieve a critical mass of students at any graduate department or school. In 2003, the foundation launched a new major initiative, the Sloan Indigenous Graduate Partnership (SIGP), with the belief that a specific focus on AI/AN scholars would allow institutions to develop critical masses, not only of AI/AN scholars, but also of faculty, staff, and administrators experienced working with and supporting AI/AN students.

Beginning in 2013, the foundation pursued a new strategy, a revised MPHD program that would concentrate its efforts to create and support University Centers for Exemplary Mentoring (UCEMs). These new centers, based at eight university campuses across the country, combine the best elements of the foundation's grant making over the years.[3] In order to qualify for a UCEM grant, the institution must demonstrate a commitment to minority graduate education, including a commitment of significant university matching funds, demonstrated buy-in from STEM department chairs and faculty mentors, and support from high-level university

---

3. The eight UCEMs are Cornell University, Duke University, the Georgia Institute of Technology, the Massachusetts Institute of Technology, Pennsylvania State University, University of California at San Diego, the University of Illinois at Urbana-Champaign, and the University of South Florida.

administrators. Moreover, UCEMs must develop minority recruitment and retention initiatives and create a variety of professional development and educational support structures designed to foster a robust community that is integrated with students and research colleagues of all ethnicities and genders and that is dedicated to facilitating success.

Supported approaches in the current program include (1) interventions that aim to increase diversity through the direct provision of needed resources and experiences to historically underrepresented students and faculty, including stipends and scholarships, mentoring, networking, leadership training programs, and support for curricular innovation; (2) interventions that aim to increase diversity through catalyzing lasting, positive change in the capacity of US educational institutions to successfully recruit, retain, and advance the careers of students and faculty from historically underrepresented groups; and (3) high-quality research into the barriers to entry to STEM and economics in higher education or into the impact of strategies for improving the performance and progression of historically underrepresented students and faculty. The program is particularly interested in interventions that incorporate novel or underexplored mechanisms for advancing diversity, equity, and inclusion.

Alumni Success

Notable alumni include Erick C. Jones, PhD (associate dean, College of Engineering, and Professor of Industrial, Manufacturing and Systems Engineering, University of Texas, Arlington); Laura K. Dassama, PhD (assistant professor of chemistry, Stanford University); and Erika T Camacho, PhD (program director, National Science Foundation's ADVANCE program, and associate professor, Arizona State University).

Research Preparation

The Sloan UCEM program is a comprehensive initiative at each participating school, which includes student support, mentoring, career development, and network development. Once graduated, Sloan MPHD scholars become part of the Sloan Scholars Mentoring Network, which is devoted to increasing the numbers and status of underrepresented populations in the academy, establishing a Sloan scholars brand that raises the public profile and prestige of the MPHD program for the benefit of the scholars, strengthening the Sloan scholar community's commitment to mentorship, and identifying and nurturing leaders to foster more inclusive and supportive cultures within academic institutions.

Workshops

Programming for the Sloan Scholars Mentoring Network includes professional development webinars, grants, academic job-market boot camps, leadership training, and networking opportunities.

Professional Development Opportunities

Sloan MPHD scholars attend the annual Institute on Teaching and Mentoring, hosted by the Compact for Faculty Diversity and the SREB. Scholars have access to a host of professional development presentations and seminars at this four-day event. Also, each MPHD UCEM campus provides yearlong professional development and mentoring activities for Sloan scholars. Professional development and mentoring activities for the SIGP program are provided at on-campus and intercampus events as well as at the annual American Indian Science and Engineering Society (AISES) conference.

Funding

All Sloan MPHD scholars receive full support for tuition and fees, stipends, and professional development funds to support research, books, and travel to conferences. Support varies based on the institution, but support for tuition, fees, and a stipend is standard.

INCLUSION AND IDENTITY

Inclusion

The success of the Sloan Foundation's UCEM and SIGP programs is predicated on institutional commitment to the recruitment, retention, and graduation of its minority scholars. This commitment is demonstrated at all levels of the institution, from high-level university administrators to graduate school deans, department chairs, and faculty mentors. Each has a role to play in building a strong environment of support for MPHD and SIGP scholars. The critical components of support include academic coursework and advising; student social engagement with peers and faculty; collaborative research environments; robust campus resources, including diversity, equity and inclusion resources; peer and faculty mentoring; professional development; and direct support from the foundation.

Identity

Each institution sponsored by the Sloan Foundation provides opportunities to strengthen self-identity and self-efficacy. Further, by attending the Compact for Faculty Diversity, Sloan mentors and their mentees bond in their experience. Sloan faculty mentors are dedicated to modeling techniques of effective communication and mentoring scholars about how to understand departmental cultures, navigate interactions within research teams, and negotiate postdoctoral training and tenure-track faculty positions.

Voice

Mentoring

Each Sloan UCEM scholar is afforded the opportunity to attend the Compact for Faculty Diversity's Institute on Teaching and Mentoring two times while earning their degree. At the four-day conference, held annually, scholars are able to participate in a host of professional development workshops and make new connections with Sloan scholars and faculty. Developing a strong community of scholars at UCEMs and across UCEMs is an initiative that is supported by the foundation, allowing current scholars to connect in and across institutions. Upon graduation, scholars have the ability to join a community of alumni through the Sloan Scholars Mentoring Network. This network provides continuing programming for Sloan scholars in postdoctoral roles or who are employed for the first time in industry, government, and academia.

In addition to financial support and recruitment strategies developed specifically for AI/AN students, SIGP institutions create strong campus communities through regular meetings of scholars and SIGP leaders, as well as through support for and involvement in AISES and similar organizations for Indigenous students. In addition, SIGP scholars are invited to attend professional development program activities at the annual Institute on Teaching and Mentoring.

Expectations

The goal of the program is to recruit and graduate URMs in STEM, with the hope that they have given careful consideration to a career in academia and may be effective role models for the next generation of college students. If academia proves not to be of interest, there are endless opportunities to mentor URM students in STEM.

Participating institutions are expected to develop a slate of professional development, mentoring, and educational support structures. These support structures are designed to foster vibrant communities for scholars and to facilitate success by integrating scholars with students and research colleagues of all ethnicities and genders.

Between 1996 and 2012, the MPHD program funded more than seventeen hundred doctoral candidates, graduating nearly one thousand, one hundred and seventy scholars through 2018. The new MPHD UCEM program, started in 2013, has funded over four hundred PhD candidates, graduating forty-five to date. Through 2018, the foundation has funded more than three hundred MS and PhD AI/AN scholars in the SIGP program, with more than one hundred and graduates.

Graduate Governmental Academic Pipeline Programs

National Institute of Health

There are multiple branches of the National Institute of Health (NIH) featured in this section. The first is the National Institute of General Medical Sciences (NIGMS) (https://www.nigms.nih.gov/training/Pages/Home.aspx), which houses community college, undergraduate, postbaccalaureate, graduate, and postdoctoral programs. We also highlight NIH programs under the National Institute on Minority Health and Health Disparities (NIMHHD) (https://www.nimhd.nih.gov/programs/extramural/research-areas/clinical-research.html) and the National Institute of Neurological Disorders and Stroke (NINDS) (https://www.ninds.nih.gov/). This section will highlight graduate programs. These initiatives are for institutions and students.

Research Training Initiative for Scientific Enhancement (RISE) Program supports research-active institutions in training a diverse pool of students to complete PhDs in biomedical fields (https://www.nigms.nih.gov /Training/RISE). Two programs are associated with RISE at the graduate level, Bridges to the Doctorate and the Graduate Research Training Initiative for Student Enhancement (G-RISE).

Minority Health and Health Disparities Research Training Program (MHRT) provides research training opportunities for undergraduate, postbaccalaureate, and graduate students as well as residents and fellows within the United States and abroad. Research settings include low-income areas where biomedical, clinical, social, or behavioral science research can be conducted. Programming is directed toward students directly through the participating institution (https://www.nimhd.nih.gov/pr ograms/extramural/domestic-international-research-trai ning.html).

Neuroscience Scholars Program provides graduate students and postdoctoral scholars with a two-year fellowship that includes professional development, mentoring, travel, live events and webinars, and access to a community of alumni. This program is administered through the Society of Neuroscience (https://www.sfn.org/initiatives /diversity-initiatives/neuroscience-scholars-program).

Ruth L. Kirschstein National Research Service Awards for Individual Predoctoral Fellowships to Promote Diversity in Health-Related Research (F31) provides multiyear research training support for diverse scholars (low-income and first-generation [LIFG] scholars, scholars from underrepresented racial/ethnic groups, and scholars with disabilities) who are pursuing a PhD or MD/PhD in the biomedical, behavioral, health, or clinical sciences (https://www.niehs.nih.gov/research/supported /training/fellowships/f31/index.cfm).

Initiative for Maximizing Student Development (T32) provides funding to train scientists earning a PhD who are underrepresented in the biomedical, clinical, behavioral, and social sciences. This initiative is an institutional training program that includes curricular programming, mentoring, research training, and professional development. The grant includes multiyear funding toward graduate study (https://grants.nih.gov/gr ants/guide/pa-files/par-19-037.html).

MCKNIGHT DOCTORAL FELLOWSHIP PROGRAM

Established in 1984, the McKnight Doctoral Fellowship (MDF) Program predates many pipeline initiatives specifically geared to URM doctoral students to prepare them to enter the professoriate. Although this program serves colleges and universities in Florida, many other programs (e.g., SREB Doctoral Scholars Program) have used this model as a standard to develop their programmatic structures.

Type

McKnight Doctoral Fellowship Program	
Place in the Pipeline	Doctoral students and junior faculty
Type of Students Served	URMs
Disciplines Served	All majors
Funding Source	Other funding: (1) endowment, (2) Florida legislature, and (3) private donations
Institutional Structure	Florida Education Fund (nonprofit organization)
Length of Time in Program	Length of doctoral program, dissertation cycle, or junior faculty
Geographic Location	Florida institutions
Institutions Served	Nine Florida institutions
Program Accepts New Sites	No (accepts new students)
Program Deadlines	McKnight Doctoral Fellowship—**January 15**; McKnight Dissertation Fellowship—usually during the **last week in May**; McKnight Junior Faculty Fellowship—**February 1**
Website	fefonline.org

History

The Florida Education Fund (FEF) was initially established through a major grant from the McKnight Foundation of Minneapolis, Minnesota, and by a challenge grant from the foundation, which required matching funds from the Florida legislature. As a not-for-profit corporation, FEF has provided avenues to ensure educational opportunities for historically underrepresented individuals. This quasi-public entity, with a statewide mission and national impact, was originally known as the McKnight Programs in Higher Education. From the onset, it was administered by the Florida Association of Colleges and Universities and served as the forerunner to what is now known as FEF. Since then, FEF has developed and now administers the MDF Program and the McKnight Junior Faculty Fellowship (MJFF) Program. The MDF program was designed to increase the pool of minorities with PhDs in an effort to diversify college and university faculty. As partner and facilitator, FEF works with doctorate-degree-granting universities to recruit, retain, and graduate students pursuing the PhD. Each year, FEF awards up to fifty fellowships.

The MJFF Program was intended to encourage excellence in teaching and research by women, African Americans, Hispanics, and Native Americans. To date, FEF has awarded 233 fellowships. At least forty-four fellows have obtained tenure, thirty-seven fellows have completed their doctorate degrees, and thirty-eight fellows have earned promotions. Notable alumni include Robin Brooks, PhD (assistant professor, Africana studies, University of Pittsburgh) and Jonathan Gayles, PhD (professor and chair of African American studies, Georgia State University).

Research Preparation

Both the MDF and MJFF Programs offer fellowships for doctoral students and tenure-track junior faculty and professional development support, which may include travel grants to participate in professional conferences, financial support for special projects and equipment, various workshops, job-recruitment fairs, professional editorial assistance, mentoring, and counseling.

Workshops and Professional Development

The FEF organizes and conducts four professional development conferences a year. The conferences are the Annual New Fellows Orientation, the Annual McKnight Fellows Meeting and Graduate School Conference, the Mid-Year Research and Writing Conference, and Summer/Fall Research & Writing Institute. Online writing workshops and editorial assistance are provided throughout the year. Each conference provides mentoring and networking components.

The conferences listed above provide the following support services: dissertation writing and research workshops; CV development and cover letter workshops; grant writing workshops and editorial assistance; conference presentation workshops through actual presentations; strategic planning for graduate school completion, job placement, and career planning; research and publication collaboration; and networking.

Inclusion and Identity

Inclusion

All of our programs are designed to assist with formulating self-identity and self-efficacy. The MDF Program strengthens inclusionary practices within institutions, academic departments, and faculty through outreach, which assures institutions follow the requirements of the program. The program promotes inclusiveness in every aspect of its programming. All programming activities provide opportunities for fellows, regardless of their race and gender, to participate fully in programming activities. Role models and mentoring activities are provided by individuals from diverse backgrounds.

Identity

All applicants to the PhD fellowship must complete an application that identifies their race and ethnicity as well as the focus of their research and the scope of their academic and work experiences. Applicants must explain why they have chosen their specific focus and to what extent their work will contribute to their professional, state, local, and international communities. The program examines their grades, writing, letters of recommendations, and other experiences to help create programming activities.

All fellows are required to participate in the following professional development activities: (1) writing and publication workshops, (2) grant writing, (3) strategic plan development, (4) conflict resolution workshops, (5) conference panels related to their research, (6) conference paper presentations, (7) conference panels where they serve as professional discussants, and (8) presentations of their research to general audiences. The program promotes and fosters collaboration on research projects and engages in network building. These activities all build an awareness of one's academic self-identity.

Voice

Every component of the MDF and MJFF Programs prepares participants to overcome barriers or obstacles in academia. Specifically, FEF allow its fellows to participate in panel discussions, develop and present plenary speeches, recommend topics for conference discussions, and assist with organizing professional development activities. Participants and alumni are intentionally provided voices, and alumni of FEF programs coach and mentor current participants, serve as workshop speakers, submit performance evaluations highlighting their successes, help with job placement, and even provide monetary support back to FEF. Participants in FEF programs are given voice through activities that promote networking as well as collaboration on research, grant writing, and publications.

Expectations

The McKnight Doctoral Fellowship Program has the following goals and expectations of its participants: strive to complete a PhD program within the five-year funding period; present conference papers at professional meetings prior to graduation; and participate in workshops on prospectus development, dissertation research and writing, job placement, conference presentations, and writing skills development. In addition, all fellows must apply for external grants, mentor other fellows, submit performance-evaluation reports three times per year, attend annual conferences, and present research at the annual research and writing conferences. Finally, it is expected that all fellows must follow their university's academic requirements, and graduates of the program must pursue an academic appointment. Since 1984, FEF has awarded 1,280 fellowships, and 726 fellows have received their PhD. A total of 405 fellows are currently matriculating, and FEF maintains an outstanding retention rate of 88 percent.

FORD FOUNDATION FELLOWSHIP PROGRAM

The Ford Foundation Fellowship Program has supported under-represented populations for years. This fellowship program has the mandate to diversify the professoriate through sponsorship, networks, and professional development. For over thirty years, this program has supported numerous students in their quest to complete the PhD. Although we focus on graduate fellowships in this section, the Ford Foundation provides postdoctoral and senior faculty fellowships.

Type

Ford Foundation Fellowship Program	
Place in the Pipeline	Doctoral students
Type of Students Served	URMs, undocumented
Disciplines Served	Computer and information sciences, engineering, humanities, life sciences, library sciences, mathematics, neurosciences, physical sciences, and social sciences
Funding Source	Ford Foundation (private foundation)
Institutional Structure	National Academies of Sciences, Engineering, and Medicine (nonprofit organization)
Length of Time in Program	Funding students annually
Geographic Location	Nationwide
Institutions Served	N/A (all); fifty to one hundred institutions per year, depending on the applicants
Program Accepts New Sites	Yes (new students)
Program Deadlines	December 1
Website	http://sites.nationalacademies.org/PGA/FordFellowships/index.htm

History

The National Academies of Sciences, Engineering, and Medicine has managed the Ford Foundation Fellowship Program since 1979. From 1979 until 2004, the Ford Foundation provided grants to the fellowship office for the administration of the Ford Foundation Fellowships for Minorities. Aimed at addressing the severe under-representation of specified ethnic and racial groups in the United States professoriate, these fellowship programs were open to US citizens from six racial and ethnic groups. In 2005, the Ford Foundation replaced these programs with the Ford Foundation Fellowships Program, broadening eligibility to include all US citizens, regardless of race, national origin, religion, gender, age, disability, or sexual orientation.

The mission of the Ford Foundation Fellowship Program is to increase the diversity of the nation's college and university faculties by increasing ethnic and racial diversity, to maximize the educational benefits of diversity, and to increase the number of professors who can and will use diversity as a resource for enriching the education of all students.

The Ford Foundation Fellowship Program was established explicitly to support efforts in producing eminently qualified and competitive candidates for faculty positions. Accordingly, the manner and extent to which fellows have been successful in this regard are considered, with particular attention to teaching, research, and service that reflects five general areas: scholarship, academic curriculum, leadership, broadening participation, and public presence and activities. These interrelated areas provide a general basis with which to identify and assess the impact of the work and other activities of the fellows, especially in their roles as academics. The number of participants over the life of the program is approximatively thirty-eight hundred students.

Alumni Success

Ford fellows are employed in the professoriate, within college administration, and at governmental agencies nationwide. Notable alumni include Keivan Stassun, PhD (Stevenson Professor of Astrophysics, College of Arts & Science, and codirector, the Fisk-Vanderbilt Master's-to-PhD Bridge Program, Vanderbilt University), Beverly Daniel Tatum, PhD (ninth president of Spelman College), Carol Anderson, PhD (Charles Howard Candler Professor and chair of African American studies, Emory University), Erika T. Camacho, PhD (program director, National Science Foundation's ADVANCE program), and Ron Mickens, PhD (recipient, 2018 Tapia Prize, Fuller E. Callaway Distinguished Professor in the Department of Physics, Clark Atlanta University).

Research Preparation

Fellow scholarship and research provide the basic knowledge for the advancement and improvement of society and its constituents and represents a principal source for social and economic vitality. Arguably, scholarship and research-informed activities ultimately reflect and provide institutional value and societal benefit. For example, 79 percent of fellows have been recognized or have received awards for groundbreaking research, patents, and the establishment of cross-disciplinary projects and programs. It is interesting to note that discussions of scholarship by fellows were mainly framed in terms of policy relevance and practical applicability. This applicability is important, especially given concerns about the societal benefits of the program. Knowledge creation was tied explicitly to broader impacts and benefits. In the same vein, 78 percent of fellows identified their roles in the creation of, among other things, new courses and workshops, research centers and institutes, and educational programs for children and youth. Research preparation also comes through a network of mentoring by other Ford Fellows at the annual Conference of Ford Fellows.

Workshops and Professional Development

At the annual Conference of Ford Fellows, scholars are given workshops on publishing, strategies to complete the dissertation, planning an academic career, and career advancement. The professional development opportunities come in the form of networking with peers and elders or face-to-face conversations with university and academic presses, paper and poster presentation comments and critiques, and interactions with established and emerging scholars.

Funding

The predoctoral program supports a stipend but not tuition. All benefits include an annual stipend of $24,000, an invitation to attend the Conference of Ford Fellows, and access to Ford Fellow Regional Liaisons (a network of Ford Fellow alumni). The predoctoral program supports doctoral study for three years. There are additional funding mechanisms to support dissertation and postdoctoral study as well. The Dissertation Fellowship award provides a $25,000 stipend for a nine- or twelve-month term.

Inclusion and Identity

When asked about the various aspects of their role as mentors, 35 percent of fellows specifically identified both formal and informal mentoring as critical contributions they make to their institutions and fields as well as to other individuals. In general, fellows have had positive experiences with mentors. Moreover, with particular emphasis on the dedication of mentors to their students, fellows discussed mentoring as a way to help the various communities with which they are involved. Many of these fellows were responsible for creating institutional and community mentoring programs, in addition to participating in them. The generation of collaborative networks—often across generational and disciplinary lines—and the building of a community of scholars have been important outcomes of the Ford Foundation Fellowship Program. The salience of this point is grounded by the number of Ford Fellows (12 percent) who are engaged in collaborative research, and it is a principal factor determining their scholarly productivity and efficacy.

Inclusion

The Ford Foundation Fellowship Program develops a sense of academic belongingness through various meetings with doctoral scholars and peer researchers, exchanges at academic conferences, and the creation of safe spaces, climates, and environments. Further, fellows have the opportunity to participate in an annual conference for first- and second-year fellows. Senior fellows hold regional meetings (alumni networking) and have support from regional liaisons.

Identity

Fellows have a network of liaisons who provide support as fellows develop their academy identities. This network consists of a directory of fellows as well as a network listserv that is managed by Ford Fellows. A Facebook page assists with various surveys and reports.

Voice

Mentoring

During the annual conferences, there is networking, mentoring, and coaching with other Ford Fellows and the Society of Senior Ford Fellows (launched in January 2019). There are also regional liaisons who are available to mentor to other Ford Fellows.

Further, many Ford Fellows have used their awards and networks to branch out. For example, 29 percent of fellows have engaged in collaboration not only within their institutions and fields, or academia in general, but also externally with individuals and organizations in both the public and private sectors. High levels of service were reported among 59 percent of fellows, with 52 percent serving in explicit leadership roles with decision-making power and impact, especially within their universities and professional associations. At least fourteen fellows have served as university presidents or provosts, and another twenty-three have held positions as vice presidents or vice provosts. At least twenty-seven have served as presidents of their national professional associations. When involved in professional associations, fellows tend to be engaged in specialized roles (e.g., organizational officer, board member, committee chair). Fellows also have engaged in leadership and service roles in other venues (e.g., tribal organizations, Young Women's Christian Associations [YWCAs], health-care facilities, community organizations, government agencies, local schools, correctional facilities). With many fellows reporting multiple positions as organizational leaders, tutors, project directors, advisory board members, and so on, fellows contribute to institutional effectiveness and beyond, with activities extending to local, national, and international levels.

The Ford Foundation Fellowship Program uses feeder pathways (e.g., existing partnerships with programs at a similar or the next level of the academic pipeline) and mentoring opportunities to instill voice among its participants. Ford mentors provide psychological and emotional support. They use their social capital to provide voice based on the exchange of social displays of scientific knowledge and practices. Further, they give their support with goal setting and career planning. Currently, Ford Fellows and alumni serve as mentors, using social media and online communications to show various academic opportunities. Collaborative discussion happens formally at the annual conference, which is considered a safe space, as well as informally between fellows. Typically, there are cohorts of fellows at larger institutions who often support one another.

Expectations

The goal of the program is to diversify the professoriate. The Ford Foundation expects fellows to complete their doctorate degree and pursue a career as a faculty member, whether teaching or researching, at a US college or university. Several fellows have received special recognition and awards for excellence in their research, teaching, and service. For example, of the 674 fellows for whom such information was available, 4,543 awards were listed in recognition of their scholarship and related activities, conferred from a variety of sources, including private foundations and government agencies. In addition, 431 fellows reported receiving 1,219 grants and contracts, again from a variety of private and public sources. Also, fifteen fellows hold forty-five patents, with an additional seven pending. Analysis of self-reports and CVs also revealed at least 185 fellows who fall into the category of public intellectuals in an even more direct sense. For example, their contributions to the media have included, among other things, serving as columnists, writing reviews, providing exclusive topic interviews, acting as expert commentators and advisors for news outlets, and developing and contributing to special informational programs and websites. While the preparation of special reports and specific service on government commissions and advisory boards have been notable, fellows also have been called upon by the courts as expert witnesses and have offered expert testimony before Congress about various public policy issues.

Evaluations are received through an annual performance report to Ford Foundation sponsors. There are regular surveys, which are often focused on the impact of the program, for quantitative and qualitative data to provide outcomes. The goal of the program is for completion of the doctorate degree and attainment of a position in academia. The Ford Foundation surveys fellows to document completion and career progression. The most recent survey data include 98 percent degree completion and 87 percent faculty positions. Key performance indicators include degree completion and career progression.

Graduate Governmental Academic Pipeline Programs

Indian Health Service
https://www.ihs.gov/

The University of North Dakota hosts yearlong (including summer) programs aimed to boost American Indian/ Alaskan Native (AI/AN) enrollment in nursing, psychology, and other health professions. Programs aim to assist AI/AN students as undergraduates through academic and professional counseling.

The Indians into Medicine (INMED) Program supports AI/ANs to pursue careers in health care. The program offers tutoring, career counseling, financial assistance, summer educational sessions, and grants to attend health-related conferences. Funding is offered for multiple years to colleges and universities (https://www.ihs.gov/dhps/dhpsgrants/indiansmedicineprogram/).

The American Indians into Nursing (RAIN) Program targets students in the field of nursing. RAIN provides academic support and assistance to AI students seeking a nursing degree, from the bachelors of nursing degree (BSN) through the doctorate (https://www.ihs.gov/dhps/dhpsgrants/americanindiansnursingprogram/).

THE NATIONAL GEM CONSORTIUM

The mission of the National GEM Consortium is to attract a pool of African American, Hispanic American, and Native American talent to careers in STEM fields by promoting the attainment of advanced degrees. Each year, GEM identifies and recruits nearly two thousand URM undergraduate students, graduate students, and working professionals for admission to advanced degree programs at the nation's top universities. Through three graduate fellowship tracks—MS in engineering, PhD in science, and PhD in engineering—participants are provided with much-needed financial support, which is often the deciding factor in pursuing graduate education. Also, all GEM Fellows work as paid summer interns while completing their graduate studies—a requirement that provides excellent career experience as well as opportunities for companies to assess and recruit talented employees. More than half of all alumni report accepting full-time employment offers from employer sponsors upon completion of their degree.

Type

The National GEM Consortium	
Place in the Pipeline	Undergraduate, graduate (master's and doctoral students)
Type of Students Served	URMs, low-income first-generation (LIFG)
Disciplines Served	Computer and information sciences, engineering, life sciences, mathematics, and physical sciences
Funding Source	Other source or multiple sponsors
Institutional Structure	Minority-serving institutions (MSIs) and predominantly white institutions (PWIs)
Length of Time in Program	Funding students annually
Geographic Location	Nationwide
Institutions Served	A consortium of over one hundred and fifty universities, employers, and national laboratories
Program Accepts New Sites	Yes
Program Deadlines	Application opens July 1 and closes mid-November
Website	http://www.gemfellowship.org/

History

The history of the National GEM Consortium extends over the past fifty years. The following describes the annual accomplishments of individuals and various initiatives associated with the program over the years:

Year	Key Accomplishment
1972	J. Stanford Smith, senior vice president, General Electric Company, calls for a tenfold increase in minority engineering graduates within ten years.
1973	The National Academy of Engineering sponsors a symposium on increasing minority participation in engineering.
1974	In April, Ted Habarth, affirmative action officer, Applied Physics Laboratory, Johns Hopkins University, drafts a national consortium proposal to increase the participation of minorities and women in engineering.
	Forty strong: In July, the University of Notre Dame hosts a meeting of forty representatives from thirteen research centers, fourteen universities, and five advocacy organizations to develop methods to increase representation.
	In the fall, the group is charged with revising Habarth's proposal based on the July meeting recommendations.
1975	The task force reconvenes, discovers, and agrees the mission should fill the graduate-education gap within the minority engineer development pipeline. The proposal is completed and sent to fifty-three institutions and organizations with a cover letter from Fr. Theodore M. Hesburgh, University of Notre Dame president.
1976	The first six master's in engineering (MS E) fellowships are awarded.
1978	Howard G. Adams, PhD, becomes executive director.
1981	Ted Habarth is appointed president.
1985	One hundred and six fellowships are awarded.
1987	Edward W. Seeberger is appointed president.
1990	Fellowships for a PhD in engineering (PhD E) and PhD in science (PhD S) are launched.
1992	GEM awards 132 MS E, fifteen PhD E, and fifteen PhD S fellowships. One hundred and five students total have graduated from the MSE program.
1993	Two hundred and fourteen fellowships are awarded, and the first two PhD E students graduate.
	John A. White is appointed president.

1995	Charles Vest is appointed president.
1996	The GEM Consortium celebrates its twentieth anniversary in Washington, DC.
	The Faculty Bridge (now Future Faculty Professionals [FFP]) Symposium is launched.
1998	GEM awards 174 MS E, nine PhD E, and forty PhD S fellowships; graduates a total of 129 MS engineers, ten PhD engineers, and seven PhD scientists.
2001	GEM wins the Exemplary Mathematics, Science, and Engineering Partnership Award by the Quality Education for Minorities (QEM) Network.
	Kurt Landgraf is appointed president.
2003	Ronald E. Goldsberry is appointed president.
2004	The Building Engineering and Science Talent (BEST) blue ribbon panel names GEM the sole exemplary graduate-focused program in *A Bridge for All: Higher Education Design Principles to Broaden Participation in Science, Technology, Engineering and Mathematics.*
2006	GEM celebrates its thirtieth anniversary in Chicago, Illinois; GRAD Lab is launched.
2007	GEM moves from the University of Notre Dame to the Educational Testing Services (ETS) offices in Washington, DC.
	Juan Andrade is appointed president.
2009	GEM secures a permanent home in Alexandria, Virginia.
	Michael L. Vaughan is appointed president.
2010	Alfred Grasso is appointed president.
2011	GEM celebrates its thirty-fifth anniversary at the National Harbor, Maryland.
2012	Eric D. Evans is appointed president.
2018	Michael Greene is appointed president.
	Four thousand men and women have achieved the MS in Engineering, PhD in engineering, and PhD in science through GEM's best-in-class graduate fellowship program.

Source: GEM Consortium.

Each year, more than three hundred graduate students on college campuses around the nation, as well as in the commonwealth of Puerto Rico, realize the dream of obtaining an advanced degree. Each is a role model who is going to work in our communities as an expert in a chosen field.

Alumni Success

There are over four thousand GEM alumni but well over one hundred thousand students have been served since its inception. Notable alumni include Ursula Burns (chief executive officer, Xerox Corporation), Frank Martinez (worldwide digital inclusion director, Intel Corporation), Darryll Pines, PhD (dean, Nariman Farvardin Professor of Aerospace Engineering, University of Maryland), Johney B. Green, PhD (associate laboratory director for mechanical and thermal engineering sciences, National Renewable Energy Laboratory), Sylvia Acevedo (commissioner, White House Initiative for Educational Excellence for Hispanics), and Lesia Crumpton-Young (founder, chief executive officer, Powerful Education Technologies).

Research Preparation

The FFP Symposium is GEM's signature career development program for future faculty members and industry professionals. The goal of the FFP Symposium is to provide graduate students with improved research and career competitiveness, tools and metrics for greater control in career planning, and access to a powerful network of peers and mentors.

Workshop and Professional Development Opportunities

Launched at the thirtieth-anniversary conference in June 2006, GRAD Lab is GEM's first programmatic offering for undergraduates, offering URM students exposure to the benefits of research and technology careers in a highly interactive one-day event. Speakers may range from current graduate students to senior managers to faculty and senior administrators. They are selected from diverse communities and disciplines to present on the following topics: "Why Graduate School," "How to Prepare for Graduate School," "Understanding the GEM Fellowship," and "Voices from the Field: Real Life Research and Internship Experiences." GRAD Lab encourages young people of color to consider graduate engineering or science education and to apply for the GEM Fellowship Program. By focusing on the global importance of research and innovation, lifelong career benefits, and real-world role models, the symposium helps each student envision his or her future as a technology leader. The symposium also helps students apply successfully for a GEM Fellowship and gain entry to a graduate program. GRAD Lab is GEM's portable and scalable solution for developing diverse technical talent with advanced degrees.

Funding and Support

GEM offers MS- and PhD-level students an outstanding opportunity as well as access to dozens of the top engineering and science firms and universities in the nation. The GEM Fellowship was designed to focus on promoting opportunities for individuals to enter the industry at the graduate level in areas such as research and development, product development, and other high-level technical careers. GEM also offers exposure to many opportunities in the academy. Admission into a STEM graduate department at a GEM-member university does not directly translate to the applicability of the GEM Fellowship. At the time of selection, a representative from the GEM-member university will confirm in writing if the GEM Fellowship can be used at their institution. The graduate program must also confirm willingness to fund an applicant as a GEM Fellow before the GEM Fellowship can be awarded.

Length of Fellowship

An MS in engineering fellow is expected to complete their master's degree in four semesters or six quarters. PhD in engineering and science fellows receive support up to the fifth year of their PhD program. After the first year of support through GEM, fellows are required to accept a research or teaching assistantship, or other financial support, through the GEM-member university.

Terms of Fellowship

Fellows are required to attend a GEM-member university, maintain satisfactory progress toward an MS or PhD degree, abide by GEM guidelines, and abide by the guidelines of the GEM employer sponsor.

Code of Conduct

Confirmed GEM Fellows are expected to conduct themselves professionally at all times. Each participant is required to work as a summer intern for the sponsoring employer for ten to twelve weeks during the summer. While on assignment with the sponsoring employer, the fellow is governed by that employer's employment policies, practices, procedures, dress code, and standards of conduct. To avoid any misunderstanding, it is recommended that fellows obtain clarification regarding such matters from employers when they begin their assignments. The employer's performance measurement process will measure a participant's performance while on assignment as an intern. Each student must receive a satisfactory (or better) performance rating for the period of the internship to retain the fellowship. Failure to do so will result in dismissal as a GEM Fellow. A summary report explaining the participant's internship experience is sent to GEM offices, with a copy sent to the supervisor, no later than two weeks after the completion of the internship.

GEM-member universities may place additional requirements on GEM Fellows, such as requiring the GEM Fellows obtain in-state residency. GEM Fellows must check with individual representatives of GEM-member universities to determine if additional requirements exist at that university.

Inclusion and Identity

Inclusion

The National GEM Consortium is a network of universities and employers. Each member has a representative who helps GEM to facilitate and promote its mission among faculty, staff, and students. Before a university can become a GEM-member institution, it must apply and provide the full details of its success with producing URM graduate students. It is the goal of the National GEM Consortium to assist with the creation of inclusive environments and safe spaces for URM doctoral students while in their academic program. Annually, GEM hosts their FFP Symposium, which is GEM's signature career-development program for junior and future faculty members as well as industry professionals. The GEM program is intentional about providing spaces to nurture and grow new URM STEM doctoral professionals.

Identity

Each year, GEM convenes a national conference and board meeting. This event has tracks for GEM Fellows, alumni, employers, universities, and prospective fellows. Each track has workshops for all of the participants. Additionally, there are technical presentations, competitions, and poster competitions for students. A gala is held to celebrate the accomplishments of the alumni, employers, and universities. Meanwhile, fellows develop relationships with other fellows and alumni and discuss their movements through the academy. This collegial environment among URM students and alumni allows for dialogue that assists with identity building, which is necessary for success in graduate study and beyond.

Fellows are admitted into graduate programs on their own merit. Additionally, they are recruited for internships due to the skill sets with which they enter the program as well as for the new abilities they learn during the program. The GEM program assists in the process of building skills that allow for competencies to thrive in the competitive workplace.

Voice

Mentoring

GEM uses its FFP program, as well as their alumni network of four thousand, to help fellows successfully matriculate through graduate school. Participants and alumni are connected through communications and events for networking and sharing experiences and professional opportunities.

Incoming fellows participate in webinars, training sessions, and conferences to ensure success in their upcoming graduate studies. Workshops include What It's Like to Be a Graduate Student, Research 101, How to Select an Advisor, How to Manage Your GEM Fellowship, and The Importance of Mentoring. The GEM Fellow success training is an excellent opportunity for students to network with other fellows. Additionally, fellows and alumni are given a voice when celebrated at the aforementioned national conference gala, which awards a GEM Fellow of the Year and Young GEM Alumnus of the Year (for both categories, a man and a woman are awarded).

Expectations

The National GEM Consortium expects fellows to complete their master's or PhD programs. The National GEM Consortium utilizes its alumni network and fellows to mentor the community of current and prospective fellows. The program is dedicated to creating more URM PhDs in STEM for faculty and industry diversity. The National GEM Consortium has supported over four thousand fellows in its forty-four-year tenure, per reporting. Further, GEM uses two metrics to evaluate performance: (1) graduate school transcripts at the conclusion of each semester and (2) internship mid-summer and end-of-summer surveys.

Graduate Governmental Academic Pipeline Programs

National Science Foundation
https://nsf.gov/

The National Science Foundation (NSF) has several divisions to assist with graduate student matriculation and success. The Division of Human Resources Development (HRD) (https://www.nsf.gov/funding/programs.jsp?org=HRD) has several programs that work with both undergraduates and graduate students. Another substantial set of initiatives for graduate students are led by the Division of Graduate Education (https://www.nsf.gov/funding/programs.jsp?org=DGE).

Bridges to the Doctorate (BD) Fellowship works with institutions who have the Louis Stokes Alliance for Minority Participation (LSAMP). These programs provide funding for master's-level students who are LSAMP graduates in various STEM disciplines (https://nsf.gov /funding/pgm_summ.jsp?pims_id=13646#:~:text=Bridge %20to%20the%20Doctorate%20(BD)%20Activity%3A%20 BD%20projects%20are,them%20to%20successfully%20ea rn%20STEM).

Alliances for Graduate Education and Professoriate (AGEP) supports underrepresented doctoral and post-doctoral students, as well as faculty, to improve pathways to STEM and STEM education disciplines. Funding is

---

granted to institutions (https://www.nsf.gov/funding/pgm_summ.jsp?pims_id=5474).

Graduate Research Fellowships Program is aimed at diversifying the workforce. The fellowship is open to STEM, psychology, an social sciences students pursuing research-based masters and doctoral degrees. The fellowship promotes STEM education and learning through financial support and a mentored research experience (https://www.nsf.gov/pubs/2018/nsf18573/nsf18573.pdf).

FISK-VANDERBILT MASTER'S-TO-PHD BRIDGE PROGRAM

The Fisk-Vanderbilt Master's-to-PhD Bridge Program is a national leader in producing African American and other URM students with doctorate degrees in STEM disciplines. The collaboration assists these two institutions, as well as many others, in the recruitment and retention of underrepresented students of color in life and physical science disciplines. For fifteen years, the program has created pipelines of diversity into doctoral programs and research and faculty posts around the country.

Type

Fisk-Vanderbilt Master's-to-PhD Bridge Program	
Place in the Pipeline	Graduate-Master's and doctoral students
Type of Students Served	URMs, LIFG
	Disability, gender, military/veteran status, race/ethnicity, religion, sexual orientation, socio-economic status (e.g., low-income)
Disciplines Served	Life sciences and physical sciences
Funding Source	Support is from the Department of Education, including Title VII and Graduate Assistance in Areas of National Need (GAANN) grants. There is also support from Bridges to the Doctorate Program grants from the National Institutes of Health (NIH) (R25), as well as from NSF grants, which are awarded to the program in general and to specific mentors. Further grants are pending with NASA.
Institutional Structure	PWIs HBCUs
Length of Time in Program	Other
Geographic Location	Nationwide
Institutions Served	Vanderbilt University and Fisk University
Program Accepts New Sites	No
Program Deadlines	April 15
Website	www.fisk-vanderbilt-bridge.org

History

Since 2004, the Fisk-Vanderbilt Master's-to-PhD Bridge Program has focused on increasing the number of underrepresented minorities earning PhDs in astronomy, biology, chemistry, materials science, and physics. For more than 135 students, the program has built a family of scholars who are committed to mentoring one another and to doing world-class research. In the first two years of the program, students work towards a master's degree at Fisk University, with access to instructional and research opportunities at both Fisk and Vanderbilt Universities. Students receive full funding, which covers tuition, fees, and a monthly stipend. The program prepares students to apply to and thrive within a PhD program of their choice, and the program works to cement valuable research connections in PhD programs to make the transition as seamless as possible. Students in the bridge family, whether at Vanderbilt or elsewhere, are supported through the PhD and beyond. Students are provided with mentorship; networking opportunities; internships at national labs; assistance with presentations; qualifying exams, thesis, and defense preparation; job talks; and job placement. As a result, Fisk has become the nation's top producer of African Americans with master's degrees in physics, and Vanderbilt has become a top producer of URM PhDs in astronomy, physics, and materials science.

The Fisk-Vanderbilt Master's-to-PhD Bridge Program was first conceived in 2002 by David Ernst, PhD (Vanderbilt University), Eugene Collins, PhD (Fisk University), and Arnold Burger, PhD (Fisk University). After Ernst met and recruited Keivan Stassun, PhD, for a faculty position at Vanderbilt, the two began to formalize the program, and Stassun and Burger were named codirectors. This initiative took on its first student in September 2004.

Alumni Success

As of 2018, the Fisk-Vanderbilt Master's-to-PhD Bridge Program has produced twenty-nine graduates with doctorates in physics, astronomy, and materials sciences, making this initiative one of the top producers of African Americans with PhDs in these disciplines. The program produced the first African American woman to graduate with a PhD in astronomy from Yale University (Jedidah Isler, PhD, astrophysicist, founder of Vanguard STEM).

Research Preparation

Students can complete their master's degree under the guidance of caring faculty mentors. Students in the Fisk-Vanderbilt

Master's-to-PhD Bridge Program develop a strong academic foundation and research skills, and one-on-one mentoring relationships foster a successful transition to the PhD While students earn their master's at Fisk University, they are provided with research skills through various scientific and professional skill-development programs. Courses are provided to address any gaps in undergraduate preparation, and research experiences allow students to develop and demonstrate their full scientific talent and potential.

The program is administered by the Graduate School, which requires all first-year graduate students to enroll in a course to enhance research and professional skills. All entering graduate students participate in a weekly ninety-minute session during their first semester, which focuses on achieving success in their graduate program. The seminar-style course, Introduction to Graduate Studies and the Responsible Conduct of Research, is coordinated by faculty and staff at Fisk University and partnering institutions. This required course will address professional topics, including, but not limited to, time management; ethics, honesty, and plagiarism; electronic bibliographic tools; the library and its digitally linked tools; the responsible conduct of research; career opportunities in the sciences outside of academia; oral and written communication; and poster presentations. The course ends with a poster presentation, where first-year students describe the overall research objectives of their research supervisor's program and the specific project or project area in which they will do their thesis research.

Workshops

Workshops are given throughout the year, are several hours in length, and focus on professional skills needed by graduate students for preparing their thesis and in achieving their next professional goals. A boot camp for students writing a thesis is held each spring, in partnership with the Fisk University Writing Center, and it will facilitate the completion of the second-year student's master's thesis.

Additional workshops will also be made available in partnership with the Office of Career Planning and Development at Fisk University. Workshops include topics like preparing a résumé and CV, as well as learning about, applying for, and interviewing for PhD programs or career positions (with mock interviews). The program also welcomes additional topics of interest to students. Many students who enter Fisk's master's program have the goal of ultimately obtaining a PhD or a discipline-focused professional degree. Though GREs are required for consideration of admission to Fisk's master's programs, some students find their scores would not be competitive for direct admission to a PhD program. Consequently, one of Fisk's missions is to maximize the career opportunities of its trainees, and master's students are encouraged to participate in Kaplan preparation programs. These preparation programs are no longer funded by the university, and students must register for them independently.

Students are given access to resources to improve their writing skills. The Fisk University Writing Center is a resource that all participants are encouraged to use. Students are encouraged to visit and meet with a tutor at any stage of the writing process, from brainstorming a topic to making final revisions.

Professional Development Sessions

There are several opportunities to enhance skills through professional development. The Fisk-Vanderbilt Master's-to-PhD Bridge Program provides seminars on the following topics: time and stress management, the transition to graduate school (PhD), lab notebooks and clarification of data ownership, mentorship, authorship, scientific writing, research misconduct, the path to tenured professor, ancestors and legacies, confidence and productivity, imposter syndrome, networking and social interaction, résumés and CVs , and online tutorials.

Funding Opportunities

Financial assistance is available to qualified students through tuition waivers granted by the university and through graduate student stipends and research assistantships, which are funded by various grants and contracts to Fisk faculty or Fisk University. Students who receive full-time stipend support are not permitted, based on the mandates of the federal funding for these stipends, to engage in part-time work. The basis for the stipend funding is to permit students to focus entirely on their learning and research discovery.

Inclusion and Identity

Students are introduced to graduate education at a minority-serving institution (specifically, an HBCU), where they are nurtured in a holding environment for learning. Participants earn their master's degree under the guidance of caring faculty mentors while developing a strong academic foundation and research skills, and they are provided with one-on-one mentoring relationships that foster a successful transition to the PhD The program is flexible and focuses on the individualized goals and needs of each student. Courses are selected to address any gaps in undergraduate preparation, and research experiences allow students to develop and demonstrate their full scientific talent and potential. Students are given the inclusive space to reach academic goals and transition into a doctoral program.

Inclusion

The Fisk-Vanderbilt Master's-to-PhD Bridge Program strives to be inclusive of all identities, recognizing that we bring our whole selves to our work. The program seeks to have culturally competent mentoring practices. Students are part of a cohort when they join the program, and the cohort supports their academic and personal success.

Identity

The Fisk-Vanderbilt Master's-to-PhD Bridge Program encourages academic and scientific self-efficacy through individualized coursework and fundamental hands-on scientific research training. In addition, the program provides a yearlong professional skills course that addresses how to build self-efficacy as well as how to manage imposter syndrome and stereotype threat. The program also provides opportunities for students to develop the skills needed to navigate the academic environment.

The Fisk-Vanderbilt program provides extensive, scaffolded mentoring, which is intended to allow students to bring their whole self to the community. One-on-one meetings are used to track student progress and provide resources and opportunities that align with student goals. They use a proactive mentoring approach to rapidly respond to a student's personal or academic needs.

Voice

Mentoring and Coaching

Students are partnered with faculty and peer mentors throughout their experience. Mentees are expected to be reviewed by mentors during their relationship. Students are evaluated on basic concepts of the research project, technical skills, independent thinking, professional conduct, ability to meet deadlines, ability to define objectives, communication skills, use of literature, ability to obtain relevant results, ability to appropriately interpret data, ability to formulate supportable conclusions, and organization. Mentorship is a hallmark of the Fisk-Vanderbilt Master's-to-PhD Bridge

Program, allowing students the holding space to find their voice and have the bandwidth to handle the rigors of a doctoral program.

Mentors are peers of the program's participants (e.g., near peer, tiered peer). Mentors provide regularly scheduled meetings with mentees, psychological and emotional support, exchanges of social displays of scientific knowledge and practices, and support with goal setting and career planning. Mentees are shown academic customs, pitfalls, departmental politics, and taboos, and mentees are allowed to attend events with mentors (e.g., dinners, social events, conferences, retreats). Mentors give support with academic- or discipline-specific knowledge through direct teaching and access to academic resources (e.g., precollegiate/collegiate/graduate/postdoctoral/faculty training, standardized test preparation, writing workshops, research workshops, tenure and promotion information). Mentees recognize the value of their mentors (e.g., coauthorship, graduate school and employment references). Further, alumni of the program serve as mentors and workshop speakers.

The program provides voice in monthly seminars, which engage the community and encourage students to share their experiences with their cohort and mentors. Students are part of steering committees, which ensures they have direct representation in improving and developing the program. Monthly newsletters celebrate achievements. Also, the program provides professional development and social events, which encourage interactions between students as well as between faculty and students. Finally, the program offers a Bridge Research Celebration Day, which brings students, faculty, and alumni together to learn about scholarship and each other.

Expectations

The goal of the program is to increase the number of URM doctoral students in STEM disciplines, where they are historically underrepresented (e.g., astronomy, biology, chemistry, materials science, physics). The program is on track to produce three to five PhDs per year, significantly bolstering the number of researchers and faculty of color in these disciplines. Fisk University has now become one of the top producers of African Americans earning master's degrees in STEM fields. Further, the Fisk-Vanderbilt Master's-to-PhD Bridge Program has an 83 percent retention rate for the PhD and a 97 percent overall retention rate while students are in the program. The program has produced over ninety master's degrees and thirty-six PhDs since 2004. Key performance indicators include student experience, degree completion, transition and retention to the PhD, PhD completion, time to degree, fellowships, student publications, grant funding, and employment.

Graduate Governmental Academic Pipeline Programs

Substance Abuse and Mental Health Services Administration
https://www.samhsa.gov

The Substance Abuse and Mental Health Services Administration (SAMHSA) was established in 1992 to reduce the effects of substance abuse and mental illness in US communities. It is part of the US Department of Health and Human Services.

The Substance Abuse and Mental Health Services Administration Minority Fellowship Program (SAMSHA MFP) is a program to develop more master's- and doctorate-level professionals who are dedicated to improving behavioral health outcomes for minority communities. The SAMSHA MFP supports graduate-level training in the four traditional mental health and substance abuse disciplines: psychiatric nursing, psychiatry, psychology, and social work. The program focuses on providing training support to members of underrepresented racial and ethnic minority groups. Professional

---

organizations provide financial support for racial and ethnic minority students. Awards are given to fellows interested in mental health or substance abuse service delivery as providers or through indirect means, such as research, teaching, or administration (https://www.samhsa.gov/minority-fellowship-program).

US Department of Agriculture
https://www.usda.gov/

The US Department of Agriculture (USDA) is a long-standing partner with nationwide graduate programs.

Minorities in Agriculture, Natural Resources and Related Sciences (MANRRS) promotes diversity in college students' academic, professional, and leadership skills. Students can participate in an internship program and the annual conference (https://info.manrrs.org/summerblminternship).

SUMMARY

Graduate and professional school academic pipeline programs prepare trainees to leverage opportunities into postdoctoral and faculty posts. Because most of the illustrated programs have existed for over twenty years, they can use their alumni networks, affiliated faculty, and institutions to find academic homes for their graduates. There are not many URM PhDs in the United States who have not had some association with at least one of the programs listed or pipeline programs highlighted in the index. These programs significantly increase the number of URM students who pursue careers in the academy. One of the critical commonalities of doctorate or graduate pipeline programs is mentorship. While many URM students are capable of handling the academic rigors of being a graduate student, they often lack interpersonal and networking skills, which are required to be successful in doctoral programs (Thomas, Willis, & Davis, 2007). Mentors enhance the silent variables of social capital, social networks, and self-efficacy that are necessary for academic and career success in advanced study (Byrd, 2016).

Another commonality of the listed pathway initiatives are the professional development and research opportunities (Young & Brooks, 2008). Because these opportunities are critical to moving URM and LIFG students into postdoctoral and faculty position, most pipeline initiatives work them into the fabric of the programming. Consistent professional development training is generally composed of workshops on conference presentations and attendance, résumés/CVs, time-management skills, imposter syndrome, academic careers, thesis and dissertation committee selection, and funding opportunities. These professional development opportunities are vital to URM and LIFG graduate students, as many are not prepared or do not know where to seek these services on their college campuses.

Moreover, academic pipeline programs provide safe spaces for underserved graduate students to find one another, share common research interests, and share stories of how they overcame similar obstacles. Graduate students from URM and LIFG groups use these programs as areas where they can develop their academic identity and voice. Peer and former mentors of these initiatives help students develop their professional skills, including organizing their academic portfolio, improving their communication abilities, using literature to ground research, and working with mentors to understanding academic culture. These pathway programs provide the spaces necessary for scholars to learn, develop, grow, and thrive in the academic world. Because so many of the students who participate in these programs are first generation, particularly when it comes to graduate and professional programs, these initiatives are necessary aids for faculty, mentors, and administrators looking to support their students in graduating from their programs. Further, students from these programs are given the skill sets to not only graduate but to also seamlessly transition into postdoctoral and faculty positions and to thrive as top scholars in the academy.

In the next chapter, we will introduce the final set of programs, which support one of the most critical segments of the pipeline. Faculty diversity is a goal for many of these initiatives, and faculty diversity is necessary for the ever-growing multicultural college classroom.

Selected Additional Graduate Academic Pipeline Programs

American Education Research Association
https://www.aera.net/

Since 1991, the American Education Research Association (AERA) has supported historically underrepresented racial and ethnic groups in higher education (e.g., African Americans, Alaska Natives, Native Americans, Asian Americans, Hispanics or Latinos, Native Hawaiian, Pacific Islanders).

AERA Minority Dissertation Fellowship Program in Education Research supports graduate students from historically underrepresented racial and ethnic groups in higher education with a stipend of $25,000 for one year. Awardees also present their research as part of an invited poster session during the annual AERA meeting and participate in a mentoring and career development workshop (https://www.aera.net/Professional-Opportunities-Funding/AERA-Funding-Opportunities/Minority-Dissertation-Fellowship-Program).

American Psychological Association
https://www.apa.org/

The American Psychological Association (APA) Minority Fellowship Program (MFP) has been supporting graduate

---

students since 1974. The goal of the MFP is to provide financial support, professional development, training, and mentoring for graduate students, postdoctoral scholars, and early-career professionals.

Dalmas A. Taylor Memorial Summer Minority Policy Fellowship was named in honor of the past president of the Society for the Psychological Study of Social Issues (SPPSI), who was very instrumental in starting the APA MFP. The fellowship is administered through SPPSI in conjunction with the APA MFP. The fellowship is designed to support a graduate student who identifies as an ethnic minority to work on public policy issues in the summer. In addition to a stipend, funding is provided to assist with housing and relocation expenses. Fellows also participate in the SPPSI conference and gain a network of mentors. Applicants are strongly encouraged apply to this fellowship and the APA MFP at the same time (https://www.spssi.org/index.cfm?fuseaction=page.viewPage&pageID=743&nodeID=1).

Interdisciplinary Minority Fellowship Program (IMFP) supports graduate students at both the master's and doctorate levels who are studying psychology, nursing, social work, marriage and family therapy, mental health counseling, or substance use and addictions counseling. Students receive a stipend, professional development, travel assistance to trainings, assistance with career planning, and networking (http://mfpapp.apa.org/docs/apa/IMFPinformationdocument-final.pdf).

Psychology Summer Institute (PSI) offers one-on-one mentorship for advanced doctoral students and early-career psychologists, with the intent that fellows will submit successful postdoctoral fellowship or grant

proposals (https://www.apa.org/pi/mfp/psychology/insti
tute).

Social Science Research Council
https://www.ssrc.org

Mellon Mays Predoctoral Research Grants support the Mellon Mays Undergraduate Fellowship Program (MMUF). Three opportunities for funding exist. Graduate studies enhancement (GSE) grants (up to $2,000) provide funding to purchase resources to support professional development (e.g., travel, books, journal subscriptions, software). Predoctoral research development (PRD) grants (up to $3,000) support small-scale research activities. Both GSE and PRD grants are open to second- to fifth-year graduate students. Dissertation completion research (DCR) grants are for graduate students who are in their seventh year or beyond. Funding assists with resources to support the professional development necessary to complete the dissertation (e.g., travel, books, journal subscriptions, software). Fellows with DCR grants also have access to the Preparing for the Professoriate Seminar, which has workshops related to CV building, job applications, fit, postdoctoral fellowships, and identity (https://www.ssrc.org/fellowships/view/mellon-mays-predoctoral-research-grants/).

Robert Wood Johnson Foundation
https://www.rwjf.org/

Health Policy Research Scholars is a fellowship for full-time doctoral students in their second year who are pursuing a research-based discipline that can impact health or build healthier and more equitable communities. Funding is provided for up to four years, with an optional nonfiscally supported fifth year. Scholars get access to a network of mentors and are involved in advocacy work as alumni (https://healthpolicyresearch-scholars.org/).

Doctoral/Graduate/Professional Program Commonalit es Using the THRIVE Index

Program	Type	History	Research	Inclusion-Identity	Voice	Expectations
Southern Regional Educational Board (SREB) Doctoral Scholars Program **Alfred P. Sloan Foundation Minority Graduate Scholarship** **McKnight Doctoral Fellowship Program** **Ford Foundation Fellowship Program** **National GEM Consortium** **Fisk-Vanderbilt Master's-to-PhD Bridge Program**	graduate and professional	average length of time each program has been in existence: ten to forty years	workshop seminars on professional development (e.g., CV development, interviews, academic writing) funding based on research and writing training in research methodologies	conferences to support each other's research and network with likeminded scholars building community of scholars understanding the logistics and politics of academic departments building self-confidence acknowledgment of successes collaborative research teams	providing mentorship (e.g, near peer, junior & senior faculty relationships) partnership between participants and alumni of programs to allow for support and conversations on how to succeed development of safe spaces for interactions among participants and faculty, administration participation in conferences, reinforcing presentation skills and professional work	high retention rates within graduate programs success placing graduates into faculty positions evaluations and annual performance reports, KPIs development of sustained networks and reinforcing networks when transitioning into faculty posts

CHAPTER 5

POSTDOCTORAL/FACULTY PROGRAMS

In this chapter, we will review programs considered the final destination of the academic pipeline. The highlighted initiatives in this postdoctoral/faculty section provide resources that reinforce the success of those who have earned a doctorate and who have connected the dots to become tenured faculty members. Key elements of these programs include establishing mentorship, navigating academic procedures and cultures, strengthening networks, and building persistence and resilience. Becoming a tenured faculty member involves maintaining a disciplined and consistent scholarly writing schedule, seizing professional development opportunities, building and maintaining networks, acculturating successfully in an academic department (without losing identity), becoming a solid research scholar/practitioner, and developing thoughtful teaching skills (Smith, Turner, Osei-Kofi, & Richards, 2004). Although there are many facets to becoming a proficient faculty member, the programs we highlight in this section have been very successful in assisting with every aspect of this arduous journey.

Faculty and administrator pipeline programs assist their participants with the iterative process of learning coping skills during times of rejection, accepting constructive criticism, building mentoring networks, and developing academic socialization skills (Robbins & LePeau, 2018). In this section, we will illustrate some of the hallmark URM faculty and postdoctoral programs (the University of California President's Postdoctoral Fellowship Program, the National Center for Faculty Development & Diversity (NCFDD) Faculty Success Program, the Sisters of the Academy [SOTA] Institute, the Rochester Institution of Technology [RIT] Future Faculty Career Exploration Program, and the Creating Connections Consortium [C3]), which have assisted many underrepresented minority (URM) postdoctoral researchers and faculty members to move successfully through their academic life journey. Each program was reviewed using the THRIVE index. Also, we have included established governmental and foundational academic pipeline programs, which provide a lens into supportive initiatives for URM PhDs in STEM, social sciences, humanities, and education fields.

UNIVERSITY OF CALIFORNIA PRESIDENT'S POSTDOCTORAL FELLOWSHIP PROGRAM

The University of California (UC) President's Postdoctoral Fellowship Program is one of the longest existing initiatives to support newly minted doctoral students in the country. This program encourages top female and minority scholars to pursue academic careers at the University of California.

Type

UC President's Postdoctoral Fellowship Program	
Place in the Pipeline	Postdoctoral PhDs
Type of Students Served	URMs, gender minorities, disabled, and LGBTQIA+
Disciplines Served	All majors
Funding Source	Funded directly by the UC
Institutional Structure	Predominantly white institutions (PWIs)
Length of Time in Program	Two years
Geographic Location	Nationwide
Institutions Served	Nationwide
Program Accepts New Sites	No
Program Deadlines	November 1
Website	https://ppfp.ucop.edu/info/

History

The UC President's Postdoctoral Fellowship Program was founded in 1984 to train promising scholars with the potential to contribute to the diversity of the UC faculty through their research, teaching, and service. The program has supported over 700 fellows. The UC President's Postdoctoral Fellowship Program works with students who have completed their doctorate degree, including terminal doctorate degrees beyond the PhD (e.g., EdD, JD, MD), as long as they are pursuing careers in university teaching and research. In 2011, the University of Michigan's President's Postdoctoral Fellowship Program (https://presidentspostdoc.umich.edu/) was formed in collaboration with the UC.

Alumni Success

Notable alumni of the program include the following: Adela de la Torre (president, San Diego State University), Cullen Bui (director of MIT's Laboratory for Energy and Microsystems), Padmini Rangamani (recipient, Presidential Early Career Award for Scientists and Engineers), Dwight McBride (president, The New School), and Janna Levin (recipient, Guggenheim Fellowship in natural sciences, PEN/Robert W. Bingham Prize).

Research Preparation

The UC President's Postdoctoral Fellowship Program prepares postdoctoral students with various scholarly opportunities as they prepare for academic careers. Scholars are required to focus full-time on research and limit other activities, such as teaching or additional employment. Participants are encouraged to spend time on research and publishing activities. Teaching commitments must align with the scholar's research and must take place in small, focused courses to allow for the scholar to strengthen their teaching skills and pedagogy.

Workshops and Professional Development

Participants are exposed to various career development workshops. Workshops include activities on writing, academic job interview preparation, negotiation assistance, faculty mentorship, and hiring incentives. The program includes a fall meeting, which brings together postdoctoral- and dissertation-year fellows for workshops and discussion groups. There is a winter writing retreat, where fellows work to develop their research toward publication (e.g., journals, books). Further, there is an academic retreat in the spring, where fellows and faculty mentors work together in various networking sessions. Also, fellows are given feedback on research papers they may present at conferences.

Funding

The UC President's Postdoctoral Fellowship Program supports approximately fifteen scholars in all areas of research. The 2018 annual salary was $48,216 (which varies based on the field of expertise), with a $5,000 stipend for research and professional development. Fellows are also provided health benefits, sick leave, maternity leave, and paid time off. In 2017–2018, the UC President's Postdoctoral Fellowship Program introduced fellowships that are either fully funded, partially funded, or unfunded (without salary compensation). These new fellowships meant the program could maximize the number of scholars it served.

Inclusion and Identity

Inclusion

The UC President's Postdoctoral Fellowship Program creates safe spaces for diverse PhDs who learn new skills to prepare for academic life. Program staff work with faculty administrators to assure equitable search practices. The fellowship program provides academic retreats, physical space, and quality time for forums to discuss diversity and inclusion issues.

Identity

This program supplies ongoing interaction with mentors and program staff who provide mentorship and guidance on post-award tenure. These experiences and spaces assist with building academic identity. The interventions established by the program create proficient new academics who are prepared for the rigors of a tenure-track position.

Voice

Mentoring

Fellows are given faculty and peer mentors to serve as strong role models, provide community, and support academic excellence. Faculty mentors are expected to be tenured faculty (associate or full professor) and serve to assist fellows in achieving their research goals, establishing a presence in the department, participating in national and international meetings, and preparing for interviews and academic life. The faculty mentor role is critical because it provides the essential networks necessary to joining the discipline's faculty ranks. Peer mentors serve as senior fellows in their second year, an important contribution to the program. These "renewed fellows" have a valuable role in the program, and they share their experiences and provide advice to the new fellows.

Program officials and mentors lend advice on job-talk preparation and negotiation. Fellows are assisted with workshops on academic culture, as well as on race, ethnicity, gender, and ability, which strengthen fellows' resolve as they pursue academic careers in fields where they are often underrepresented. The program activities and mentor relationships empower these new scholars, which allows them to feel confident as they start out in the academic community.

Expectations

The UC President's Postdoctoral Fellowship Program has both long-term and short-term goals. Overall, their primary goal is to transition fellows to tenure-track faculty positions in the UC system. Participants are selected based on their desire to pursue a career in the academy and receive mentorship and guidance to support this goal. Fellows choose academic mentors to work with during their fellowship. They receive other mentoring from participating faculty and administrators within the UC system. These students are groomed to become highly effective researchers, faculty, and administrators within some of the finest institutions in the nation.

Some current initiatives and goals within the program include strategic planning with UC advisory committees, developing hiring incentives for the health sciences, and including national partner institutions to expand the network of scholars across the nation.

Postdoctoral/Faculty Governmental Academic Pipeline Programs

National Institutes of Health
https://www.nih.gov/

We highlight examples of the National Institutes of Health (NIH) initiatives provided through the National Institute of General Medical Sciences (NIGMS) (https://www.nigms.nih.gov/training/Pages/Home.aspx).

Maximizing Opportunities for Scientific and Academic Independent Careers (MOSAIC; K99/R00 and UE5) helps postdoctoral researchers transition into the faculty workforce. The award has both an individual (K99/R00) and an institutional (UE5) component (https://www.nigms.nih.gov/training/careerdev/Pages/MOSAIC.aspx).

National Institute on Drug Abuse (NIDA) Scientific Director's Fellowship for Diversity in Research (SDFDR) Postdoctoral Fellows offers scholars who have received terminal degrees (PhD, MD, DDS, or equivalent) within five years of application a mentored research experience. Activities include professional development (e.g., seminars, individual development plans, research presentation) and a group community project (https://irp.drugabuse.gov/organization/diversity/sdfdr-postdoc/).

The National Science Foundation (NSF) has several initiatives to support faculty, from undergirding research projects to providing professional development and mentoring. Many of these programs are geared for URM faculty at different stages of their academic career. A common theme of these programs is that participants must submit a proposal to obtain the resources of the program. Divisions of education and human resources (EHR) houses many programs that are geared toward underrepresented students and faculty. The two listed in this section specifically work with URM faculty.

Faculty Early Career Development Program (CAREER) highly encourages women, members of URM groups, and persons with disabilities to apply. The CAREER is considered one of the NSF's most prestigious awards. CAREER supports early-career faculty who are future role models in research education within their department or organization. The goal of this program is to provide early-career faculty with a firm foundation of leadership skills for the life of their career (https://www.nsf.gov/funding/pgm_summ.jsp?pims_id=503214).

ADVANCE: Organizational Change for Gender Equity in STEM Academic Professions seeks a more diverse STEM workforce by looking at gender, racial, and ethnic equity. The NSF ADVANCE program seeks to implement evidence-based change and strategies promoting equity in STEM. This program supplies grants to institutions to support equity and inclusion by mitigating the systemic factors that create inequities in the academy and workplace, particularly in STEM. The award supports STEM,

social, behavioral and economic sciences (https://www
.nsf.gov/funding/pgm_summ.jsp?pims_id=5383&org=EH
R&from=home).

NATIONAL CENTER FOR FACULTY DEVELOPMENT & DIVERSITY FACULTY SUCCESS PROGRAM

The National Center for Faculty Development & Diversity (NCFDD) Faculty Success Program is one of the most innovative programs to directly affect the composition and adaptability of diverse faculty in the academy. The program has evolved into a national initiative to assist diverse graduate students, postdoctoral researchers, junior faculty, tenured faculty, administrators, and institutions of higher learning in their quest to incorporate diversity into the college classroom.

Type

National Center for Faculty Development & Diversity (NCFDD) Faculty Success Program	
Place in the Pipeline	Collegiate faculty members and Graduate-doctoral students
Type of Students Served	URMs and gender minorities
Disciplines Served	All majors
Funding Source	Other funding; universities sponsor faculty members as a part of their professional development
Institutional Structure	Nonprofit; works with institutions and individuals
Length of Time in Program	Twelve weeks
Geographic Location	Nationwide
Institutions Served	Nationwide
Program Accepts New Sites	No
Program Deadlines	No deadline, but participants must be tenure track or tenured faculty and register during designated time frames for fall, spring, or summer programs. Dissertation Success Curriculum—no deadline, based on demand. Graduate students at NCFDD institutions can participate for free in the program. Graduate students at nonparticipating institutions can get sponsored or pay the fee of $240.
Website	https://www.facultydiversity.org/fsp-boot camp; https://www.facultydiversity.org/dissertation -success-public

History

The Faculty Success Program, founded in 2010 by Kerry Ann Rockquemore, PhD, helps support tenure-track faculty on their path toward tenure. More than six thousand faculty have participated in the Faculty Success Program, and the most recent cohort is the largest ever, with more than four hundred faculty participating. The program represents those who are URMs (e.g., racial gender) within the faculty.

The Dissertation Success Curriculum, established in 2016, helps graduate students with support toward the progression and completion of their dissertation. The NCFDD has more than one hundred and ninety members, and all their graduate students get access to this program for free.

Alumni Success

Alumni from the Faculty Success Program are better equipped to handle work–life balance, research and writing agendas, and the tenure system. Notable alumni include Deanna L. Fassett, PhD (professor and chair, San Jose State University) and Tamara Beauboeuf-Lafontant, PhD (professor and director, DePauw University).

Research Preparation

The Faculty Success Program is all about learning the secrets to increasing research productivity, getting control of time, and living a full and healthy life beyond campus. As NCFDD's signature program, the Faculty Success Program is specifically designed to transform personal and professional life. The program is for tenure-track and tenured faculty who are looking for the perfect combination of empirically tested methods to improve research productivity through intense accountability, coaching, and peer support. Further, NCFDD looks to propel work–life balance and personal growth to a whole new level.

Workshops and Professional Development

The Dissertation Success Curriculum is designed to provide the skills, strategies, and support that advanced graduate students need to overcome the three most significant obstacles to finishing the dissertation: perfectionism, procrastination, and isolation. The community of graduate students in NCFDD are part of a supportive community and help to keep one another on track and accountable. The focus is on time management and effective writing habits to complete the dissertation. The accountability instruction is built from NCFDD's twelve "dissertation success training modules," facilitated by Kerry Ann Rockquemore, PhD. The NCFDD core curriculum trainings includes a moderated discussion forum for peer mentoring and tracking daily writing. Participants are assigned an "accountability buddy match" for additional support through the program.

Funding

NCFDD primarily provides professional development, training, and mentoring communities for graduate students, postdoctoral trainees, faculty, and administrators. No financial support is provided.

Inclusion and Identity

The NCFDD program was designed for underrepresented faculty to obtain mentorship beyond their institutions. Every week, a tenured faculty member leads a small group session with four faculty members, which enables them to get mentorship and to communicate in a safe, inclusive space.

Inclusion

The NCFDD Faculty Success Program provides structured dialogues and interactions (e.g., one-on-one sessions, virtual dialogues), personalized counseling services, and a sense of belongingness. The Faculty Success Program deliberately creates safe spaces and climates for newly minted PhDs to become fully functioning academics.

Identity

By helping graduate students complete their dissertation, the NCFDD program enables them to learn habits to start their academic journey. While the skills learned through the NCFDD program can help all graduate students, the program was developed to support URMs and gender minorities. The delivery of the program is on demand, and the mentor relationships are external, enabling safe environments for personal and professional development. Also, there are self-completed surveys, which are provided to participants to determine their strengths and levels of need.

Voice

Completing the dissertation is an important milestone to help start a faculty career. This program helps underrepresented groups learn the correct skills and habits to enable them to finish. By doing so, NCFDD is able to support each participant's career and academic journey.

Mentoring

The program assists participants to overcome the barriers faced by underrepresented faculty members. Administrators provide mentorship for underrepresented faculty, which they may not receive or which may not be available at their institution. Senior faculty serve as mentors for postdoctoral trainees and junior faculty, assisting them in the nuances of the tenure track. Program participants are coached and mentored while also learning to become independent, successful, and productive faculty members.

EXPECTATIONS

The Faculty Success Program is all about learning the secrets to increasing research productivity, getting control of your time, and living a full and healthy life beyond campus.

The NCFDD Dissertation Success Curriculum is designed to provide the skills, strategies, and support advanced graduate students need to overcome the three biggest obstacles to finishing their dissertation: perfectionism, procrastination, and isolation. The program is built on the premise that there is only one way to complete a dissertation: to write it. These skills are learned through various program surveys.

Faculty Governmental Academic Pipeline Programs

National Endowments of the Humanities
https://www.neh.gov/grants

The National Endowment for the Humanities (NEH) is an independent federal agency that funds humanities programs in the United States. In order to strengthen teaching and learning in schools and colleges, NEH provides grants to support colleges, universities, and individual scholars. Support from NEH facilitates research, publication, opportunities for lifelong learning, and access to cultural and educational resources. Faculty can apply for the support to strengthen the institutional base of the humanities. Awards include categories for faculty who serve minority-serving institutions.

SISTERS OF THE ACADEMY INSTITUTE

Sisters of the Academy (SOTA) Institute was created to facilitate the success of Black women in the academy. This initiative targets the creation of educational networks for Black female faculty, with a focus on teaching, scholarly inquiry, and service to the community. Further, SOTA aims to facilitate collaborative scholarship and enhance professional development among women of color in higher education.

Type

Sisters of the Academy (SOTA) Institute	
Place in the Pipeline	Postdoctoral-Faculty University and college faculty and instructors
Type of Students Served	URMs, gender minorities, low-income and first-generation (LIFG)
Disciplines Served	All majors
Funding Source	Funded through registration fees, foundations, federal agencies, and other private donors
Institutional Structure	Predominantly white institutions (PWIs) and other institutions, based on members
Length of Time in Program	Two years
Geographic Location	Nationwide
Institutions Served	Nationwide
Program Accepts New Sites	Yes (fifteen to thirty new participants per year)
Program Deadlines	Research BootCamp: May 1
Website	www.sistersoftheacademy.org

History

Founded in 2001, the SOTA Institute has a mission to facilitate the success of Black women in the academy. Specifically, the organization aims to create an educational network of Black women in higher education in order to foster success in the areas of teaching, scholarly inquiry, and service to the community; facilitate collaborative scholarship among Black women in higher education; and facilitate the development of relationships to enhance members' professional development. The institute hosts a variety of programs, including the Signature Research BootCamp, the Writing Retreat, and the Intensive Grantsmanship Workshop. SOTA represents both postdoctoral researchers and faculty within the educational pipeline.

Alumni Success

Notable alumni of the program include Rihana S. Mason, PhD (research scientist, Georgia State University) and Felica Moore Mensah, PhD (professor of science and education, associate dean, Columbia University).

Research Preparation

A variety of programs are offered by SOTA, including signature programs like the Signature Research BootCamp, the Writing Retreat, and the Intensive Grantsmanship Workshop. Most of SOTA programming is centered around research, mentorship, collegiality teaching, scholarly inquiry, and service and network building within the community of Black women scholars.

Workshops and Professional Development

The workshops and opportunities provided by SOTA begin with the Priming the Pipeline program, which focuses on mentorship, leadership, and community engagement for women of color who are undergraduate and graduate students. These future scholars are invited to network with SOTA members at the BootCamp, discuss future scholarly activities, participate in mentoring sessions, develop team action plans, and participate in leadership training sessions. In 2017, the Black Male Research BootCamp was created to assist Black male doctoral students with their research aspirations. Senior scholars are invited to interact with Black male scholars during their journey to become new academics. The initiative also provides an Intensive Grantsmanship Workshop, which includes plenary sessions, group and breakout discussions, and collaborative proposal writing. Junior and senior-level faculty, as well as doctoral students, are provided information on the proposal-writing process, budget development, practical and fundable research, and submission processes. Members are invited to participate in biennial writing retreats. Participants receive assistance with their writing endeavors, including dissertations, manuscripts, reports, or book chapters. Finally, SOTA has its Signature Research BootCamp. This long-standing biennial initiative is a one-week program to assist doctoral students and junior scholars to develop their research projects. Senior scholars are made available to facilitate workshops to assist new Black women scholars in conceptualizing and designing components of their dissertation. Senior scholars cultivate mentoring relationships with junior scholars and provide networks for the academic journey.

Funding and Support

Membership dues are $80 annually. Membership also includes membership in the Textbook and Academic Authors Association, free webinars, writing resources, grants, and a monthly newsletter.

Inclusion and Identity

Inclusion

Programming is "for us, by us" (FUBU, https://fubu.com/), which means it is designed and implemented by Black women for Black women. Sister circles are another successful attribute of the SOTA community because they allow for individual and small-group mentoring.

Identity

The SOTA Institute develops scholar and researcher identity, self-confidence, and confidence in research for all participants. By focusing on each woman's development and helping her to reach her full capacity, SOTA enables women to feel supported, confident, and highly competent. It is understood that diverse faculty contribute significantly to higher education as an enterprise; therefore, SOTA is changing the academy by working through individual faculty.

Voice

Mentoring

All SOTA programs assist with overcoming various obstacles and empower Black women during their journey as tenure-track faculty. Through programs, SOTA demystifies much of the academy's inner workings for Black women who are new to or unfamiliar with academia. In providing culturally responsive professional development, SOTA centers Black women's identity in all of their programming. By centering Black women, SOTA enables participants to see themselves and their perspectives reflected in their fellow participants, in the coordinators, in the implementers, and in the programs' foundations and framing.

Expectations

The primary goal of SOTA is to facilitate the success of Black women in the academy. The institute is intentional in building networks of scholarly inquiry, strengthening teaching, facilitating collaborative scholarship, and enhancing professional development among its members. Much of this intentional work is done through the SOTA framework of "results-based accountability" (RBA), which is used for teaching, learning, and program-administration training in order to facilitate program management and improvement for SOTA members.

Finally, SOTA truly exemplifies the pipeline process. By working with undergraduate students, connecting them with those in the doctoral phase of the pipeline, linking those in the doctoral phase with those who have earned their PhD, and, lastly, connecting junior nontenured faculty with senior tenured faculty, SOTA seeks to complete the academic network circle for aspiring Black women scholars. This nuanced program has found a successful method, which can be used among similar initiatives.

Faculty Foundation Academic Pipeline Programs

American Educational Research Association
https://www.aera.net/Professional-Opportunities-Funding

American Educational Research Association Fellowship Program on the Study of Deeper Learning (AERA-SDL) is designated for early-career education researchers and postdoctoral scholars and is designed to enhance the use of deeper learning data sets. Scholars are expected to foster excellence and rigor for the next generation of faculty, researchers, and scholars. Women and URM researchers are encouraged to apply for these grants. Fellows are provided funding, data training workshops, research conferences, networking opportunities, and a research institute held at the AERA annual meeting (https://www.aera.net/Professional-Opportunities-Funding /AERA-Funding-Opportunities/AERA-Fellowship-Program-on -the-Study-of-Deeper-Learning).

American Psychological Association
https://www.apa.org/

Leadership and Education Advancement Program (LEAP) for Diverse Scholars is designed for early-career professionals in various fields (e.g., anthropology, psychology, public health) who conduct research related to the mission of the National Institute of Diabetes and Digestive Kidney Diseases (NIDDK) and who have not been supported by R01 funding. The

---

program provides professional-development support related to grant submission and mentoring through a network of senior-level professionals (https://www.apa.org/pi/mfp/leap).

Postdoctoral Fellowship in Mental Health and Substance Abuse Services (MHSAS) supports early-career professionals for up to two years through funds from SAMSHA. Eligible applicants include individuals who demonstrate interest in service or policy related to behavioral health or the psychological well-being of ethnic minorities. Awards support travel and related expenses, professional development, and mentoring through a network of professionals who are engaged in research related to ethnic minorities (https://www.apa.org/pi/mfp/psychology/postdoc).

Social Science Research Council
https://www.ssrc.org/

Sloan Scholars Mentoring Network Grants provides three different types of grants to alumni of the Alfred P. Sloan Minority PhD Program. Grants can be used for conference travel (up to $1,500), mentoring activities (up to $5,000), and seed funding for research (up to $10,000) (https://www.ssrc.org/fellowships/view/ssmn-grants/).

Robert Wood Johnson Foundation
https://www.rwjf.org/

Harold Amos Medical Faculty Development Program is a fellowship designed to increase the number of faculty from URM backgrounds who reach senior-level faculty positions in the disciplines of medicine, dentistry, and nursing. Participating scholars receive a stipend, a grant to support research activities, and faculty mentoring for multiple years. Scholars attend an annual meeting (https://www.amfdp.org/).

ROCHESTER INSTITUTE OF TECHNOLOGY FUTURE FACULTY CAREER EXPLORATION PROGRAM (FFCEP)

The Rochester Institute of Technology (RIT) Future Faculty Career Exploration Program (FFCEP) has been one of the leading faculty diversity initiatives in the country for over fifteen years. In order to help new URM PhDs transition to become faculty members, RIT FFCEP assists them with establishing meaningful relationships, developing a curriculum, networking, and taking advantage of employment opportunities. The program is set up for the recruitment and retention of diverse faculty at RIT, a university with a proud teaching and research philosophy, and the program allows for participants to engage RIT deans and department chairs, based on their academic work and career interests. The initiative is one of a handful of dedicated faculty diversity programs at the university level in the nation.

Type

RIT Future Faculty Career Exploration Program

Place in the Pipeline	University and college faculty and instructors
Type of Students Served	URMs
Disciplines Served	Business management, communication, computer and information sciences, engineering, humanities, life sciences, mathematics, physical sciences, and social sciences
Funding Source	Other sources
Institutional Structure	PWI
Length of Time in Program	One-week or two-year postterminal degree fellowship positions
Geographic Location	Applicants from nationwide institutions
Institutions Served	RIT
Program Accepts New Sites	No
Program Deadlines	May (second week in May)
Website	https://www.rit.edu/academicaffairs/facultyrecruitment/future-faculty-programs/future-faculty-career-exploration-program

History

In the early 2000s, the president of RIT saw the need for faculty diversity, based on disparities among faculty of color at the institution. After physically witnessing the lack of diversity when welcoming a new cohort of faculty, the president developed the concept for this program in 2003. The president was told that search committees could not find historically underrepresented scholars—that they did not exist. This program proved that there are methods for recruiting and retaining reliable postdoctoral scholars and faculty members. This program serves as a pipeline-building program to bring URM scholars to campus and showcase their teaching and research. It provides a unique and exciting opportunity to explore future career choices through opportunities for mutual exchange, presentations, and meetings with deans, department heads, and administration and provides campus and community tours. Since the inception of the FFCEP program fifteen years ago, it hit the following milestone: over three hundred and thirty scholars have participated in the program, 11 percent of whom have been offered faculty or postdoctoral positions at RIT.

Alumni Success

Notable alumni include Dr. Kim Renee Ramsey-White (director of undergraduate programs, clinical professor, School of Public Health, Georgia State University); Dr. Robert C. Osgood, program director, associate professor of Biomedical Sciences, RIT.

Research Preparation

The program gives participants a glimpse into what is involved in the faculty search process. The graduate students and newly minted PhD who are involved in the program must prepare similar documents to apply for the program as they would for a faculty position. Additionally, participants have several exploratory interviews with faculty and administration and give a job talk on their research, just as they would during an on-campus interview.

Workshops and Professional Development

Participants are involved in workshops to gain presentation, networking, and interviewing skills. They can take in feedback and make adjustments without the full pressure of being in an actual interview. The program offers opportunities to build relationships with peers and faculty and to cultivate potential partnerships for future research collaborations. The program has many intangible benefits, but some of the key components that participants gain are interviewing, networking, and presentation skills. Participants hear from current faculty regarding the tenure and promotion process, search and selection process, mentorship, the balancing act of service, research and teaching, salary and start-up negotiations, grant writing, and parental and family leave policies, which make participants well prepared for pending job searches.

Funding

If selected for FFCEP, participants are provided travel, lodging, and meal expenses for the weekend visit to Rochester, New York. There is also an RIT Future Faculty Fellowship Program (FFFP) that provides a two-year post-graduate degree fellowship position to see if the candidate would be a good match with RIT.

Inclusion and Identity

Inclusion

While at FFCEP events, selected participants have interactions with RIT URM faculty and graduate students to reveal the campus culture and community of Rochester. The Division for Diversity and Inclusion at RIT, which has a mission to create environments of learning and support for prospective URM faculty, hosts FFCEP events and provides connections and networks for those who attend. The Division for Diversity and Inclusion is deliberate about faculty diversity and fostering an inclusive environment for RIT students. As a champion of diversity in thinking, research, and science, RIT believes having innovative URM faculty will enrich the learning experience for everyone on campus.

One of the guiding principles of FFCEP is relationship building. The program brings together faculty and promising scholars to forge relationships and build upon time spent together to network and share experiences. Mutual exchange is beneficial for scholars because it allows them to receive feedback, explore mentorship opportunities, and discuss diversity and inclusion issues they encounter in academia. The practices employed throughout the program strengthen each scholar's candidacy for future tenure-track positions.

Identity

Throughout the application process, RIT FFCEP affirms and acknowledges the different identities of participants by learning about them in their teaching, learning, and diversity statements. When selected candidates come to campus, RIT officials are able to better understand the needs of each. Further, program participants meet with the university's administration, deans, faculty, staff, and students to gain a better understanding of the culture and expectations of incoming faculty, with the intention of developing an inclusive environment.

Voice

As part of the program, participants essentially go through a faculty search process. Although no job is on the line, the program provides a supportive environment where participants can receive feedback and input for future interviews. Each participant partakes in exploratory interviews, gives a job talk, and meets with students and faculty to gain a better sense of the culture at RIT and within the department. Former participants have equated the program to a dry run for the job market, as it enhances their interview skills. Additionally, participants gain an understanding of the expectations of being a tenure-track faculty member.

Mentoring

Participants of RIT FFCEP have opportunities to network with RIT's president, provost, deans, and department chairs, who are very interested in their research and promote opportunities to teach on campus. Those invited to attend FFCEP are encouraged to formally present their research during the weekend to see if their interests align with RIT's academic departments. Senior faculty engage with prospective faculty by establishing meaningful dialogue and relationships, and those who find a match with their research interests are brought back for the FFFP, a two-year post-terminal degree fellowship that allows selected URM candidates an opportunity to be mentored and assisted with their teaching, which enhances their scholarly excellence.

In order to be intentional about celebrating the voice of each participant, there are several programmatic events that lend to discussions about a participant's journey. Most importantly, the program also provides an opportunity for participants to share their research with a broader audience, which takes place on an informal level during many social events, like at lunch or dinner.

Expectations

The program works to prepare and identify scholars for future faculty positions, whether at RIT or another institution. The goal of FFCEP is to expand pipelines of diversity into academia by encouraging URM graduate students and PhDs to further their research interests and learn the nuances of academic living. The potential for success is possible for URM PhDs, but initiatives like RIT FFCEP allow for comprehensive faculty diversity. The ultimate metric is gainful employment in faculty roles, whether at RIT or another institution.

CREATING CONNECTIONS CONSORTIUM

The Creating Connections Consortium (C3) was developed to address issues of diversity and inclusion within higher education by devoting resources and building capacity in URMs pursuing graduate degrees to become faculty. Partnerships were developed among liberal arts institutions by diversity officers, and these partnerships promote the creation of new strategies to diversify students and faculty by working with likeminded research institutions. What is innovative about C3 is their organic pipeline program, which bridges undergraduate research, graduate school support, faculty cohort building, and institutional transformation.

Type

Creating Connections Consortium	
Place in the Pipeline	University and college faculty and instructors, as well as graduate and undergraduate students
Type of Students Served	URMs
Disciplines Served	Communications, humanities, social sciences
Funding Source	Private foundation (Andrew W. Mellon Foundation)
Institutional Structure	PWIs
Length of Time in Program	Other
Geographic Location	Nationwide and specific institutions
Institutions Served	Specific institutions served
Program Accepts New Sites	No
Program Deadlines	Faculty funding, New Scholars Series—November 1 and May 1
Website	http://c3transformhighered.org

History

In 2012, C3 was created by representatives from three liberal arts colleges (Connecticut College, Middlebury College, and Williams College) and two research universities (Columbia University and UC Berkeley). This group applied for funding from the Andrew W. Mellon Foundation to build on the visits already offered by the Liberal Arts Diversity Officers (LADO) consortium to UC Berkeley. In 2015, C3 welcomed Bates College as the fourth liberal arts college partner. In 2016, it welcomed the University of Chicago and the University of Michigan as the third and fourth partner research universities.

Research Preparation

C3 provides summer research fellowships to URM undergraduate scholars who are interested in going to graduate school. Among the mentorship and research experiences these students receive are workshops on applying to graduate school and studying for the GRE. The goal is for these students to attend graduate school and potentially become faculty members at one of the liberal arts institutions that are part of the consortium.

Professional Development

In the C3/LADO visits to partner research universities, faculty members from LADO institutions provide graduate students with information on applying to and working at liberal arts colleges. They also have one-on-one meetings with graduate students to go over job application materials. Workshops and panels are also offered to graduate students at the C3 Summit and Pathways to Academia: Visits and Experiences (PAVE) program visits to liberal arts college partners.

Funding

Liberal arts institutions that are part of the consortium can apply for funding to support the first two years of a tenure-track position, plus start-up funds for research and travel. Through its New Scholar Series and Faculty Funding programs, C3 provides financial support to liberal arts colleges in the LADO consortium who are interested in learning about cutting-edge research by URM scholars (New Scholar Series), as well as to those departments or programs who want to diversify their curricular offerings (Faculty Funding).

Inclusion and Identity

To facilitate building inclusive campuses, C3 also creates new models or modifies existing ones to create new programming that can be implemented on any campus. The PAVE program is a new model, and the New Scholar Series is an existing model they modified. Through the New Scholars Series, affiliated liberal arts institutions are provided funds to support short-term visits to their campuses by URM graduate students or new graduates of doctorate-granting institutions. Through these visits, potential URM candidates provide new and diverse perspective for curricula and pedagogy.

Inclusion

To understand institutional and school cultures and expectations, C3 provides networking events and conversations with undergraduates, doctoral students, postdocs, and faculty. They also offer conferences, with workshops on curricula and pedagogical practices, as well as discussions about the specific challenges faced by underrepresented members of the academy.

Identity

In order to promote identity development, C3 offers various interactions with mentors, including professional development and coaching with feedback. In fact, C3's success depends on acknowledging students where they are, whether in conversations, in workshops for career and research development, with mentorships with faculty from underrepresented backgrounds, or at biannual conferences that build on inclusion and identity.

Voice

In the Faculty Funding program offered to C3 liberal arts institutions, support is given to institutions who seek new perspectives on their curricular offering and pedagogy and who see value in engaging doctoral candidates from URM groups. Many institutions do not invest in different perspectives in teaching and learning, and this program rewards institutions with financial support for being deliberate in hiring URM doctoral graduates.

Mentorship

Newly minted PhDs or MFAs can participate in the C3 Postdoctoral Fellowship program at one of the liberal arts institutions. Participants are mentored on how to build their teaching portfolios, advance their scholarship, and prepare for tenure-track positions. Mentors are available with this cohort model program. Further, candidates can be selected for open tenure-track faculty positions, where mentorship continues with two years of support from the Mellon Foundation.

Mentors are used in a variety of ways. This includes providing time for meetings, support, and information about academic culture. Further, mentors offer support with goal setting and career planning, assistance with academic- or discipline-specific knowledge through direct teaching, as well as awareness of academic resources (e.g., tenure and promotion information). Typically, mentees recognize the value of the mentor (e.g., coauthorship, graduate school and employment references) for their continued success on the journey to the professoriate. Alumni of the C3 program serve as workshop speakers and submit performance evaluations highlighting their successes. Participants are able to collaborate at conferences with various constituencies and have opportunities for mentorship and engagement with undergraduates, graduate students, staff, postdoc, faculty, and administrators.

Expectations

The goal of the C3 initiative is to create an organic academic pipeline, with undergraduate liberal arts students from consortium institutions eventually earning terminal degrees from the research institutions at which they did their summer undergraduate research. Then, after those students have earned their doctorate degrees, they have the opportunity, if selected, to teach and conduct research at a consortium institution. This symbiotic relationship achieves the goals of all of the institutions involved.

Underrepresented undergraduate students get research experience at a highly regarded university. These research universities have a pool of vetted prospective URM doctoral students from which to choose and the liberal arts institutions have fully invested, quality URM doctoral graduates to join their faculty. This program can indeed be a model for other institutions who are invested in diversifying academia at all levels.

Between 2014 and 2018, the Postdoctoral Fellowship program welcomed twenty-nine fellows from Columbia University, UC Berkeley, the University of Chicago, and the University of Michigan (twenty-two of whom have accepted tenure-track faculty positions.) These two-year positions provide postdoctoral fellows with an immersive experience in a liberal arts environment, which allows fellows to build their teaching portfolios, advance their scholarship, and prepare for a tenure-track position while also benefiting from a supportive mentoring and cohort program. These fellows were in residence at one of the four partner liberal arts colleges.

Program outcomes are based on surveys from all program participants, site visits to programs at various campuses, and annual reports to the funder (the Mellon Foundation). Most recent outcomes data on the C3 program include 2,004 total program participants as of August 2019, thirty-seven institutions who have participated in events, thirty-one former undergrad fellows who are enrolled in graduate school, and twenty-two of twenty-nine former postdoctoral fellows who hold tenure-track jobs. Key performance indicators include admission to graduate school, participant employment, and documentation of whether or not programming meets C3's goals and objectives.

SUMMARY

One of the common denominators of the faculty pipeline programs is mentorship. Mentoring opportunities start as soon as precollegiate programs, but the networks, as well as the cultural and social capital of these relationships, are essential through to the tenure of faculty members (Montgomery, 2017). It is critical for these initiatives to use established networks within their own groups and institutions to create environments that foster inclusivity and sustainability for new URM faculty. For example, several of these programs use elements of doctoral and postdoctoral networks to use as organic pipelines into the faculty ranks. Through mentoring, relationships, and networks, participants can polish their research, teaching, and writing skills as they are bridged into faculty positions within the same institution or at another institution. Participants can work through issues, like imposter syndrome, as many of these new scholars are first generation and not aware of the rigors of the professoriate. At this stage, most of the scholars of color brought through these programs can do the work. However, they need guidance on the nuances of navigating academic departments, staying on track through the tenure process, and not obliging oneself to outside service projects. Because there are so few diverse faculty members to serve as mentors, these programs have been used to supplement this deficit.

Specifically, programming provided by postdoctoral and faculty initiatives include developing interview skills, preparing mock job talks, developing diverse curricula and pedagogy, preparing for tenure and promotion, developing daily writing practices, managing time as an academic, writing for publication, and supporting dual-career families (Ancarana, 2019). Faculty initiatives provide the final steps to having a successful and robust academic career.

The final chapter will illustrate how these programs can be navigated seamlessly and work with each other to develop organic pipeline programming. Further, we will conclude by showing the common threads of these programs, how they provide the self-efficacy necessary for the vast number of URM students entering college, and how to use these initiatives to survive in the academy. Finally, we will demonstrate how these programs can assist in diversifying the professoriate in the new multicultural classroom.

Postdoctoral/Faculty Program Commonalities Using the THRIVE Index

Program	Type	History	Research	Inclusion-Identity	Voice	Expectations
UC President's Postdoctoral Fellowship Program National Center for Faculty Development and Diversity (NCFDD) Sisters of the Academy (SOTA) Rochester Institute of Technology (RIT) Future Faculty Career Exploration Program Creating Connections Consortium (C3)	Post-doctoral and faculty	average length of time each program has been in existence: eight to thirty years	workshops and seminars on professional development (e.g., negotiating salary, developing interview skills, developing effective writing skills for scholars) cultivating research collaborations learning about the tenure and promotion process postdoctoral fellowships to support those pursuing faculty posts	development of safe spaces for interactions with other scholars and mentors creating scholar, researcher identity understanding logistics and politics of academic departments networks and relationship building acknowledging participants where they are in their development as a scholar mentorship from faculty and peers	providing mentorship (e.g., near peer, junior and senior faculty relationships) understanding job talk preparation various faculty mentor role model relationships formal and informal gatherings to interact with senior administrators, department chairs, and senior faculty who show the ropes	successful track record of entering into tenure-track positions and earning tenure building networks and accountability to sustain new faculty in positions evaluations and annual performance reports, KPIs expand pipelines of URM faculty entering and sustaining themselves in positions

CHAPTER 6

CLOSING THOUGHTS

INTRODUCTION

> *Democracy cannot flourish in a nation divided into haves and have nots, and education plays a critical role in improving social mobility, carrying the potential to undermine the perpetuation of intergenerational inequality. For this reason, providing educational opportunities for everyone—not just the privileged—is essential for our nation's economy, and more importantly, for our democracy.*
> —Pasqueralla, aacu.org/liberaleducation/2018/winter/pasqucralla

Academic pipeline programs extend specific educational opportunities to everyone. Individuals acquire skills, resources, and networks through participation in academic pipeline programs. The cradle of academic persistence and retention among URM college students in the last twenty years has been through various research-based pathways or pipeline programs. Educational-enrichment programs provide academic services, financial support, and key programmatic components to sustain URM students, particularly in their formative years (Pender, Marcotte, Sto Domingo, & Maton, 2010).

Institutions of higher learning are regularly using national academic pipeline program models (e.g., McNair Scholars; the PhD Project) to assist URM students with creating mentoring relationships with faculty and administrators and to demystify academic success among students who may be the first generation to attend college or graduate/professional school (Minefee, Rabelo, Stewart, & Young, 2018). Programs that are tailored toward supporting postdoctoral scholars and faculty are gaining more popularity and aligning with programs at the early levels of the pipeline. Each academic pipeline program described in the book operates using a training model to promote academic and career success. Academic pipeline programs are operating as more than just *interventions*: they are building *culturally enriching communities of academic practice*.

In earlier chapters, we offered a glimpse into opportunities available to support URM students as they progress through the pipeline. Through our review of the hallmark programs, we uncovered that many academic pipeline programs operate similarly to the culture of liberal arts colleges (LAC). It has been suggested that the success of LACs lies in direct personal access to faculty, inclusion in partnerships in laboratories and fieldwork, opportunities to gain a breadth of skills, and exposure to diverse perspectives. By creating an environment that values learning for learning's sake, LACs allow students to discover their talents and calling (Scoggin, 2017). The same holds true for academic pipeline programs.

Through their longevity, these programs also demonstrate exceptional stewardship of fiscal resources and matriculation of numerous diverse scholars into the academy. Fiscal support serves as a foundation for programming to operate and as an extrinsic motivation for participation. Given the class differences and family commitments many URM students and faculty face, we recognize that one of the most salient components is financial support. As part of academic pipeline programs, financial support is offered in the form of meals, stipends, scholarships, fellowships, and travel awards, to name a few. Financial incentives in the context of academic pipeline programs are effective because they are also tied to activities that develop a greater sense of self, alongside the skills required for success (Stephens et. al., 2015). The programs we have highlighted have longevity. All but one program has supported students for ten years or more. Cumulatively, these programs have impacted around 60,000 URMs (the average of all the participants served across the highlighted programs).

The existence of so many successful programs demonstrates that the landscape of the academy is amenable to change. But change is slow. We understand that bringing awareness to these programs is neither the cure nor the only way to solve the issue of diversifying the academy. Creating this resource is one way to dispel the notion that it is hard to find well-prepared, diverse candidates for positions within the academy. We also acknowledge that there are several other factors contributing to how one navigates the academy, including financial preparation, attitudinal predispositions, family obligations, short-term and long-term goal changes, and policy changes, which influence career decisions and training outcomes (American Institutes for Research, 2014; Gándara, 2006).

More importantly, by bringing awareness to programs, we provide students and program directors with the opportunity to coordinate with one another and across programs. Research demonstrates that the greater the length of exposure to pipeline programming, the greater the likelihood for gains in academic success for program participants (see Williams, Ari, & Dortch, 2010, 2011 for precollegiate example). These programs provide evidence of successful interinstitutional partnerships, which include feeder programs between colleges and universities, government agencies, and not-for-profit organizations. The remainder of chapter 6 is organized into three sections: (1) how the Appreciative Inquiry (AI) framework relates to THRIVE and academic pipeline program best practices, (2) how to leverage academic pipeline programs as a consumer (e.g., parent, student, faculty, or administrator), and (3) how to change institutions or organizations by creating, cataloging, and coordinating programs.

APPRECIATIVE INQUIRY AND ACADEMIC PIPELINE PROGRAMS BEST PRACTICES

The academic pipeline programs highlighted in chapters 2–5 provide unique but interrelated contexts to develop people in ways that promote their success as professionals. Throughout the book, we have used the THRIVE Index as a centerpiece to illustrate the capacity of each program and to showcase their best practices. Because our tool focuses on the core strengths of these initiatives and highlights positive attributes, we have used appreciative inquiry (AI) to build the framework of THRIVE. AI asks positive questions of organizations and invites transformative dialogues with relevant actions of various human systems (Ludema, Cooperrider, & Barrett, 2001). Using AI as a framework for THRIVE allowed us to benchmark the achievements, unexplored potentials, traditions, values, and innovations of each of our programs (Cooperrider & Whitney, 2001). The THRIVE Index aligns with AI's positive 4-D cycle, which includes: (1) **discovery**, or identification of the best of what is; (2) **dream**, or imagination of what could be; (3) **design**, or creation of what will be; and (4) **destiny**, or enactment of change in learning to become what we hope for (Ludema & Fry, 2008). Below we illustrate the common themes of our twenty-one hallmark academic pipeline programs in relation to both THRIVE and AI's 4-D cycle.

Table 6.1. THRIVE dimensions and academic pipeline program best practices mapped to AI framework.

Appreciative Inquiry 4-D	THRIVE Dimensions	Common Programmatic Elements Across Highlighted Academic Pipeline Programs
Discovery	**Type**—what level the program is in the pipeline, based on their focus **History**—what the background, characteristics, mentors and alumni of the program are	discipline, level in the pipeline longevity, number of participants impacted by the program, reflecting on the best of programming and organizations that support pipeline programs
Dream	**Research**—what preparation, skills, and methodologies are learned; roles and responsibilities	research experiences, professional development opportunities, developing intellectual property, pipeline program organization's vision and routines of what to do
Design	**Inclusion/Identity**—how the program provides safe spaces for URMs to develop; promotes self-efficacy; grow future potential of URMs	specialized pedagogical practices and curricula, orientations, counseling, sense of belongingness, affirming social identity, programming for URMs
Destiny	**Voice**—how the program provides mentorship, networks, and social capital **Expectations**—what will be gained from the program	empowerment, mentorship, transferring of social and cultural capital, networking, collaborative discussions involving alumni and participants' perspectives external review, site visits, annual performance reports, surveys, key performance indicators

LEVERAGING ACADEMIC PIPELINE PROGRAMS AS A CONSUMER

How to Leverage Academic Pipeline Programs as a Parent (or Precollegiate Student)

This book is adding to a limited set of resources designed to assist parents with choosing the right academic pipeline program for their child. Choosing the right program is a complex decision. The decision to enroll a child in any program is based on several factors, including demographic characteristics, timing, cost, interest, and location. The THRIVE Index is a unique addition to currently available database listings and between college and university websites that addresses these factors.

Weighing the Cost of the Program

Academic pipeline programs have different price tags associated with them. Many are free or offer a financial incentive. However, some programs have a tuition cost. It is essential to read the application requirements to determine if there is a financial commitment. We encourage parents to consider the additional benefits like research preparation, inclusionary practices, identity enhancement, and voice when making a final decision regardless if there is a cost.

Choosing the Right Program for Your Child

Determining the right program for your child is dependent upon their individual characteristics and career interests. Many programs have eligibility requirements. Even though most programs are not restricted to certain groups, there are exceptions. Programs may only enroll students from a certain region or state. Sometimes enrollment may be based on prior exposure to certain classes or school-based experiences (e.g., course or extracurricular offerings in STEM). Some programs may pose certain constraints on your schedule. For example, some programs are only offered for a few weeks in the summer or maybe be offered during the academic year on weekends. Programs may also be designed for only commuters or residential students. You can locate initiatives that align with your child's needs within appendix A (p. 251).

Another restricting factor is career interest. If your child has not yet expressed interest in certain types of activities, take the time to discover their career interest using free, student-friendly resources (e.g., Forsyth Elementary Career Inventory [https://www.forsyth .k12.ga.us/cms/lib3/GA01000373/Centricity/Domain/3152/Inte rest%20Inventory%20itsLearning%20Make%20up.pdf], Career Clusters Activity [http://www.educationplanner.org/students/car eer-planning/find-careers/career-clusters.shtml], O-NET Interest Profiler [https://www.mynextmove.org/explore/ip], REL Southeast Career Readiness resource [https://ies.ed.gov/ncee/edlabs/in fographics/pdf/REL_SE_Career_Readiness_Preparing_the_Stude nt.pdf], and the Careeronestop Interest Assessment [https://www .careeronestop.org/toolkit/careers/interest-assessment.aspx]). The best resource for determining your child's career interest in middle school, high school, or college is through consultation with a guidance counselor or the career services office. These school-based professionals have access to other psychological and personality assessments, like Paws in Jobland (https://www.xap.com /paws/) and the Myers-Briggs Strong Interest Inventory (https:// www.themyersbriggs.com/en-US/Products-and-Services/Strong). They can also help you interpret the results. The use of inventories, like the Holland Code, is demonstrated to predict college retention (Nguyen, Williams, & Ludwikowski, 2017).

Utilizing Your Network to Find out More about Various Programs

Networking with teachers, other parents, and parent groups can help you to seize opportunities and determine whether programs may be a good fit. Teachers often get notifications of new or recurring programs through email or word of mouth. Parents are a resource to find out what programs they have liked and whether programs were supportive of students with similar characteristics and interests as your child. Social media parent groups often post about programs ahead of when they are offered or near the time of application deadlines. Start early when building your network. You may need to save programs for the future when your child meets the eligibility requirements.

How to Leverage Academic Pipeline Programs as a Student (Collegiate, Graduate/Professional)

Academic pipeline programs are designed to prepare you for the next stage of your academic journey. In order to take advantage of all they have to offer, you need to assess where you are and where you want to go academically in the future. Participating in academic pipeline programs will help you develop your existing skills further and to develop an action plan to help you obtain your future goals. Read Howard G. Adams's (2008) *Career Management 101: A Primer for Career and Life Planning*, which provides a guide for planning your career and can serve as a great foundation to considering which academic pipeline programs are best suited for your training.

Choosing the Right Program for You

Step back and assess where you are on your academic journey and determine what experiences you have yet to discover. Use the common programmatic themes mentioned above as examples of experiences to which you may or may not have yet had exposure. Follow the seven-step process outlined by Collier and Mason (2014) below:

1. **Understand your personal traits.** Where are you in your academic journey? How much time is left before you obtain your degree? Determine your course and what pathway fits with your current circumstances.

2. **Identify your personal values.** What is your purpose, passion, and position? Who do you want to be known as, how do you want to be remembered, and what are you already doing that is preparing you to take the next step? Find a new experience that can propel your further.

3. **Calculate your economic needs.** Does your current financial aid cover all of your expenses? What is the source of your financial aid? Can you leverage additional financial aid or incentives? Identify a program that can assist with offsetting costs for the remainder of your academic journey.

4. **Explore your long-term goals.** Where do you see yourself in five to ten years? Engage in a process called visioning. Visioning means to "see yourself in the future with giving thoughts to what your future career and life objectives you want to achieve" (Adams, 2008, p. 9).

5. **Specify your skill base (set).** What are the skills and attributes you already possess? Select a program that fits with your major or minor area of study.

6. **Recognize your preferred skills.** What can you offer to other students and teams? Give effort and attention to the things that matter most to you.

7. **Assess the skills that need further development.** Which skills and attributes do you want to improve? Choose a program that offers programmatic activities that will help you to improve your skill set.

If you are undecided on your major or future career, consult with your career services office on your college or university campus in order to complete psychological and personality assessments, like the Myers-Briggs Strong Interest Inventory (https://www.themyer sbriggs.com/en-US/Products-and-Services/Strong) and the Myers-Briggs Type Indicator (https://www.myersbriggs.org/my-mbti-pe rsonality-type/mbti-basics/home.htm?bhcp=1). If you have chosen a career or major, check to make sure the program you have selected is appropriate for your discipline of study. Read the eligibility requirements and see if your discipline of study is supported. If the listing is generic and you are unsure, contact the program director of the academic pipeline program for more details. Read more about your potential careers in the US Bureau of Labor and Statistics Occupational Outlook Handbook (https://www.bls.gov /ooh/).

We understand that there may be multiple ways to achieve your career goals. We suggest that you learn about the different types of research opportunities across disciplines, campus departments, and groups. Become comfortable asking questions about the scenario that bests suits your needs. Do not set limits on the number of programs you can participate in. It is possible to take advantage of multiple programs, especially if they are enhancing different skill sets or are designed for different phases of your academic journey.

Completing the Program Application

You cannot participate in an academic pipeline program if you do not apply. Start the application process early. Now that you are aware these programs exist, do not wait to check out the program listings and look up the program application deadlines. Ask for help with completing the application and proofreading any writing samples. Apply to multiple programs that are appropriate for your discipline. Do not be afraid of rejection. If you do not get accepted on the first try, get feedback on your application. Either apply again to the same program or apply a year later to a similar program that will accept you where you are. Complete the applications by the deadline. Do not expect that exceptions will be made for late applicants.

Balancing Your Other Interests and Commitments

Programs have different levels of time commitments. Programs are offered at different times and may pose certain constraints on your schedule. For example, some programs are only offered for a few weeks in the summer or may be offered on weekends during the academic year. Programs may be residential or designed to connect you with a campus outside of your home institution.

It is possible to balance extracurricular activities (e.g., athletics, sorority/fraternity, major-specific clubs, work) with the require-ments of academic pipeline programs. Get access to schedules early and synchronize your calendar. If your other activities involve travel, make sure you work with the program director to plan for potential schedule conflicts in advance. Discuss your involvement or future involvement in an academic pipeline program with your mentors and family members. Use the Institute for Broadening Participation's Pathways to Science guide (https://www.pathway stoscience.org/pdf/SummerResearch_DiscussingWithYourFamily .pdf) as a resource for those conversations.

How to Leverage Academic Pipeline Programs as a Faculty Member

Academic pipeline programs connect to faculty diversity by how they utilize initiatives that support senior doctoral students, newly minted PhDs, postdoctoral students, junior faculty, and beyond. As discussed in chapter 5, programs such as Sisters of the Acad-emy (SOTA) or the National Center for Faculty Development and Diversity (NCFDD) center around familiarity with academic culture and mentorship. At this level of the pipeline, individuals have mastered their scholarship and persistence; however, there are likely drastically few peers of similar backgrounds and ethnicities. Therefore, these academic pipeline programs may be the only spaces where URM faculty can discuss their scholarship and get advice on advancing in their careers and handling departmental politics.

The retention of diverse faculty in the academy often hinges on participation in these supportive faculty academic pipeline programs due to elements of the climate. Phelps (1995) argues that there is a phenomenon called "pet to threat." According to this phenomenon, you are initially embraced, like a *pet*, as someone who is beloved for your new ideas and expertise. This level of admiration shifts as your level of success is elevated to the status of *threat*. Faculty may begin to experience more toxic relationships on campus as their status changes. Young and Hines (2018) liken toxic campus cultures to spirit killers. Academic pipeline programs are designed for and can be leveraged by postdoctoral scholars and faculty to provide strategies for empowerment and encouragement to overcome these elements of college/university environments.

Academic Pipeline Programs and Networks for Faculty

If your campus does not have any diversity initiatives, or only has a few, to support your academic growth, there are several external agencies (e.g., the National Science Foundation, National Center for Faculty Development & Diversity, the Sisters of the Academy) that can support your journey. Also, you can be creative on your own campus. Align yourself with senior faculty or administrators (e.g., chief diversity officers, LBGTQIA+ director) who have a track record on diversity issues. Further, faculty who would like to participate in URM initiatives should make themselves available, especially if they are non-URM faculty or URM faculty who have never participated in this type of programming. There are reasons why non-URM faculty and URM faculty who have achieved success without participating in academic pipeline programs should consider participating in academic pipeline programs at any of the levels we have discussed. Even if they have never participated in an academic pipeline program, URM faculty are a part of the community of role models that other URMs need to engage with on college and university campuses. These URM faculty have valuable lessons and experiences that are invaluable to new URM faculty, such as building alliances and allies, gaining tenure in nondiverse departments, and building and maintaining a research agenda. Non-URM faculty who are committed to diversity and inclusion in the academy can serve as allies to these programs and provide insider information for navigating the ranks.

Faculty Looking to Start Academic Pipeline Programs

If your academic unit, division, school, or college is looking to start a pathway program for student or faculty diversity, there are several ways to go about this process. First, there must be some sort of needs assessment to produce the data that substantiates the rationale for such a program. Pokphanh and Augusto (2011) developed the *Faculty Roadmap to Training Grants: Proposal Preparation, Administration, & Evaluation*, which is listed later in this chapter, to assist faculty in assessment. Further, later in this chapter, we have given several examples of how to build institutional or external support to develop these kinds of programs. In order to leverage various academic pipeline programs, faculty must first determine the need for a program through local data collection (e.g., student experiences, diversity population percentages, cultural competency checklists, etc.), institutional support (particularly from senior administration), and, depending on the desired outcome, a team of departmental or interdisciplinary peers to assist in the proposal. Ultimately, the goal of increasing diversity takes dedicated allies because the success of student and faculty diversity is predicated on buy-in and involvement from as many on campus as possible. Moreover, the rational for diversifying the professoriate is to create an environment necessary to complement the complexity of the increasingly diverse college classroom.

Faculty Who Are Alumni of Academic Pipeline Programs

The acquisition or transfer of knowledge by faculty is not just important for equipping students but is also helpful for transforming institutional and community cultures. Participating in an engaged campus culture may help mitigate some of the negative consequences of becoming a successful URM in the academy. Once you successfully enter the academy, revisit not only your purpose for making new creative contributions but also reflect on the roads that made your pathway possible.

Your success story should be shared with those below you in the pipeline. We encourage you to participate in any capacity that keeps the programming within existing and newly created academic pipelines relevant to all participants. Consider serving as a mentor, research lab sponsor, invited speaker, workshop presenter, curriculum trainer, or application reviewer. Research has demonstrated that when faculty share narratives that match the experiences of low-income, first-generation (LIFG) students, LIFG students increase their level of institutional commitment (Herrmann, 2019). To achieve the goal of diversifying the academy you can become a mentor to work with URM students so that they will also thrive in the academy.

How to Leverage Academic Pipeline Programs as an Institution

The trend is for all disciplines, institutions, and organizations to utilize research and enrichment programs in order to enhance the success of URM students as they enter college and beyond.

Although many institutions use national programs to assist in these goals, some savvy institutions are institutionalizing and developing their own set of pipeline initiatives.

As mentioned in earlier chapters, examples of institutionally developed programs include the UMBC Meyerhoff Scholars Program, FAMU Graduate Feeder Program, Fisk-Vanderbilt Master's-to-PhD Bridge Program, and the Creating Connections Consortium. Some of these programs have been developed with the financial support of foundations (e.g., private donors, the National Science Foundation, the Mellon Foundation) while others are supported through groups of institutions or thoughtful university officials who have found a need for them on their campus. Whether you develop these initiatives through external support or organically on campus, they should be created based on the structure of the institution. Often, the success of your program is based on your institutional culture and/or the support from senior administration. In the following sections, we have highlighted an organic set of programs coordinated and sponsored on campuses, which create pathways to graduate school, and beyond, for URM students. Then, we discuss how institutions can use externally sponsored programs to develop an academic pipeline program specific to the needs of their individual campus.

UGA Pipeline Initiatives, Created by Coauthor
Curtis D. Byrd, PhD

In the mid-1990s, the dean of the Graduate School at the University of Georgia (UGA) gained support from the University System of Georgia (USG) to sponsor a summer undergraduate research program (SURP) for URM students. The statewide initiative supported twenty-five scholars from state historically Black colleges and universities (HBCUs) (Albany State University [ASU], Fort Valley State University, Savannah State University) and URM students from UGA. This local program was designed to increase diversity in graduate programs at UGA by bringing top URM scholars to UGA to conduct research with faculty. In 2001, one year into my tenure as director of minority graduate recruitment and retention at UGA, I wrote a proposal to expand the SURP to include all URM students from any institution and to begin a series of programs to diversify our graduate programs. As not to reinvent the wheel, I studied successful programs at the Rackham Graduate School at the University of Michigan, the Graduate School at the University of Florida, and the Graduate School of the University of North Carolina. Armed with data about the success of these initiatives, I was able to gain support (financial and programmatic) from the graduate dean and provost of UGA to create a set of local pipeline programs, complementing the SURP, and to recruit and retain URM graduate students. The programs included the following:

1. **Junior/Senior Workshop:** A workshop series was provided to URM students from UGA or any institution to show the process of applying to graduate study. This program was offered in the fall and spring semesters to illustrate the components needed to get into graduate school (e.g., obtaining a letter of recommendation, developing a solid personal statement, finding a mentor, and conducting undergraduate research).

2. **Visitation Day Weekend:** Twenty to fifty URM senior students were invited to campus but had to apply to graduate programs at UGA. Application fee waivers were provided, along with assistance applying. Students were required to have a GPA of 3.0 to 3.25. Students were also required to have taken the GRE, to have the first draft of their personal statement, and to be seriously considering UGA graduate programs. Students were provided room and board, and there were tours of campus and arranged visits to all academic departments.

3. **Summer Bridge Program:** Ten to twenty URM students who needed additional support as they transitioned into

graduate programs were provided this opportunity. The Graduate School worked with academic departments to create safe spaces for these students to familiarize themselves with the campus. A three-credit course (e.g., directed study, research, writing skills) was also required. Students were given professional development workshops on the socialization of graduate school, time management, and citation management. Finally, they were provided mentors (peer and faculty) throughout the program and, if needed, throughout their time at UGA.

4. **Graduate Recruitment Opportunities (GRO) Assistantship Program:** Ten to twenty-five admitted URM graduate students were eligible for the Graduate Recruitment Opportunities (GRO) Assistantship program. This program supported master's and doctoral students for the life of their stay at UGA. The cost was shared with academic departments (the first year of a master's program was sponsored by the Graduate School and the second year by the academic department, while the Graduate School sponsored the first two years of the doctoral program and the academic department the third and fourth, with doctoral students eligible for dissertation fellowship in their final year). The shared cost provided buy-in and accountability from academic departments. All GRO participants were assigned peer and academic mentors in their first year of the program to assist with their transition into graduate study, particularly as many of these students were coming from minority-serving institutions and/or were first-generation students in graduate study. Academic advisors were faculty in the student's home department and often became their research or major advisor.

5. **UGA Graduate Feeder Program:** Three to five URM students per institution (FAMU, Spelman College, Morehouse College, and ASU) were the first to be provided academic and financial support throughout their graduate career at UGA.

In 2001, UGA partnered with the FAMU Graduate Feeder Scholars Program (mentioned in chapter 3) to support three to five students in graduate school. In 2003, I received support to create a feeder program with several other minority-serving institutions in Georgia. UGA then agreed to support the same number of students per institution at ASU and Morehouse and Spelman Colleges. Since then, UGA has created several more arrangements to support students from other minority-serving institutions, including Fort Valley State and North Carolina A&T State Universities. Similar programming is provided to these students as is provided to the GRO Assistantship recipients.

Although the SURP program no longer exists at UGA, the Graduate School has partnered with other summer research programs to support recruits in their journey to graduate school at UGA. The Graduate School has also created several other programs to support URM students, such as their workshop series Graduate School 101 and Transitions: MSI to PWI. The original set of programs was developed to work together to create pipelines and pathways into graduate school. This seamless recruitment and retention effort for URM students into graduate study doubled the number of African American doctoral students in the first five years it was developed. Further, this set of programming keeps UGA in the top ten of all institutions in the nation, across various disciplines, for graduating URM doctoral students. Most of the programs created in the early 2000s still exist today, although the names have changed. The longevity of these programs shows the continued success of these URM initiatives. The UGA pipeline program was intentionally designed with early recruitment, mentoring, experiential training, familiarity to systems, and repetition in mind. Figure 6.1 is an illustration of the pathway of this pipeline program.

Figure 6.1. UGA graduate pipeline programming.

Institutional Academic Pipeline Programs Based on External Support

Several other institutions have developed organic academic pipeline programs that have external sponsorship. Among the aforementioned academic pipeline programs, there are two standouts: one based on its longevity and success in recruiting URM students in STEM and the other based on its design and outcomes. First, the UMBC Meyerhoff Scholars Program (mentioned in chapter 2) was created by Freeman Hrabowski, PhD, and the Robert and Jane Meyerhoff Foundation in 1988 at the University of Maryland, Baltimore County. The outstanding attributes of this program include over thirty years of longevity, 312 Meyerhoff scholars who have earned PhDs, fifty-nine who have joint MD/PhDs, 141 who have earned MDs, and nearly forty who hold tenure-track positions. Further, this program has significantly increased the number of students who have earned master's degrees in STEM, and several replica programs have been modeled after the Meyerhoff Scholars Program at other institutions. Examples of programs modeled after the Meyerhoff Scholars Program are the Millennium Scholars Program at Penn State University (https://www.millennium.psu.edu/) and the Chancellor's Science Scholars Program at the University of North Carolina (https://chancellorssciencescholars.unc.edu/). Both programs are open to high-achieving students who are interested in pursuing STEM careers. Both programs include a summer bridge component. Similarly, the Howard Hughes Medical Institute (HHMI) funds six research universities, following the Meyerhoff model, to ensure more URM students pursue STEM degrees. Also, CZI (a California-based company founded by the CEO of Facebook Mark Zuckerberg and his wife Priscilla Chan) announced a $6.9 million grant in April 2019 to create a program similar to the Meyerhoff Scholars Program at the University of California, Berkeley, and the University of California, San Diego, with an emphasis on academic and workplace diversity (Mervis, 2019).

Another standout program is the Creating Connections Consortium (C3), which developed a set of programs to guide URM students from some of the nation's most highly regarded liberal arts institutions to careers in academe. These students are then recruited back to the liberal arts schools they attended after they have earned terminal degrees from partner research institutions. Many of these liberal arts institutions are members of Lever Press, and the URM students from the C3 program are diversifying the curriculum and bringing new ideas to these campuses. The institutions who are affiliated with both C3 and Lever Press are the following: Amherst College, Berea College, Bowdoin College, Denison College, Furman College, Lafayette College, Middlebury College, Oberlin College, Sarah Lawrence College, Skidmore College, Smith College, St. Olaf College, Trinity University, Union College,

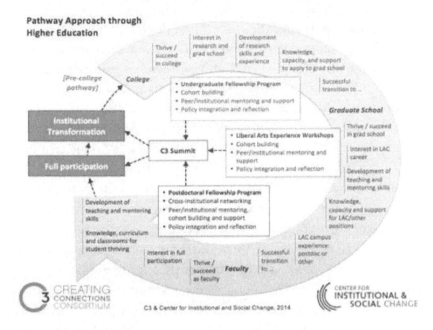

Figure 6.2. Creating Connections Consortium pathway approach through higher education.

Whitman College, and Williams College. This set of programming makes this consortium of liberal arts schools a pioneer in multi-institutional URM pathway initiatives.

The significance of this model is the iterative model by which C3 brings scholars through a thrive/succeed process throughout the pipeline (see figure 6.2). The C3 programming works with selected research institutions in the Undergraduate Fellowship Program. Those same students are encouraged to apply for doctoral programs at the host institution when they graduate from their liberal arts school. The C3 program tracks doctoral scholars and has them attend an annual summit, where institutional representatives, faculty, undergraduates, graduate students, and postdoctoral researchers from liberal arts schools all convene for a weekend of networking and discussions on inclusion and diversity in the academy.

Also, while pursuing their doctorate degrees, C3 scholars are visited by the chief diversity officers (CDOs) of the participating liberal arts institutions. The CDOs visit member research universities to cultivate interest in their institutions as well as in teaching opportunities. As discussed earlier, the success of this program lies with the number of students who enter postdoctoral programs. Eventually, over 75 percent of those who receive a PhD land tenure-track positions at one of the liberal arts institutions.

All of these initiatives are examples of successful approaches to academic pipeline programs and pathways to the professoriate. Whether the programming is supported by institutional funds, and/or by external sources, these initiatives can be configured to work seamlessly. What drives much of these programs is institutional support. In order to encourage institutional support and change (e.g., curriculum, pedagogy) on college campuses, HHMI has created a program that ties change to funding (see the box below).

HHMI Inclusive Excellence Initiative

The goal of the HHMI Inclusive Excellence initiative is to help colleges and universities build their capacity for inclusion of all students, especially those students who belong to groups underrepresented in science. For more information, please see the 2019 ie3 program announcement (https://www.hhmi.org /sites/default/files/programs/inclusive/ie3-program-announce ment-final.pdf).

The Inclusive Excellence initiative is guided by the following:

- Scientific excellence depends on having a diverse population of scientists.

- The power of diversity is only realized through inclusion so that all who are engaged feel that they belong and that the system expects them to succeed.

- The responsibility for creating an inclusive learning environment rests primarily with the colleges and universities where the students find themselves. Rather than a "fix the student" mentality, we believe the emphasis should be on the institution stepping up and exercising its responsibility.

- Faculty play a central role in establishing an inclusive campus culture. Among all of the persons who interact with a student, it is the faculty that is most closely identified as the representative of the institution.

- Faculty and staff should understand what inclusive excellence means on their campus, and they should be provided opportunities to learn the skills of inclusion.

- Making the learning environment more inclusive includes changes to institutional structures, including the curriculum, pedagogy, faculty rewards and incentives, and policies and procedures.

- HHMI grants should be made to schools that demonstrate their understanding of their institutional challenges and their readiness to change, and not based only on their past track records.

- Measuring progress requires faculty and campus leaders to engage in continuous reflection on how the institution is changing with respect to inclusion.

Finding comprehensive institutional support for URM academic pipeline programs can be a challenge on some college and university campuses. There must be intentional institutional reforms and commitment from campus leadership, along with diversity among faculty and administration, to see transformations at colleges and universities (Whittaker & Montgomery, 2013). However, when campuses do find individuals to step up, create policies, and develop programming to support URM students, changes among senior university officials (e.g., presidents, chief diversity officers) may pose challenges. When a champion of diversity initiatives leaves the campus, there may be problems if the policies and programs are not reinforced and interwoven into the institution. The success and longevity of URM academic programs on college campuses are often tied to strong, committed institutional leadership (Allen-Ramdial & Campbell, 2014). As institutions look to establish systems of pathway programs to support URM students within undergraduate programs, to develop an interest in graduate study, to recruit and retain graduate students, and to advocate for research, postdoctoral opportunities, and placement in tenure-track positions, they must enlist a variety of allies. These individuals include chief diversity officers, principal investigators of established enrichment programs (e.g., research experiences for undergraduates, the Louis Stokes Alliances for Minority Participation, McNair Scholars), research faculty mentors, diversity recruitment officers, and institutional research officers who can provide access to the necessary data to demonstrate need.

As colleges/universities and organizations demonstrate need, it opens the door to valuable external agencies that support URG/URM academic enrichment. These funding sources are relative to the needs of the campus and their students. As faculty, administrators, and institutions are searching for opportunities to gain support for academic pipeline programs, or in more technical terms "training grants," they have to look for comprehensive sites illustrating these programs. *A Faculty Roadmap to Training Grants* by Roberta Pokphanh and John Augusto (2011, https://graduate.ku.edu/sit es/graduate.ku.edu/files/docs/TrainingGrantsGuide.pdf) gives a self-reflective analysis of the "why" behind the decision to initiate a training grant. The resource helps to plan, write, and coordinate institutional resources during the formation of training grants at any given institution. *A Faculty Roadmap to Training Grants* helps the prospective "principle investigator" (PI) identify their rationale

Table 6.2. Examples of external funding sources for institutions to start URM academic pipeline programming.

Howard Hughes Medical Institute (HHMI) (https://www.hhmi.org/science-education/programs/diversity-and-inclusion)

Andrew W. Mellon Foundation (https://mellon.org/grants/)

National Science Foundation (NSF) (https://www.nsf.gov/funding/azindex.jsp)

National Institutes of Health, National Institute of General Medical Sciences Building Infrastructure Leading to Diversity (BUILD) Initiative (https://www.nigms.nih.gov/training/dpc/Pages/build.aspx)

Department of Health and Human Services Initiative for Maximizing Student Development (IMSD, T32) (https://grants.nih.gov/grants/guide/pa-files/par-19-037.html)

National Institutes of Health Support of Competitive Research (SCORE) Program (https://www.nigms.nih.gov/Research/DRCB/SCORE)

Alfred P. Sloan Foundation (https://sloan.org/grants/apply)

Amgen Foundation (https://www.amgen.com/responsibility/amgen-foundation)

US Department of Education Federal TRIO Programs and minority-serving institution grants) (https://www2.ed.gov/about/offices/list/ope/trio/index.html, https://www2.ed.gov/about/offices/list/ope/hccrfmsi.html)

and resources to develop successful proposals. Specifically, this publication identifies five steps to assist researchers: (1) exploration and identification, (2) proposal preparation, (3) proposal writing, (4) "I've Been Funded. Now What?," and (5) evaluation, progress reports, and renewal. Pokphanh and Augusto (2011) provide a host of resources (e.g., the National Center for Educational Statistics; the US Census; ideas on developing solid proposals; listings of funding agencies) for new and continuing PIs to locate and obtain support and to bring grants onto college campuses, particularly if they are looking to reinforce programming for URM students. Other types of comprehensive external funding sources for faculty, administrators, and institutions to support URM programming are listed below (table 6.2).

Early Adopters of the THRIVE Index Tool

In 2019 and 2020, the THRIVE Index were used by two different institutions to build their capacity to understand their diversity efforts and how they support URG students, faculty, and staff. Our work began with Morehouse College and their HBCU STEM Undergraduate Success Research Center. Morehouse College is the only liberal arts HBCU for African American men in the nation. The major objective of the STEM-US Center collaboration (http://hbcu.academicpipelinedatabase.net/) was to design and populate a database and interactive web platform that transfers knowledge of STEM academic pipeline programs housed at HBCUs to parents, students, faculty, and college/university administrators. The combination of technology tools brings awareness to programs and initiatives that were created to assist STEM-career-focused HBCU students in building a compelling academic (research) portfolio, successfully matriculating through college/university degree programs, and diversifying the professoriate. The Morehouse College HBCU STEM-US Center received a National Science Foundation award for $9 million in fall 2020, which included the usage of the THRIVE Index as a way to transfer knowledge gained from center activities with the mission to tell success stories about HBCUs .

Furthermore, we used the THRIVE Index in summer 2020 to develop Georgia State University's first Diversity Database (https://dei.gsu.edu/diversity-database/). The diversity database includes over one hundred and fifty listings across the entire Georgia State University campus. We have taken the THRIVE index beyond just reviewing individual programs and developed the instrument to accommodate a catalog of institutional diversity, equity, and inclusion (DEI) initiatives. In this next step, we developed "strategic priorities" categories (e.g., academic initiatives, multicultural programming and policies), and we will eventually use the tool to provide informed standards of DEI initiatives as they reach toward inclusive excellence. The use of THRIVE at Morehouse College and Georgia State University demonstrate how institutions both small and large can take stock of what already exists within a department, institution, or organization.

Quad 4P Academic Pipeline Program Rubric

Using the THRIVE Index to catalog existing initiatives as discussed also simplifies the task of comparing common features across initiatives. The use of THRIVE allows you to collect program information using a common language in a way that makes comparison possible. In chapters 2–5, we demonstrated how the THRIVE Index can be used to catalog academic pipeline programs. The THRIVE Index tool can also be used to catalog DEI programs, events, initiatives, and policies at institutions of higher education, as well as in organizations, more generally. One of the benefits of cataloging programs is that you can capitalize on your existing resources to foster more disciplinary and interdisciplinary innovation and to create platforms for the intersections of various diverse groups. It may also uncover natural ways to bring synergy between programs and increase recruitment and retention efforts. Lastly, cataloging decreases the risk of duplicating existing efforts and inefficiently allocating resources.

Once cataloging is complete, you can go a step further by gauging the level of success of programs. We developed the Quad 4P Academic Pipeline Program rubric (Mason & Byrd, 2021) for evaluating academic pipeline programs, or DEI initiatives more broadly, using THRIVE dimensions in table 6.3. You can use the Quad 4P Academic Pipeline Program rubric to make comparisons at each level of the pipeline, as well as within disciplines, within units/departments or across an institution. This rubric can be used to classify programs along a continuum from a program's starting point (*participating*) to its ultimate goal of building inclusive capacity (*partnering*). This rubric can be used as a baseline, with the goal of completing other audits or analyses of the environment in

Table 6.3. A rubric for comparing programs within an institution or organization.

Analysis of Programs Using THRIVE	
4. Partnering	To be classified as **partnering**, a DEI initiative must have consistently implemented (**H**) activities that (**R, I, V**) are backed by a department, institution, or funding agency for enough time to demonstrate participant success outcomes (**E**) for multiple diverse groups across multiple units/departments/institutions.
3. Producing	To be classified as **producing**, a DEI initiative must have consistently implemented (**H**) activities that (**R, I, V**) are backed by a department, institution, or funding agency for enough time to demonstrate participant success outcomes (**E**) for multiple diverse groups.
2. Performing	To be classified as **performing**, a DEI initiative must have implemented (**H**) activities (**R, I, V**) that are backed by a department, institution, or funding agency for enough time to demonstrate participant success outcomes (**E**) for at least one diverse group.
1. Participating	To be classified as **participating**, a DEI initiative must be implementing (**H**) activities (**R, I, V**) that are backed by a department, institution, or funding agency to demonstrate its existence. Project-specific success outcomes are not yet present (**E**).

which programs operate. See Mason and Byrd (2021) for an example version of the Quad 4P Academic Pipeline Program rubric. The example illustrates how each component of the THRIVE Index can be translated into a numeric indicator.

Once your catalog is completed, it can also be used to make data-informed decisions. For example, you could examine whether a hub for diversity initiatives is needed at a certain level of the pipeline, whether new programs need to be created to fill a gap for a particular URM, or whether sufficient partnership has been reached. As institutions are building out their capacity on DEI initiatives, it is important to research peer and aspirational institutions on their efforts to support URM students with various types of programming. The earlier example, in the section "UGA Pipeline Initiatives," of how programs were created by Dr. Byrd, can also be used to form interinstitutional agreements, partnerships, and alliances with this data.

How to Leverage Academic Pipeline Project and THRIVE as a Nonacademic Group

In the near future, we plan to use the *Academic Pipeline Programs* book and the THRIVE Index to organize and develop initiatives for nonacademic entities (e.g., corporations, nonprofits, nongovernmental organizations). Plans are underway to work with several groups to establish benchmarks with their leadership through a profile questionnaire and to gain awareness of their DEI goals. The *E* of THRIVE will be used to determine smart goals and a timeline for organizational change. Then, we will deploy the THRIVE Index and Quad 4P Academic Pipeline Program rubric to measure where the organization falls based on the initial benchmarks. Finally, recommendations will be suggested based on the AI organization development model.

CONCLUSION

As academic spaces and workplaces steadily become more ethnically and culturally diverse, colleges and universities are compelled to create a more multicultural environment. Research has shown that one of the most effective ways to accomplish this goal is through faculty diversity (Smith, Turner, Osei-Kofi, & Richards, 2004). Diverse faculty often bring more multicultural concepts and strategies to enhance the overall learning environment, provide support and mentorship opportunities deemed more suitable for the academic success of URM students, particularly at majority campuses (Fries-Britt, Rowan-Kenyon, Perna, Milem, & Howard, 2011).

Many URM students who attend predominantly white institutions (PWIs) are first-generation and having faculty from similar backgrounds and racial ethnicities can provide the voice and support necessary for them to succeed in hostile institutional environments (Felder, 2010). Therefore, there is a dire need for faculty diversity to support URM students. However, we have discussed how there is a shortage of URM faculty, the cause of which ranges from the lack of diversity among students earning doctorates to the difficulty diverse faculty face surviving the tenure process. Academic pipeline programs are necessary to reach this goal. Ultimately, these programs provide the required pathways for URM students, faculty, and administrators to succeed in academic life, particularly at majority campuses.

Academic Pipeline Programs: Diversifying Pathways from the Bachelors to the Professoriate is quite unique, as there are no national clearinghouses of URM pathway programs that detail the best practices, commonalities, and templates of success. The THRIVE Index helps to situate all programs thematically and allows us to align these initiatives based on their place within the pipeline while also illustrating the components (e.g., mentorship, financial support, appreciation for the intersections of a URM student's identities, guidance to instill self-efficacy, and attention to voice) that make their participants successful. Our goal was to show how successful programs have woven a tapestry of diversity initiatives in the twenty-first-century educational system. Further, we have illustrated best practices that can be used by various types of institutions in partnering, developing, and sustaining pathway programs for URM students.

The promise of the future will be the expansion of the visualization of these and other pipeline programs nationwide in our interactive database. It is our hope that, as trends in education and workforce development evolve, this publication, in keeping with the AI framework, will serve as a roadmap to the best of what is (*discovery*), will help to build the best of what could be (*dream*), will create what will be (*design*), and will become what we most hope for (*destiny*).

AFTERWORD

Ansley A. Abraham Jr., PhD

Academic Pipeline Programs is an ambitious and sorely needed resource that captures the authors' understanding and foresight into the research, literature, and programs around efforts to improve underrepresented minority academic achievement at the postsecondary level. The authors are commended for recognizing the lack of a cohesive, comprehensive, single-source publication that captures for secondary educators, higher-education administrators, faculty, students, and families the array of program options available to boost academic achievement and outcomes at the higher-education level.

The literature is replete with research and publications that describe any one of the programs covered by this book. Rarely, however, have the goals, objectives, methodologies, and outcomes across multiple programs been compared. The use of the THRIVE (type, history, research, inclusion/identity, voice, and expectations) Index is brilliantly deployed by the authors as a classification system and tool to understand, discuss, and compare and contrast an array of pipeline programs. THRIVE is important to understanding the elements of these programs that make them work to inform and improve outcomes for the students and faculty they serve.

The authors brought this book and its usefulness into the twenty-first century by linking academic pipeline programs that are not highlighted in the book to an interactive geographic information system (GIS) mapping system and database. This database allows readers to examine pipeline programs using the THRIVE Index to review a condensed profile of each program.

The American Council on Education (ACE) (American Council on Education, 2019) released its comprehensive report, *Race and Ethnicity in Higher Education: A Status Report.* The report contains multiple indicators about the state of race/ethnicity in higher education and an analysis of trends over a twenty-year period. The range of topics covered include secondary-school completion, undergraduate enrollment and graduation, graduate enrollment and completion, student financing of their education, faculty and staff composition, and the relationship of educational attainment to employment and earnings.

The report is a stark reminder that over the years, even with all the attention, resources, and legislative and programmatic actions to narrow gaps in achievement and participation for minority groups, gains have been made. But, these gains are tempered by knowledge of the persistent/frustrating gaps in achievement that persist.

One of the bright spots of the study is students of color attending college at higher rates. From 1996 to 2016, the percentage of undergraduate students of color increased from 29.6 percent to 45.2 percent, driven almost exclusively by the near doubling of the percentage of Hispanic students. A similar pattern was also found at the postbaccalaureate level: underrepresented minority students represented 21 percent of all graduate students in 1996 compared to 32 percent in 2016.

The study's findings are less complementary of the racial disparities in college completion rates. For example, among the 2011 student cohort entering four-year public college, 75.8 percent of Asian students and 71.1 percent of white students completed their degree within six years. By contrast, the six-year completion rates were 55.7 percent for Hispanic students and 46 percent for black students. At private four-year colleges, the completion rates were higher overall, but the gaps still persist.

According to the ACE study, minority graduates were found, more often than not, to be burdened with greater debt—no surprise here. In 2016, among bachelor's degree recipients, 86.4 percent of black graduates had borrowed money to finance their education compared to 70.3 percent of white students, 67.3 percent of Hispanic students, and 58.7 percent of Asian students. The implications and damage of the debt burden on the individual student or their family's ability to build generational wealth is devastating.

The ACE study reinforced research that fields of study are still linked to a graduates' race. Black students are significantly less likely to complete a degree in a STEM discipline—which is typically linked to greater job prospects and higher compensation. These disparities probably help explain why black graduates tend to have higher unemployment rates and lower salaries than other graduates.

The last finding from this study and most relevant to the goal of the Southern Regional Education Board (SREB) Doctoral Scholars Program (2017) is the lack of diversity among college faculty. Of the more than seven hundred thousand full-time higher-education faculty in 2016, 73.2 percent were white and 21.1 percent were faculty of color (the largest components being Asian, 9.3 percent; black, 5.7 percent; Hispanic, 4.7 percent; and Native Americans less than 1 percent). To understand just how devastating these statistics are, consider:

- These percentages are less than half the percentage representation of the students the faculty teach.
- By removing those faculty who teach at historically black

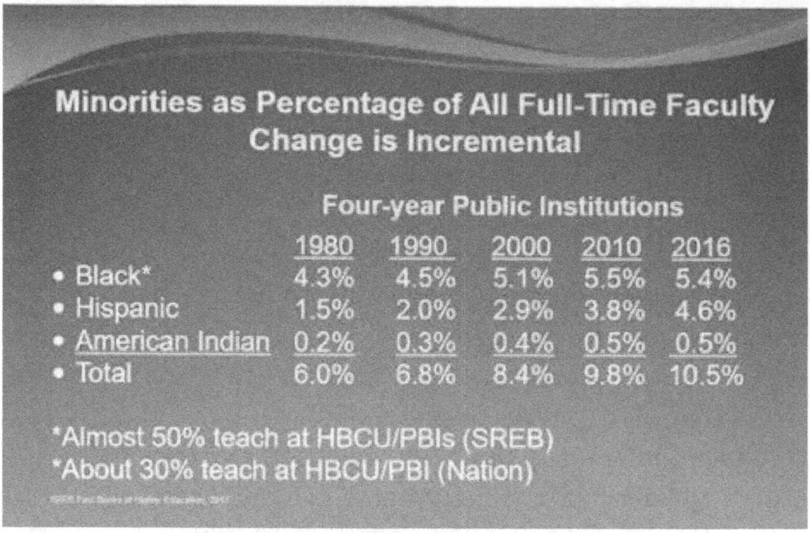

Figure 11. SREB Fact Book on Higher Education.

colleges and universities (HBCUs) or Hispanic-serving institutions (HSIs) from the calculation, the representation of
minority faculty who teach on predominantly white campuses would be reduced by 1 to 2.5 percentage points. Mean-
ing, the representation of faculty of color on predominantly
white campuses is even smaller than the data imply.

- Data taken from the SREB Fact Book on Higher Education (2017) show how change is incremental (see figure A.1)
in minority faculty representation over the thirty-six-year
period between 1980 and 2016. At this pace, it will take more
than one hundred years before these groups achieve parity
with their representation in the population.

The findings from the ACE study and others, especially this last
finding, affirm the importance and need for programs highlighted
in this book. Two recent studies, one from the Pew Research Center (2019) and the other an article in the *Hispanic Journal of Law
and Policy* (Vasquez, Wong, Barros, Carlton, & Barceló, 2019) show
the same results.

It is hoped that this book serves as a convenient, informative, and inspirational project that works as a useful resource for educators, researchers, students, administrators, and policy makers to understand and recognize the value of these pipeline programs to close gaps in minority-student participation and achievement. Further, it is the goal that this resource manifests itself as a tool to assisting those invested in diversifying the professoriate. Clearly, this book is a great start, but it is important that it serve as a catalyst for lasting changes to take root.

Ansley A. Abraham
Director
SREB Doctoral Scholars Program

Appendix A

While one of our goals of authoring this book was to provide a comprehensive resource, we are aware it would take an overwhelmingly large number of pages to include all of the programs and their accomplishments. In an effort to not *shortchange* our audience, we created an interactive appendix. This interactive appendix includes a database portal linked to geographic information system (GIS) information. It was created to allow users to quickly identify programs for collegiate students, faculty, administrators, and even K–12 administrators, teachers, and parents.

The interactive appendix is displayed as a website portal with search functionality. The web portal is searchable by the program name or academic institution and characteristics of the programs, including where they are located in the United States (i.e., Northeast, Northwest, Southeast, Southwest, Western), the level of the academic pipeline the program supports (i.e., precollegiate, collegiate, graduate, faculty), and primary academic disciplines of interest (i.e., education, health, humanities, law, social sciences, STEM, etc.). The search functionality is adaptive in the sense that it suggests other programs you may be interested in based on your search history. The interactive appendix accommodates the listing of programs irrespective of the length of time they have been in operation, their funding source, and the degree to which they support individuals. The appendix does not include programs that only offer monetary incentives (e.g., scholarship- or fellowship-only programs). The appendix includes the government-funded programs highlighted throughout chapters 2–5. Additional government funded fellowship, summer research, and internship opportunities can be found at clearinghouse sites for undergraduate students (https://stemundergrads.science.gov/) and graduate students (stemgradstudents.science.gov).

Table A.1 below provides a snapshot of some of the additional programs supporting special-interest groups (e.g., community college students, undocumented, gender minorities, sexual minorities, professional groups- medical, dental, law, and business).

Table A.1. Additional academic pipeline programs.

Level of Pipeline	Program Name	Specific Underrepresented Minority Group	Discipline
K–12	Advancement Via Individual Determination (AVID) https://www.avid.org/		most disciplines
K–12	Hidden Genius Project http://www.hiddengenius project.org/	males	technology, entrepreneurship
K–12	Raise Me https://www.raise.me/	high school students and community college students	most disciplines
K–12	Verizon Innovative Learning Girls https://www.nacce.com /verizon	girls	STEM
K–12	Verizon Innovative Learning Programs for Minority Males https://www.verizon.com /about/responsibility/veriz on-innovative-learning/	males	STEM
K–12 Collegiate/ Graduate Faculty	National Association for Community College Entrepreneurship (NACCE) https://www.nacce.com/		most disciplines
K–12, Collegiate	PUENTE https://www.thepuentepr oject.org/	community college students	most disciplines
K–12, Collegiate	Student National Medical Association Institute http://www.snma.org/ind ex.php?pID=170		medicine

K–12 Collegiate/ Graduate/ Postdoctoral/ Professionals/ Faculty	American Indian Science and Engineering Society (AISES) http://aises.org/	Native Americans and Alaska Natives	STEM
Collegiate	Amgen Scholars Program https://amgenscholars .com/	open to all URGs and international students	STEM
Collegiate	Associated Colleges of the Midwest Graduate School Exploration Fellowship https://www.acm.edu/st udent_programs/GSEF .html		humanities/ humanistic social sciences/arts
Collegiate	Big Academic Alliance Summer Research Opportunities Program (SROP) http://www.btaa.org /SROP		nonlaw, medical, and MBA careers
Collegiate	Bonner Scholars http://www.bonner.org/		most disciplines
Collegiate	Council on Undergraduate Research (CUR) https://www.cur.org/		most disciplines
Collegiate	Cuban American Alliance for Leadership & Education (CAALE) http://caale.org/	Cuban Americans	most disciplines
Collegiate	First Islander's Scholars Academy Program https://casa.tamucc.edu/ac ademic_guidance/first_is lander_scholars_academy /index.html	Low-income first generation (LIFG)	all disciplines
Collegiate	MBA Consortium https://cgsm.org/		business and MBA education

Collegiate	Pre-Law Undergraduate Scholars (PLUS) Program https://www.lsac.org/disc over-law/diversity-law-sch ool/prelaw-undergraduate -scholars-plus-programs		law
Collegiate	Summer Health Profes-sions Education Program http://www.shpep.org/	undocumented	health
Collegiate	Training and Recruitment Initiative for Admission to Leading Law Schools (TRIALS) https://trials.atfoundati on.org/		law
Collegiate	Woodrow Wilson-Rockefeller Brothers Fund Fellowship for Aspiring Teachers of Color https://scholarship.ousf .duke.edu/woodrow-wils on-rockefeller-brothers-fu nd-fellowships-aspiring-te achers-color		education
Collegiate/ Graduate	Campus Pride https://www.campuspri de.org/	gender and sexual minorities	most disciplines
Collegiate/ Graduate	Entry Point! https://www.aaas.org/pro grams/entry-point	persons with disabilities	STEM
Collegiate/ Graduate/ Professional/ Faculty/ Administra-tors	Consortium of Higher Education LGBTQ resource Professionals http://www.lgbtcampus .org/	gender and sexual minorities	most disciplines
Collegiate/ Graduate/ Postdoctoral/ Faculty	National Mentoring Research Network https://nrmnet.net/		most disciplines

Collegiate/ Graduate/ Professional/ Faculty	PhD Project https://www.phdproject .org/		business
Collegiate/ Graduate/ Postdoctoral/ Faculty	Society for Advancement of Chicanos/Hispanics and Native Americans in Science (SACNAS) http://sacnas.org/	Chicanos/Hispanics/ Native Americans	STEM
Collegiate/ Graduate/ Postdoctoral/ Faculty	Committee for Equality and Professional Opportu-nity (CEPO) http://www.sepaonline .com/cepo-about.html	gender and sexual minorities, URGs, women	psychology
Collegiate/ Graduate/ Postdoctoral/ Faculty	Lawrence Livermore National Laboratory https://st.llnl.gov/opport unities	Veterans	STEM
Collegiate/ Graduate/ Postdoctoral/ Faculty	Oak Ridge National Laboratory https://www.ornl.gov/		STEM
Collegiate/ Graduate/ Postdoctoral/ Faculty	Spark Society https://www.sparksocie ty.org/	Black/African Ameri-cans, Latinx, and Native Americans	cognitive neurosci-ence, cognitive psychology, cogni-tive science, linguistics
Graduate/ Professional/ Faculty/ Administra-tors	Graduate Management Admissions Council https://www.gmac.com/re ach-and-recruit-students /recruit-students-for-your -program/diversify-your -candidate-pool/diversity -resources-2		business

Graduate/ Professional	National Congress of American Indians Native Graduate Health Fellowship http://www.ncai.org/get -involved/internships-fello wships/native-graduate-he alth-fellowship	Native American/ Alaska Native	dentistry, medicine, pharmacy, public health
Graduate/ Postdoctoral	Preparing Future Faculty (PFF) https://preparing-faculty .org		STEM/humanities/ communication/ social sciences
Graduate/ Faculty	Robert Wood Johnson Foundation https://www.rwjf.org/		Behavioral and social sciences/ health
Graduate/ Faculty	500 Women Scientists https://500womenscienti sts.org/		Most disciplines
Graduate/ Faculty	Providing Opportunities for Women in Education Research (POWER) http://www.womeninedre search.com/	gender minority and women	child development and education
Graduate/ Professionals	Women In Medicine http://www.womeninmed icine.org/	lesbian and other sexual minorities	medicine
Postdoctoral	Howard Hughes Medical Institute Hanna H. Gray Fellows Program https://www.hhmi.org/pro grams/hanna-h-gray-fello ws-program#Overview		biomedical and life science disciplines

You can navigate to the interactive appendix at http://www.ac ademicpipelinedatabase.net. The initial landing page is shown in figure A.1. There are multiple options to search for programs. Clicking on the pipeline program project listings will allow you to find programs nationwide at various institutions and organizations.

Either of the navigation options takes you to our listings. The website has markers for each program displayed on the landscape of a GIS map of the United States (see figure A.2 below). You have the option to click on a marker or search for a program name or institution name in the search bar.

Figure A.1. Interactive appendix landing page.

Each program that has completed the THRIVE Index tool has information for the various dimensions of acronym. Each of the letters in THRIVE reveals best practices of the program. Figure A.1 shows an example for one program. Program descriptions are generated from information gathered using the THRIVE Index tool or are publicly available information on each program's website. Programs can be filtered by the following: region of the United States, institution type, discipline, and level of pipeline (i.e., precollegiate, collegiate, graduate, postdoctoral, faculty).

If you are a parent or student looking to participate in a program:

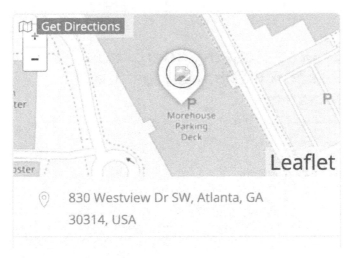

Figure A.2. GIS map with markers.

- We recommend students and parents review use the GIS map to find programs in their area and to contact the administrative personnel of these programs.
- Be aware that pipeline programs are not all the same and do not offer the same benefits.
- Financial incentives range from none to free service to stipend offered to tuition/fee-based.

If you are a faculty member or administrator implementing an existing program:

- We also recommend program directors use the GIS map to search for other programs at their institution to understand other supports guiding incoming students into their programs and for help in looking ahead of the needs of students to be successful in programs further up the academic pipeline.
- We recommend you search our appendix to find neighboring institutions engaged in similar programming

Home / Collegiate / Course-Based Undergraduate Research Experiences (CURE) Program

Course-Based Undergraduate Research Experiences (CURE) Program

Spelman College

The CURE program uses undergraduate academic research as a mechanism of student retention and engagement. We employ early career postdoctoral fellows and faculty teams to develop course-based research experiences (CRE) as a comprehensive institutional mechanism of student development. This project increases the quality and quantity of research opportunities available to Spelman students, as well as enhances the curriculum offerings related to STEM disciplines. This project is funded by the National Science Foundation's HBCU-UP Implementation Projects Program.

Figure A.3. Example academic pipeline program description.

- Go beyond our resource and use the partners directory and institution hub on http://www.pathwaystoscience.org to identify contacts at institutions, programs, and minority-serving organizations in your area.

APPENDIX B

ACADEMIC PIPELINE
PROJECT WEBSITES

Name of Program	Website
Precollegiate	
University of Maryland Baltimore County (UMBC) Meyerhoff Scholars Program	https://meyerhoff.umbc.edu/
Kits for Kids, Phoenix Student Architecture Program, Knowledge Is Power Program (KIPP), and KIPP Soul Academy	https://www.kipp.org/
College Advising Corps	https://advisingcorps.org/
United Negro College Fund, Gates Millennium Scholars Program	https://uncf.org/
Collegiate	
Annual Biomedical Research Conference for Minority Students	https://www.abrcms.org/
California Pre-Doctoral Program—Sally Casanova Scholarship	https://www2.calstate.edu/csu-system/faculty-staff/predoc
Howard Hughes Medical Institute	https://www.hhmi.org/science-education/programs/inclusive-excellence
Mellon Mays Undergraduate Fellowship Program	https://www.mmuf.org/
Florida A&M University Graduate Feeder Scholars Program	https://www.famu.edu/index.cfm?graduatestudies&GraduateFeederScholarsProgram
The Institute for Recruitment of Teachers	https://www.andover.edu/about/outreach/irt
The Leadership Alliance	https://www.theleadershipalliance.org/
Graduate/Professional	
SREB Doctoral Scholars Program	https://www.sreb.org/doctoral-scholars-program
Alfred P. Sloan Minority Graduate Scholarship Programs	https://sloan.org/fellowships/
The National GEM Consortium	https://www.gemfellowship.org/
McKnight Doctoral Fellowships	https://www.fefonline.org/mdf.html
Ford Foundation Fellowship Programs	https://sites.nationalacademies.org/PGA/FordFellowships/index.htm

Fisk-Vanderbilt Master's-to-PhD Bridge Program	https://www.fisk-vanderbilt-bridge.org/
Faculty Postdoctoral Program	
Rochester Institute of Technology Future Faculty Career Exploration Program	https://www.rit.edu/diversity/future-faculty-career-exploration-program
National Center for Faculty and Development Diversity	https://www.facultydiversity.org/
Sisters of the Academy Institute	https://sistersoftheacademy.org/
UC President's Postdoctoral Fellowship Program	https://ppfp.ucop.edu/info/
Creating Connections Consortium (C3)	https://c3transformhighered.org/home/

Chapter 1

RTI International	https://firstgen.naspa.org/research-and-policy/national-data-fact-sheets-on-first-generation-college-students/national-data-fact-sheets#:~:text=Highlight%3A%20As%20of%20academic%20year,family%20to%20go%20to%20college
Boys & Girls Clubs of America	https://www.bgca.org/about us/annual-report

Chapter 2

Centers for Disease Control and Prevention (CDC)	https://www.cdc.gov/
The Office of Minority Health and Health Equity (OMHHE)	https://www.cdc.gov/about/leadership/leaders/omhhe.html
CDC Science Museum Detective Camp	https://www.cdc.gov/museum/camp/detective/index.htm
National Aeronautics and Aerospace Administration	https://www.nasa.gov/
NASA Minority University Research and Education Project (MUREP) Aerospace Academy	https://www.nasa.gov/stem/murep/MAA/about/index.html
National Institutes of Health	https://www.nih.gov/research-training/training-opportunities

Summer Internships in Biomedical Research for High School Students (HS-SIP)	https://www.training.nih.gov/programs/hs-sip
Research Assistantships for High School Students (RAHSS)	https://www.nsf.gov/funding/pgm_summ.jsp?pims_id=500035
Pathways to Science	https://www.pathwaystoscience.org/k12.aspx
Common App—Find a College	https://www.commonapp.org/
US Department of Agriculture	https://www.usda.gov/
Jr. Minority in Agriculture, National Resources, and Related Sciences (MANRRS) Pre-College Initiative Program	https://www.manrrs.org/jr-manrrs-membership
US Department of Education	https://www.ed.gov
Gaining Early Awareness and Readiness for Undergraduate Programs (GEAR UP)	https://www2.ed.gov/programs/gearup/index.html
Talent Search	https://www2.ed.gov/programs/triotalent/index.html
Upward Bound	https://www2.ed.gov/programs/trioupbound/index.html
Upward Bound Math and Science	https://www2.ed.gov/programs/triomathsci/index.html
US Department of Agriculture	https://www.usda.gov/
USDA Summer Internship Program	https://www.usda.gov/internships
US Department of Energy K–12 Programs	https://www.energy.gov/eere/education/opportunities-k-12-students

Chapter 3

Centers for Disease Control and Prevention (CDC)	https://www.cdc.gov/
The Office of Minority Health and Health Equity (OMHHE)	https://www.cdc.gov/about/leadership/leaders/omhhe.html
CDC Undergraduate Public Health Scholars Program (CUPS)	https://www.cdc.gov/healthequity/features/cups/index.html

Maternal Child Health Careers/ Research Initiatives for Student Enhancement Undergraduate Program (MCHC/RISE-UP) at Kennedy Krieger Institute	https://www.kennedykrieger.org/training/programs/center-for-diversity-in-public-health-leadership-training/mchc-rise-up
Kennedy Krieger Institute Maternal and Child Health Leadership Education, Advocacy, and Research Network (MCH-LEARN)	https://www.kennedykrieger.org/training/programs/center-for-diversity-in-public-health-leadership-training/mch-learn
Dr. James A. Ferguson Emerging Infectious Diseases Research Initiatives for Student Enhancement (RISE) Fellowship Program	https://www.kennedykrieger.org/training/programs/center-for-diversity-in-public-health-leadership-training/ferguson-rise
Morehouse College Public Health Sciences Institutes Project Imhotep	https://www.morehouse.edu/academics/centers-and-institutes/public-health-sciences-institute/project-imhotep/
Morehouse College CDC Public Health Leaders Fellowship Program (PHLFP)	https://www.umass.edu/sphhs/2020-public-health-leaders-fellowship-program
Columbia University Medical Center- Summer Public Health Scholars Program (SPHSP)	https://www.ps.columbia.edu/sphsp
University of Michigan School of Public Health Future Public Health Leaders Program (Michigan FPHLP)	https://sph.umich.edu/fphlp/
UCLA Public Health Scholars Training Program	https://ph.ucla.edu/prospective-students/ucla-public-health-scholars-training-program
Kennedy Krieger Public Health Leadership and Learning Undergraduate Student Success (PLLUSS)	http://www.ugresearch.umd.edu/documents/PLLUSSProgram.pdf
Association of State Public Health Nutritionists (ASPHN) Health Equity Internship Program	https://asphn.org/health-equity-internship-program/
Hispanic Association of Colleges and Universities (HACU) National Internship Program (HNIP)	https://www.hacu.net/hacu/HNIP.asp

Mellon Mays Predoctoral Grants	https://www.ssrc.org/fellowships/view/mellon-mays-predoctoral-research-grants/
Woodrow Wilson National Fellowship Foundation	https://woodrow.org/fellowships/mellon/
Health and Human Services	https://www.hhs.gov/
Health Careers Opportunity Program (HCOP)	https://www.hrsa.gov/grants/find-funding?status=All&bureau=640
American Indians Into Psychology Programs (Indians Into Psychology Doctoral Education)	https://www.ihs.gov/dhps/dhpsgrants/americanindianpsychologyprogram/
National Institutes of Health	https://www.nih.gov/
NIH Bridges to the Baccalaureate (R25)	https://www.nigms.nih.gov/Research/Mechanisms/Pages/BridgesBaccalaureate.aspx
NIH Research Training Initiative for Scientific Enhancement (RISE) Program	https://www.nigms.nih.gov/Training/RISE
Maximizing Access to Research Careers Undergraduate Student Training in Academic Research (MARC U-STAR T34)	https://www.nigms.nih.gov/Training/MARC/Pages/USTARAwards.aspx
Minority Health and Health Disparities Research Training Program (MHRT)	https://www.nimhd.nih.gov/programs/extramural/domestic-international-research-training.html
Postbaccalaureate Research Education Program (PREP)	https://www.nigms.nih.gov/training/PREP/Pages/default.aspx
National Institute of Diabetes and Digestive Kidney Diseases (NIDDK) Diversity Summer Research Training Program (DSRTP)	https://www.niddk.nih.gov/research-funding/research-programs/diversity-programs/research-training-opportunities-students/diversity-summer-research-training-program-dsrtp
National Institute on Drug Abuse (NIDA) Intramural Research Program (IRP)	https://irp.drugabuse.gov/organization/diversity/recruitment-under-represented-populations/
Leadership Alliance	https://www.theleadershipalliance.org/
Mellon Mays Undergraduate Fellowship Program	https://www.mmuf.org/

Ronald E. McNair Postbaccalaureate Achievement Program	https://mcnairscholars.com/
Gates Millennial Scholars Program	https://gmsp.org/
Bonner Scholars Program	http://www.bonner.org/
Woodrow Wilson Rockefeller Brothers Fund (WW-RBF) Fellowships for Aspiring Teachers of Color	https://woodrow.org/fellowships/
National Aeronautics and Aerospace Administration (NASA)	https://www.nasa.gov/
NASA Science and Engineering Mathematics and Aerospace Academy (SEMAA)	https://www.nasa.gov/education/semaa
Minority University Research and Education Project (MUREP)	https://www.nasa.gov/stem/murep/home/index.html
National Science Foundation (NSF)	https://www.nsf.gov/
NSF Broadening Participation in Engineering (BPE)	https://www.nsf.gov/funding/pgm_summ.jsp?pims_id=505632
Historically Black Colleges and Universities Undergraduate Program (HBCU-UP)	https://hbcu-up.org/
Louis Stokes Alliance for Minority Participation (LSAMP)	https://www.nsf.gov/funding/pgm_summ.jsp?pims_id=13646
Significant Opportunities in Atmospheric Research and Science (SOARS)	https://soars.ucar.edu/
US Department of Agriculture	https://www.usda.gov/
Minority in Agriculture, Natural Resources, and Related Sciences Program (MANRRS)	https://info.manrrs.org/summerblminternship
Student Support Services (SSS)	https://www2.ed.gov/programs/triostudsupp/index.html
Ronald E. McNair Postbaccalaureate Achievement Program	https://mcnairscholars.com/
Veterans Upward Bound	https://www2.ed.gov/programs/triovub/index.html
US Department of Commerce	https://www.commerce.gov/

National Oceanic and Atmospheric Administration (NOAA) Educational Partnership Program with Minority Serving Institutions (EPP/MSI) Undergraduate Scholarship	https://www.noaa.gov/office-education/epp-msi/undergraduate-scholarship
US Department of Energy	https://www.energy.gov
Office of Environmental Management Minority Serving Institutions Partnership Programs (MSIPP)	https://www.anl.gov/education/minority-serving-institutions-partnership-program
Robert Wood Johnson Foundation	https://www.rwjf.org/
Summer Health Professions Program	http://www.shpep.org/
Chapter 4	
US Health and Human Services	https://www.hhs.gov/
Centers of Excellence	https://www.hrsa.gov/grants/find-funding/hrsa-17-065
Area Health Education Centers	https://www.hrsa.gov/grants/find-funding?status=All&bureau=640
Graduate Psychology Education Program (GPE)	https://www.hrsa.gov/grants/find-funding/hrsa-19-002
Health Resources & Services Administration Health Workforce Public Health Training Centers (PHTC)	https://bhw.hrsa.gov/grants/publichealth
American Indian Science and Engineering Society (AISES)	https://www.aises.org/
National Institute of General Medical Sciences (NIGMS)	https://www.nigms.nih.gov/training/Pages/Home.aspx
National Institute on Minority Health and Health Disparities (NIMHHD)	https://www.nimhd.nih.gov/programs/extramural/research-areas/clinical-research.html
NIH Research Training Initiative for Student Enhancement (RISE) Program	https://www.nigms.nih.gov/Training/RISE
Minority Health and Health Disparities Research Training Program (MHRT)	https://www.nimhd.nih.gov/programs/extramural/domestic-international-research-training.html

Neuroscience Scholars Program	https://www.sfn.org/initiatives/diversity-initiatives/neuroscience-scholars-program
Ruth L. Kirschstein National Research Service Awards for Individual Predoctoral Fellowships to Promote Diversity in Health-Related Research (F31)	https://www.niehs.nih.gov/research/supported/training/fellowships/f31/index.cfm
Department of Health and Human Services Initiative for Maximizing Student Development (T32)	https://grants.nih.gov/grants/guide/pa-files/par-19-037.html
Indian Health Service (IHS)	https://www.ihs.gov/
IHS Indians into Medicine (INMED)	https://www.ihs.gov/dhps/dhpsgrants/indiansmedicineprogram/
IHS Retention of American Indians into Nursing (RAIN)	https://www.ihs.gov/dhps/dhpsgrants/americanindiansnursingprogram/
National Science Foundation (NSF)	https://nsf.gov/
NSF Division of Human Resource Development	https://www.nsf.gov/funding/programs.jsp?org=HRD
NSF Division of Graduate Education	https://www.nsf.gov/funding/programs.jsp?org=DGE
NSF Bridges to the Doctorate (BD)	http://sas.fiu.edu/nsf-bridge-doctorate-fellowship/#:~:text=The%20NSF%20Bridge%20to%20the,programs.
NSF Alliances for Graduate Education and the Professoriate (AGEP)	https://www.nsf.gov/funding/pgm_summ.jsp?pims_id=5474
NSF Graduate Research Fellowship Program (GRFP)	https://www.nsf.gov/funding/pgm_summ.jsp?pims_id=6201
Substance Abuse and Mental Health Services Administration (SAMSHA)	https://www.samhsa.gov/
SAMSHA Minority Fellowship Program (SAMSHA MFP)	https://www.samhsa.gov/minority-fellowship-program
US Department of Agriculture	https://www.usda.gov/
Minority in Agriculture, Natural Resources, and Related Sciences Program (MANRRS)	http://info.manrrs.org/summerblminternship

American Education Research Association (AERA)	https://www.aera.net/
AERA Minority Dissertation Fellowship in Education Research	https://www.aera.net/Professional-Opportunities-Funding/AERA-Funding-Opportunities/Minority-Dissertation-Fellowship-Program
American Psychological Association (APA)	https://www.apa.org/
Dalmas A. Taylor Memorial Summer Minority Policy Fellowship	https://www.spssi.org/index.cfm?fuseaction=page.viewPage&pageID=743&nodeID=1
Interdisciplinary Minority Fellowship Program (IMFP)	http://mfpapp.apa.org/docs/apa/IMFPinformationdocument-final.pdf
Psychology Summer Institute (PSI)	https://www.apa.org/pi/mfp/psychology/institute
Society for Neuroscience	https://www.sfn.org/
Neuroscience Scholars Program	https://www.sfn.org/initiatives/diversity-initiatives/neuroscience-scholars-program
Social Science Research Council	https://www.ssrc.org/?gclid=CjoKCQjwy8f6BRC7ARIsAPIXOjgByMVQ-1oXl6meyM-QwyTbjJeWc6ZhGZcZvtn7nihvGVjLZCmpj-QaAjtsEALw_wcB
Mellon Mays Predoctoral Research Grants	https://www.ssrc.org/fellowships/view/mellon-mays-predoctoral-research-grants/
Robert Wood Johnson Foundation	https://www.rwjf.org/
Health Policy Research Scholars	https://healthpolicyresearch-scholars.org/
Chapter 5	
University of Michigan's President's Postdoctoral Fellowship Program	http://presidentspostdoc.umich.edu/
National Institutes of Health (NIH)	http://nih.gov/
NIH National Institute of General Medical Sciences (NIGMS)	https://www.nigms.nih.gov/training/Pages/Home.aspx

NIH Maximizing Opportunities for Scientific and Academic Independent Careers (MOSAIC, K99/R00 and UE5)	https://www.nigms.nih.gov/training/careerdev/Pages/MOSAIC.aspx
National Institute on Drug Abuse (NIDA) Scientific Director's Fellowship for Diversity in Research (SDFDR) Postdoctoral Fellows	https://irp.drugabuse.gov/organization/diversity/sdfdr-postdoc/
National Science Foundation (NSF)—Education and Human Resources	https://www.nsf.gov/dir/index.jsp?org=EHR
NSF Faculty Early Career Development Program (CAREER)	https://www.nsf.gov/funding/pgm_summ.jsp?pims_id=503214
NSF ADVANCE: Organizational Change for Gender Equity in STEM Academic Professions	https://www.nsf.gov/funding/pgm_summ.jsp?pims_id=5383&org=EHR&from=home
National Endowments of the Humanities	https://www.neh.gov/grants
American Educational Research Association (AERA)	https://www.aera.net/Professional-Opportunities-Funding
AERA Fellowship Program on the Study of Deeper Learning (SDL)	https://www.aera.net/Professional-Opportunities-Funding/AERA-Funding-Opportunities/AERA-Fellowship-Program-on-the-Study-of-Deeper-Learning
American Psychological Association (APA)	https://www.apa.org/
APA Leadership and Education Advancement Program (LEAP) for Diverse Scholars	https://www.apa.org/pi/mfp/leap
Mental Health and Substance Abuse Services (MHSAS) Postdoctoral Fellowship	https://www.apa.org/pi/mfp/psychology/postdoc
Social Science Research Council	http://ssrc.org/
Sloan Scholars Mentoring Network Grants	https://www.ssrc.org/fellowships/view/ssmn-grants/
Robert Wood Johnson Foundation	https://www.rwjf.org/

Harold Amos Medical Faculty Development Program	http://www.amfdp.org/about

Chapter 6

Forsyth Elementary Career Inventory	https://www.forsyth.k12.ga.us/cms/lib3/GA01000373/Centricity/Domain/3152/Interest%20Inventory%20itsLearning%20Make%20up.pdf
Education Planner.org Career Clusters Activity	http://www.educationplanner.org/students/career-planning/find-careers/career-clusters.shtml
O-Net Interest Profiler	https://www.mynextmove.org/explore/ip
REL Southeast Career Readiness Resource	https://ies.ed.gov/ncee/edlabs/infographics/pdf/REL_SE_Career_Readiness_Preparing_the_Student.pdf
Careeronestop Interest Assessment	https://www.careeronestop.org/toolkit/careers/interest-assessment.aspx
Paws in Jobland	https://www.xap.com/paws/
Holland Code (RIASEC) Test	https://openpsychometrics.org/tests/RIASEC/
Myers-Briggs Strong Interest Inventory	https://www.themyersbriggs.com/en-US/Products-and-Services/Strong
Myers-Briggs Type Indicator	https://www.myersbriggs.org/my-mbti-personality-type/mbti-basics/home.htm?bhcp=1
US Bureau of Labor Statistics Occupational Outlook Handbook	https://www.bls.gov/ooh/
National Science Foundation's Pathways to Science Guide	https://www.pathwaystoscience.org/pdf/SummerResearch_DiscussingWithYourFamily.pdf
Penn State Millennium Scholars Program	https://www.millennium.psu.edu/
Chancellor's Science Scholars Program at the University of North Carolina	https://chancellorssciencescholars.unc.edu/
Howard Hughes Medical Institute (HHMI) Inclusive Excellence Initiative	https://www.hhmi.org/science-education/programs/inclusive-excellence

HHMI Inclusive Excellence Program Announcement	https://www.hhmi.org/sites/default/files/programs/inclusive/ie3-program-announcement-final.pdf
A Faculty Roadmap to Training Grants: Proposal Preparation, Administration, & Evaluation	https://graduate.ku.edu/sites/graduate.ku.edu/files/docs/TrainingGrantsGuide.pdf
Howard Hughes Medical Institute (HHMI)	https://www.hhmi.org/science-education/programs/diversity-and-inclusion
Andrew Mellon Foundation	https://mellon.org/grants/
Department of Energy Office of Minority Programs	https://www.energy.gov/diversity/office-minority-programs
National Science Foundation (NSF)	https://www.nsf.gov/funding/azindex.jsp
National Institutes of Health (NIH) Building Infrastructure Leading to Diversity (BUILD) Initiative	https://www.nigms.nih.gov/training/dpc/Pages/build.aspx
NIH Initiative for Maximizing Student Development (IMSD, T32)	https://grants.nih.gov/grants/guide/pa-files/par-19-037.html
NIH Support of Competitive Research (SCORE) Program	https://www.nigms.nih.gov/Research/DRCB/SCORE/pages/SCOREUpdateFAQ.aspx
Alfred P. Sloan Foundation	https://sloan.org/grants/apply
Amgen Foundation	https://www.amgen.com/responsibility/amgen-foundation/
US Department of Education Federal TRIO Programs	https://www2.ed.gov/about/offices/list/ope/trio/index.html
US Department of Education MSI Grants	https://www2.ed.gov/about/offices/list/ope/idues/eligibility.html
Academic Pipeline Project/THRIVE Index, STEM-US Collaboration	https://academicpipeline.web.app/index.html
Georgia State University Diversity Database	https://dei.gsu.edu/diversity-database/

APPENDIX C

CONTRIBUTORS TO THE THRIVE INVENTORY

Name	Program
Ansley Abraham, Director	Southern Regional Education Board Doctoral Scholars Program[1]
David Asai, Senior Director, Science Education, Howard Hughes Medical Institute	Howard Hughes Medical Institute[2]
Armando Bengochea, Senior Program Officer and Director of MMUF, the Andrew W. Mellon Foundation	Mellon Mays Undergraduate Fellowship Program[3]
Elizabeth Boylan, Program Manager	Alfred P. Sloan Graduate Scholarship Programs[4]
LaShawnda Brooks, Executive Director	Institute for Recruitment of Teachers[5]
Donathan Brown, PhD, Assistant Provost and Assistant Vice President for Faculty Diversity and Recruitment	Rochester Institute of Technology Future Faculty Career Exploration Program[6]
Lu Duong, Director	Program is UNCF Fund II Foundation, HBCU Innovation - Silicon Valley
Reginald K. Ellis, PhD, Assistant Dean for the School of Graduate Studies and Research	Florida A&M University Graduate Feeder Scholars Program[7]
H. Ray Gamble, PhD, Director, Fellowships Office	Ford Foundation Fellowship Program[8]
Medeva Ghee, PhD, Executive Director	The Leadership Alliance[9]
Keith M. Harmon, Director	University of Maryland, Baltimore County, (UMBC) Meyerhoff Scholars Program[10]
Shaundra Holmes, Fellowship Program Coordinator	Annual Biomedical Research Conference for Minority Students[11]
Freeman A. Hrabowski III, President	UMBC[12]
Irene V. Hulede, Senior Manager, Education	Annual Biomedical Research Conference for Minority Students[13]
Rachel Hynson, PhD, Director	Creating Connections Consortium (C3)[14]
Johnny Ray James II, MEd, Director of Extended Learning; Assistant Principal	Kits for Kids, Phoenix Student Architecture Program, Knowledge Is Power Program (KIPP)[15]; KIPP Soul Academy
Maridith A. Janssen, PhD, Director	California Pre-Doctoral Program's Sally Casanova Scholarship[16]

Tamara Bertrand Jones, PhD, Research BootCamp Chair, Associate Professor/ Interim Chair, College of Education, Florida State University	Sisters of the Academy Institute[17]
Mark A. Lawson, PhD, Director	UC President's Postdoctoral Fellowship Program[18]
Brennon Marcano, CEO	The National GEM Consortium[19]
Robin Mohapatra, CEO	National Center for Faculty Development & Diversity[20]
Lawrence Morehouse, PhD, President and CEO	McKnight Doctoral Fellowship Program[21]
Yarbrah Peeples, Senior Regional Director-East	College Advising Corps[22]
Aarron Stallworth, Senior Relationship Manager	United Negro College Fund Gates Millennium Scholars Program[23]
Dina Stroud, PhD, Executive Director/Executive Director of the Vanderbilt TLSAMP Bridge to the Doctorate	Fisk-Vanderbilt Master's-to-PhD Bridge Program[24]

Note: Each contributor provided the content related to their respective programs.
1. https://www.sreb.org/doctoral-scholars-program
2. https://www.hhmi.org/science-education/programs/inclusive-excellence
3. https://www.mmuf.org/
4. https://sloan.org/fellowships/
5. https://www.andover.edu/about/outreach/irt
6. https://www.rit.edu/diversity/ffcep
7. https://www.famu.edu/index.cfm?graduatestudies&GraduateFeederScholarsProgram
8. https://sites.nationalacademies.org/PGA/FordFellowships/index.htm
9. https://theleadershipalliance.org/
10. https://meyerhoff.umbc.edu/
11. https://www.abrcms.org/
12. https://www.abrcms.org/
13. https://www.abrcms.org/
14. https://c3transformhighered.org/
15. https://www.kipp.org/?gclid=CjwKCAjwg6b0BRBMEiwANd1_SJJXYyj44klMAAqmeVm8C5XVTEdbeAtFAabfS2f0ZftsdqCXJkxDWBoC2AkQAvD_BwE
16. https://www2.calstate.edu/csu-system/faculty-staff/predoc
17. http://sistersoftheacademy.org/
18. https://ppfp.ucop.edu/info/
19. https://www.gemfellowship.org/
20. https://www.facultydiversity.org/
21. https://www.fefonline.org/mdf.html
22. https://advisingcorps.org/
23. https://uncf.org/events?gclid=CjwKCAjwg6b0BRBMEiwANd1_SLbfxB6DiEIN6tShVrvgsg62VDy5kBWCLXIxyhNa7sO2gcJwl0XmihoCEQMQAvD_BwE
24. https://www.fisk-vanderbilt-bridge.org/

Bibliography

Abraham, A. (2013). A generation of success—The SREB-State Doctoral Scholars Program celebrates 20 years. Retrieved from http://publications.sreb.org/20 13/13E10_Gen_Success.pdf

Adams, H. G. (2008). *Career management 101: A primer for career management.* Norfolk, VA: Howard Adams.

Allen-Ramdial, S. A., & Campbell, G. (2014). Reimagining the pipeline: Advancing STEM diversity, persistence, and success. *BioScience, 64*(7), 612. doi:10.1093 /biosci/biu076

American Council on Education. (n d). Postsecondary faculty and staff. Retrieved from https://www.equityinhighered.org/data_table_category/postsecondary -faculty/

American Council on Education. (2019). Equity in higher ed. Retrieved from https://www.equityinhighered.org/

American Institutes for Research. (2014). Early academic career pathways: Do gender and family status matter? Washington, DC: Author. Retrieved from https://www.air.org/sites/default/files/STEM%20PhD%20Early%20Academ ic%20Career%20Pathway_March%202014.pdf

Ancarana, E. (2019). Supporting dual-career families: It takes a village, or maybe just a good, strong bicycle wheel. received from national center for faculty development and diversity. Retrieved from https://www.facultydiversity.org /news/dual-career-families

Angrist, J. D., Dyanarski, S. M., Kane, T. J., Pathak, P. A., & Walters, C. R. (2011). Who benefits from KIPP? *Institute for the Study of Labor: Discussion Paper Series.* Germany: University of Bonn.

Arao, B., & Clemens, K. (2013). From safe spaces to brave spaces: A new way to frame dialogue around diversity and social justice. In L. Landreman (Ed.), *The art of effective facilitation: Reflections from social justice educators* (pp. 135–150). Sterling, VA: Stylus.

Bajaj, M. (2014). Lanterns and street signs. *The truly diverse faculty* (pp.235–263). New York, NY: Palgrave MacMillan.

Bandura, A., & Schunk, D. H. (1981). Cultivating competence, self-efficacy, and intrinsic interest through proximal self-motivation. *Journal of Personality and Social Psychology, 41*(3), 586–598.

Beilke, J. R. (1997). The changing emphasis of the Rosenwald Fellowship Program, 1928–1948. *The Journal of Negro Education, 66*(1), 3–15.

Blockett, R.A., Felder, P. P., Parrish III, W., & Collier, J.N. (2016). Pathways to the professoriate: Exploring black doctoral student socialization and the pipeline to the academic profession. *Western Journal of Black Studies, 40*(2), 95.

Bourdieu, P. (1977). *Outline of a theory of practice*. London: Cambridge University Press.

Brady, S. T., Cohen, G. L., Jarvis, S. N., & Walton, G. M. (2020). A brief social-belonging intervention in college improves adult outcomes for black Americans. *Science Advances, 6*(18), eaay3689. doi:10.1126/sciadv.aay3689

Brock, T. (2010). Young adults and higher education: Barriers and breakthroughs to success. *The Future of Children, 20*(1), 109–132. doi:10.1353/foc.0.0040

Brown, C. L., & Bergen, M. (2018). Amgen scholars: Best practices in summer undergraduate research programs. Retrieved from https://amgenscholars.com/about/

Burke, L. (2014). Reauthorizing the higher education act—Toward policies that increase access and lower costs. Retrieved from https://www.heritage.org/education/report/reauthorizing-the-higher-education-act-toward-policies-increase-access-and-lower

Bushe, G. R., & Kassam, A. F.(2005). When is appreciative inquiry transformational? A meta-case analysis. *The Journal of Applied Behavioral Science, 41*,(2), 161–181. doi:10.1177/0021886304270337

Byrd, C. D. (2016). *Diversifying the professoriate* (Doctoral dissertation, University of Georgia). Retrieved from http://purl.galileo.usg.edu/uga_etd/byrd_curtis_d_201605_edd

Carpi, A., Ronan, D. M., Falconer, H. M., & Lents, N. H. (2017). Cultivating minority scientists: Undergraduate research increases self-efficacy and career ambitions for underrepresented students in STEM. *Journal of Research in Science Teaching, 54*(2), 169–194. doi:10.1002/tea.21341

Carruthers, C., & Wanamaker, M. (2013). Closing the gap? The effect of private philanthropy on the provision of African-American schooling in the U.S. south. *Journal of Public Economics, 101,* 53–67. doi:10.1016/j.jpubeco.2013.02 .003

Casad, B. J., Chang, A. L., & Pribbenow, C. M. (2016). The benefits of attending the Annual Biomedical Research Conference for Minority Students (ABRCMS): The role of research confidence. *CBE-Life Sciences Education, 15*(ar46), 1–11. doi:10.1187/cbe.16-010048

Center for Minority Serving Institutions (2021). A brief history of MSIs. Retrieved from https://cmsi.gse.rutgers.edu/content/brief-history-msis.

Chemers, M. M., Zurbriggen, E. L., Syed, M., Goza, B. K., & Bearman, S. (2011). The role of efficacy and identity in science career commitment among underrepresented minority students. *Journal of Social Issues, 67*(3), 469–491. doi:10.1111 /j.1540-4560.2011.01710.x

Clewell, B. C., Cohen, C. C., Tsui., L., Forcier, L., Gao, E., Young, N., Deterding, N., & West, C. (2005). Evaluation of the National Science Foundation Louis Stokes Alliances for Minority Participation. Retrieved from https://www.nsf .gov/funding/pgm_summ.jsp?pims_id=13646

Colby, S. L., & Ortman, J. M. (2015). Projections of the size and composition of the U.S. population: 2014 to 2060. Retrieved from https://www.census.gov/conte nt/dam/Census/library/publications/2015/demo/p25-1143.pdf

Coleman, J. S. (1988). Social capital in the creation of human capital. *The American Journal of Sociology, 1.* doi:10.2307/2780243

Coleman, J. S. (1990). *Foundations of social theory.* Cambridge, MA, and London: Harvard University Press.

Collier, C., & Mason, R. S. (2014). *Thinking critically about your career in psychology.* E-book. Retrieved from goes with Collier and Mason reference above for the E-book.

Cooperrider, D.L., & Srivastva, S. (1987). Appreciative inquiry in organizational life. In R. Woodman and W. Pasmore (Eds.), *Research in organizational change and development* (pp. 129–169). Stamford, CT.

Cooperrider, D. L., & Whitney, D. A. (2005). Appreciative inquiry: A positive revolution in change. San Francisco: Berrett-Koehler Publishers.

DesJardins, S. L., & McCall, B. P. (2014). The impact of the Gates Millennium Scholars Program on college and post-college related choices of high ability, low-income minority students. *Economics Education Review, 38,* 124–138. doi:10.1016/j.econedurev.2013.11.004

Domingo, M. R. S., & Sathy, V. (2019). Here's how to increase diversity in STEM at the college level and beyond. Retrieved from https://www.higheredjobs.com /Articles/articleDisplay.cfm?ID=1934

Domingo, M. R. S., Sharp, S., Freeman, A., Freeman Jr., T., Harmon, K., Wiggs, M.,

Sathy, V., Panter, A. T., Oseguera, L., Sun, S., Williams, M. E., Templeton, J., Folt, C. L., Barron, E. J., Freeman III, A. H., Maton, K. I., Crimmins, M., Fisher, C. R., & Summers, M. F. (2019). Replicating Meyerhoff for inclusive excellence in STEM. *Science, 364*(6438), 335–337.

Duffus, W. A., Trawick, C., Moonesinghe, R., Tola, J., Truman, B. I., & Dean, H. D. (2014). Training racial and ethnic minority students for careers in public health sciences. *American Journal of Preventive Medicine, 47*(5 Supplement 3), S368–375.

Farmer-Hinton, R. L., & Adams, T. L. (2006). Social capital and college preparation: Exploring the role of counselors in a college prep school for black students. *The Negro Educational Review, 57*(1–2), 101–116.

Felder, P. (2010). On doctoral student development: Exploring faculty mentoring in the shaping of African American doctoral student success. *The Qualitative Report, 15,* 455–474.

Fleming, L., & Saslaw, R. (1992). Rockefeller and general education board influences on vocationalism in education, 1880–1925. (Report No. CE062065). Chicago, IL: Midwestern Educational 171 Research Association.

Fries-Britt, S. L., Rowan-Kenyon, H. T., Perna, L. W., Milem, J. F., & Howard, D. G. (2011). Underrepresentation in the academy and the institutional climate for faculty diversity. *Journal of the Professoriate, 5*(1), 1–34.

Gándara, P. (2006). Strengthening the academic pipeline leading to careers in math, science, and technology for Latino students. *Journal of Hispanic Higher Education, 5*(3), 222–237. doi:10.1177/1538192706288820

Gee, J. P. (2000). Identity as an analytic lens for research in education. *Review of Research in Education, 25*(1), 99–125. doi:10.3102/0091732X025001099

Gilbert, C. K., & Heller, D. E. (2013). Access, equity, and community colleges: The Truman Commission and federal higher education policy from 1947 to 2011. *The Journal of Higher Education, 84*(3), 417–443. doi:10.1080/00221546 .2013.11777295

Gonzalez Quiroz, A., & Garza, N. R. (2018). Focus on student success: Components for effective summer bridge programs. *Journal of Hispanic Higher Education, 17*(2), 101–111. doi:10.1177/1538192717753988

Hall, A. K., Miklos, A., Oh., A., & Gaillard, S. D. (2016). Educational outcomes from the Maximizing Access to Research Careers Undergraduate Student Training in Academic Research (MARC U-STAR) program. Retrieved from https://www .nigms.nih.gov/News/reports/Documents/MARC-paper031416.pdf

Haggard, D. L., Dougherty, T. W., Turban, D. B., & Wilbanks, J. E. (2011). Who is a mentor? A review of evolving definitions and implications for research. *Journal of Management, 37,* 280–304. doi:10.1177/0149206310386227

Herrmann, S. D. (2019). Crossing class cultures: Understanding first-generation college students' transitions. *Eye on Psi Chi, 23*(4), 23–25. doi:10.24839/2164-9 812.Eye23.4.22

Hunter, I., Dik, B. J., & Banning, J. H. (2010). College students' perceptions of calling in work and life: A qualitative analysis. *Journal of Vocational Behavior, 76*, 178–186. doi:10.1016/j.jvb.2009.10.008

KIPP. (2017). Alumni survey results. Retrieved from https://www.kipp.org/appro ach/kipp-through-college/kipp-alumni-survey-results/

Kitchen, J. A., Sonnert, G., & Sadler, P. M. (2018). The impact of college- and university-run high school summer programs on students' end of high school STEM career aspirations. *Science Education, 102*(3), 529–47. doi:10.1002/sce .21332

Krim, J. S., Cote, L. E., Schwartz, R. S., Stone, E. M., Cleeves, J. J., Barry, K. J., Burgess, W., Buxner, S. R., Gerton, J. M., Horvath, L., Keller, J. M., Lee, S. C., Locke, S. M., & Rebar, B. M. (2019). Models and impacts of science research experiences: A review of the literature of CUREs, UREs, and TREs. *CBE Life Sciences Education, 18*(65), 1–14. doi:10.1187/cbe.19-03-0069

Jordan, T. C., Burnett, S. H., Carson, S., Caruso, S. M., Clase, K., DeJong, R. J., Dennehy, J. J., Denver, D. R., Dunbar, D., Elgin, S. C. R., Findley, A. M., Gissendanner, C. R., Golebiewska, U. P., Guild, N., Hartzog, G. A., Grillo, Hollowell, G. P., Hughes, L. E., Johnson, A., King, R. A., Lewis, L. O., Rosenzwieg, L. W., Rubin, M. R., Saha, M. S., Sandoz, J., Shaffer, C. D., Taylor, B., Temple, L., Russell, D. A. , Cresawn, S. G., Lopatto, D., Bailey, C. P., & Hatfull, G. F. (2014). A broadly implementable research course in Phage discovery and genomics for first-year undergraduate students. *mBio, 5*(1). doi:10.1128/mBio.01051-13

Joskow, P. L. (2016). Diversity & inclusion initiatives at the Alfred P. Sloan Foundation (1950–2016), 2016 president's letter. Alfred P. Sloan Foundation. Retrieved from https://sloan.org/programs/higher-education/diversity-equity-inclusi on/minority-phd-program

Lamont, M., & Lareau, A. (1988). Cultural capital: Allusions, gaps and glissandos in recent theoretical developments. *Sociological Theory, 6*(2), 153–168.

Lareau, A., & Weininger, E. B. (2003). Cultural capital in educational research: A critical assessment. *Theory and Society, 32*(5–6), 567–606.

Linn, M. C., Palmer, E., Berenger, A., Gerard, E., & Stone, E. (2015). Undergraduate research experiences: Impacts and opportunities. *Science, 347*, 6222. doi:10.11 86/science.1961757

Liu, S-N. C., Brown, S. E. V., and Sabat, I. E. (2019). Patching the "leaky pipeline": Interventions for women of color faculty in STEM academia. *Archives of Scientific Psychology, Advancing Gender Equality in the Workplace, 7*(1), 32–39. doi:10 .1037/arc0000062

Ludema, J. D., Cooperrider, D., & Barrett, F. (2001). Appreciative inquiry: The power of the unconditional positive question. In P. Reason & H. Bradbury (Eds.). *Handbook of action research: Participative inquiry and practice* (pp. 189–199). London: Sage.

Ludema, J. D., & Fry, R. E. (2008). The practice of appreciative inquiry. In P. Reason & H. Bradbury (Eds.), *The sage handbook of action research: Participative inquiry and practice* (pp. 280–297). London: Sage.

Lunsford, L. G., Crisp, G., Dolan, E. L., & Wutherick, B. (2017). Mentoring in higher education. In D. A. Clutterbuck, F. K. Kochan, L. Lunsford, N. Dominguez, & J. Haddock-Millar (Eds.). *Sage handbook of mentoring* (pp. 316–334). Washington, DC: Sage.

Markets Insider. (2018). UNCF announces third class of UNCF® STEM scholars through $48 million investment from Fund II Foundation. Retrieved from https://markets.businessinsider.com/news/stocks/uncf-announces-third-class-of-uncf-stem-scholars-through-48-million-investment-from-fund-ii-foundation-1027364028#

Mathematica. (2015). The consortium: 2015 year in review. Retrieved from https://www.mathematica-mpr.com/our-publications-and-findings/publications/the-consortium-stimulating-selfsufficiency-and-stability-scholarship-year-in-review

Mason, R. S., & Byrd. C. D. (2021). 4P academic pipeline program rubric. Atlanta, GA: Academic Pipeline Project, LLC. doi:10.17605/OSF.IO/5NZ4M

Mason, R. S. (2020). Mentoring as discipleship at historically black colleges and universities (HBCUs). In A. Bradley (Ed.), *Black lives matter in community: On renewing African American and other communities on the margins*, 93–102. Wheaton, IL: Crossway Publications.

Maton, K. I., & Hrabowski, F. A. III. (2004). Increasing the number of African American Ph.D.s in the sciences and engineering: A strengths-based approach. *American Psychologist, 59*(6), 547–556. doi:10.1037/0003-066X.59.6.547

Maton, K. I., Hrabowski, F. A., & Schmitt, C. L. (2000). African American college students excelling in the sciences: College and postcollege outcomes in the Meyerhoff scholars program. *Journal of Research in Science Teaching, 37*, 629–654. doi:10.1002/1098-2736(200009)37:7<629::AID-TEA2>3.0.CO;2-8

McCay, J., & Bruns, S. (2015). Project AWESOME: Advancing welfare and family self-sufficiency research. Retrieved from https://www.mathematica-mpr.com/our-publications-and-findings/publications/the-consortium-stimulating-selfsufficiency-and-stability-scholarship-year-in-review

Mervis, J. (2019). Vaunted diversity program catches on. *Science, 365*(6451), 308–309.

Montgomery, B. L. (2017). Mapping a mentoring roadmap and developing a supportive network for strategic career advancement. *Sage Journals, 7*(2). doi.org/10.1177/2158244017710288

Montgomery, B. L., Dodson, J. E., & Johnson, S. M. (2014). Guiding the way: Mentoring graduate students and junior faculty for sustainable academic careers. *SAGE Open, 4*(4). doi:10.1177/2158244014558043

McCray, V. (2018). Gates Foundation grant to help Atlanta students find the best fit. Retrieved from http://www.kipp.org/news/gates-foundation-grant-help -atlanta-students-find-best-college-fit/

McElroy, E., & Arnesto, M. (1998). TRIO and Upward Bound: History, programs, and issues—Past, present, and ruture. *The Journal of Negro Education, 67*(4), 373–380. doi:10.2307/2668137

McLeod, J. (2011) Student voice and the politics of listening in higher education. *Critical Studies in Education, 52*(2), 179–189, doi:10.1080/17508487.2011.572830

Minefee, I., Rabelo, C. R., Stewart, O. J. C., & Young, N. C. J. (2018). Repairing leaks in the pipeline: A social closure perspective on underrepresented racial/ethnic minority recruitment and retention in business schools. *Academy of Management Learning & Education, 17*(1), 79–95. doi:10.5465/amle.2015.0215

Murphy, M. C., Gopalan, M., Carter, E. R., Emerson, K. T. U., Bottoms, B. L., & Walton, G. M. (2020). A customized belonging intervention improves retention of socially disadvantaged at a broad-access university. *Science Advances* 6(29), 1–7. doi:10.1126/sciadv.aba4677

National Center for Education Statistics. (2020). Projections of education statistics to 2028. Retrieved from https://nces.ed.gov/programs/PES/section-3.asp #5

National Research Council. (2018). *Identifying and supporting productive STEM programs in out-of-school settings.* Washington, DC: National Academies Press.

National Center for Education Statistics. (2019). Digest of education statistics. Table 219.30. Retrieved from https://nces.ed.gov/programs/digest/d19/tables /dt19_219.30.asp

National Science Foundation, National Center for Women, Minorities, and Persons with Disabilities in Science and Engineering. (2019a). Employment. Retrieved from https://ncses.nsf.gov/pubs/nsf19304/digest/employment

National Science Foundation, National Center for Women, Minorities, and Persons with Disabilities in Science and Engineering. (2019b). Field of degree: Minorities. Retrieved from https://nces.ed.gov/programs/digest/d18/tables/dt 18_306.10.asp

Nora, A., & Crisp, G. (2007). Mentoring students: Conceptualizing and validating the multi-dimensions of a support system. *Journal of College Student Retention: Research, Theory & Practice, 9*(3), 337–356. doi:10.2190/CS.9.3.e

Nguyen, T. L. K., Williams, A., & Ludwikowski, W. M. A. (2017). Predicting student success and retention at an HBCU via interest-major congruence and academic achievement. *Journal of Career Assessment, 25*(3), 552–566. doi:10.11 77/1069072716651870

Nishii, L. N. (2017). *A multi-level process model for understanding diversity practice effectiveness* (CAHRS Research Link No. 5). Ithaca, NY: Cornell University, ILR School, Center for Advanced Human Resource Studies.

Palmer, R. T., Maramba, D. C., & Dancy, T. E. (2011). A qualitative investigation of factors promoting the retention and persistence of students of color in STEM. *Journal of Negro Education, 80*(4), 491–504.

Pell Institute. (2018). Indicators of higher education equity in the United States. Retrieved from http://pellinstitute.org/downloads/publications-Indicators _of_Higher_Education_Equity_in_the_US_2018_Historical_Trend_Report .pdf

Pender, M., Marcotte, D. E., Sto Domingo, M. R., & Maton, K. I. (2010). The STEM pipeline: The role of summer research experience in minority students' Ph.D. aspirations. *Education policy analysis archives, 18*(30), 1–36.

Perna, L. (2015). *Improving college access and completion for low-income and first-generation students: The role of college access and success programs.* University Park, PA: University of Pennsylvania Graduate School of Education.

Perna, L., Wagner-Lundy, V., Drezner, N. D., Gasman, M., Yoon, S., Bose, E., & Gary, S. (2009). The contribution of HBCUs to the preparation of African American women for STEM careers: A case study. *Research in Higher Education, 50,* 1–23.

Pew Research Center. (2012). Most parents expect their children to attend college. Retrieved from https://www.pewresearch.org/fact-tank/2012/02/27/most-par ents-expect-their-children-to-attend-college/

Pew Research Center. (2019). Fact tank. Retrieved from https://www.pewresearch .org/fact-tank/2019/07/31/us-college-faculty-student-diversity/

Phelps, R. E. (1995). What's in a number: Implications for African American female faculty at predominantly white colleges and universities. *Innovative Higher Education, 19*(4), 255–268.

Pierre, P.A. (2015). A brief history of the collaborative minority engineering effort: A personal account. In J. B. Slaughter, Y. Tao, & W. Pearson, Jr. (Eds.), *Changing the face of engineering: The african american experience* (pp 13–35). Baltimore, MD: Johns Hopkins University Press.

Pokphanh, R., & Augusto, J. (2011). A faculty roadmap to training grants: Proposal preparation, administration, & evaluation. Retrieved from https://graduate .ku.edu/sites/graduate.ku.edu/files/docs/TrainingGrantsGuide.pdf

Puritty, C., Strickland, L. R., Alia, E., Blonder, B., Klein, E., Kohl, M. T., McGee, E., Quintana, M., Ridley, R. E., Tellman, B., & Gerber, L. R. (2017). Without inclusion, diversity initiatives may not be enough. *Science, 357*(6356), 1101–1102. doi:10.1126/science.aai9054

Rutgers Graduate School of Education. (2014). Penn Center for Minority Serving Institutions.

Rincon, B. E. (2018). Does Latinx representation matter for Latinx representation in STEM. *Journal of Hispanic Higher Education, 9*(4), 437–451. doi:10.1177/153 8192718820532

Rine, J. P. (2015). *Expanding access and opportunity: How small and mid-size independent colleges serve low-income and first-generation students.* Washington, DC: Council of Independent Colleges and Universities.

Robbins, C. K., LePeau, L. A. (2018). Seeking better ways: Early-career faculty researcher development. *Studies in Graduate and Postdoctoral Education, 9*(2), 113–126. doi:10.1108/SGPE-D17-00029

Rockquemore, K. A. (2013, July 22). A new model of mentoring. *Inside Higher Education.* Retrieved from https://www.insidehighered.com/advice/2013/07/22/es say-calling-senior-faculty-embracenewstyle-mentoring

RTI International. (2019). First-generation college students: Demographic characteristics and postsecondary enrollment. Washington, DC: NASPA. Retrieved from https://firstgen.naspa.org/files/dmfile/FactSheet-01.pdf

Russell, S. H., Hancock, M. P., & McCullogh, J. (2007). Benefits of undergraduate research experiences. *Science, 316,* 548–549.

Scandura, T. A., & Williams, E. A. (2004). Mentoring and transformational leadership: The role of supervisory career mentoring. *Journal of Vocational Behavior, 65,* 448–468. doi:10.1016/j.jvb.2003.10.003

Schultz, P. W., Hernandez, P. R., Woodcock, A., Estrada, M., Chance, R. C., Aguilar, M., & Serpe, R. T. (2011). Patching the pipeline: Reducing educational disparities in the sciences through minority training programs. *Educational evaluation and policy analysis, 33*(1), 95–114. doi:10.3102/0162373710392371

Scoggin, D. (2017). The lasting value of a classical liberal arts education. Thomas B. Fordham Institute. Retrieved from https://fordhaminstitute.org/national /commentary/lasting-value-classical-liberal-arts-education

Smith, D. L., Turner, C. S., Osei-Kofi, N., & Richards, S. (2004). Interrupting the usual: Successful strategies for hiring diverse faculty. *The Journal of Higher Education, 74*(2), 133–160. doi:10.1080/00221546.2004.11778900

Southern Regional Education Board. (2017). SREB fact book on higher education. Retrieved from https://www.sreb.org/sites/main/files/file-attachments/2019f actbook_web.pdf?1561062852

Stephens, N. M., Hamedani, M. H., & Destin, M. (2014). Closing the social-class achievement gap: A difference-education intervention improves first-generation students' academic performance and all students' college transition. *Psychological Science, 25,* 943–953. doi:10.1177/0956797613518349

Stephens, N. M., Townsend, S. S. M., Hamedani, M. G., Destin, M., & Manzo, V. (2015). The difference-education intervention equips first-generation college students to thrive in the face of stressful college situations. *Psychological Science, 26*(10), 1556–1566. doi:10.1177/0956797615593501

Strayhorn, T. L. (2011). Bridging the pipeline: Increasing underrepresented students' preparation for college through a summer bridge program. *American Behavioral Scientist, 55*(2), 142–159. doi:10.1177/0002764210381871

Thomas, K. M., Willis, L. A., & Davis, J. (2007). Mentoring minority graduate students: Issues and strategies for institutions, faculty, and students. *Equal Opportunities International, 26*(3), 178–192. doi:10.1108/02610150710735471

Toldson, I. A. (2019). Cultivating STEM talent at minority serving institutions: Challenges and opportunities to broaden participation in STEM at historically black colleges and universities. In L. L. Winfield, G. Thomas, L. M. Watkins, & Z. S. Wilson-Kennedy (Eds.). *Growing diverse STEM communities: Methodology, impact, and evidence.* Washington, DC: American Chemical Society.

Tull, A. (2019). Applying student development theories holistically: Exemplar programming in higher education. In K. Branch, J. S. Hart-Steffes, and C. M. Wilson (Eds.), *Journal of College Student Development, 60*(5), 637–639. doi:10.1353/csd.2019.0058

US Census Bureau. (n.d.). Quick facts: Table. Retrieved from https://www.census.gov/quickfacts/fact/table/US/PST045219

US Census Bureau. (2020). CPS historical time series tables. Table A-2. Retrieved from https://www.census.gov/data/tables/time-series/demo/educational-attainment/cps-historical-time-series.html

US Department of Homeland Security. (2012). What is community college? Retrieved from https://studyinthestates.dhs.gov/2012/03/what-is-community-college

Valentine, H. A., Lund, P. K., & Gammie, A. E. (2016). From the NIH: A systems approach to increasing diversity of the biomedical research workforce. *CBE Life Science Education, 15*(3), ii. doi:10.1187/cbe.16-03-0138

Valla, J. M., & Williams, W. M. (2012). Increasing achievement and higher-education representation of under-represented groups in science, technology, engineering, and mathematics fields: A review of current K–12 intervention programs. *Journal of Women Minor Science and Engineering, 18*(1), 21–53. doi:10.1615/JWomenMinorScienEng.2012002908

Vasquez, J. H., Wong, I. F., Barros, A. E. S., Carlton, J. B., and Barceló, S. M. (2019). Considering the ethnoracial and gender diversity of faculty in United States college and university intellectual communities. *Hispanic Journal of Law and Policy*, 1–31. Retrieved from https://www.dropbox.com/s/9ijhhx37niz8jf5/2019%20ISSUE%20Heilig%201-31.pdf?dl=0

Whittaker, J., & Montgomery, B. (2014). Cultivating institutional transformation and sustainable STEM diversity in higher education through integrative faculty development. *Innovative Higher Education, 39*(4), 263–275. doi:10.1007/s10755-013-9277-9

Williams, R. S., Ari, O., & Dortch, C. (2010). African American high school student's reading performance as a function of academic enrichment program exposure. *Black in America: A scholarly response to the CNN documentary-Policy brief series.* 101–114.

Williams, R. S., Ari, O., & Dortch, C. (2011). The relationships between human capital, implicit views of intelligence, and literacy performance: Implications for the Obama education era. *Urban Education, 46*(4), 563–587. doi:10.1177/0042085910377514

Williams, D. A., & Wade-Golden, K. C. (2013). *The chief diversity officer: Strategy, structure, and change management.* Sterling, VA.: Stylus Publishing.

Worthington, R. L. (2012). Advancing scholarship for the diversity imperative in higher education: An editorial. *Journal of Diversity in Higher Education, 5*(1), 1–7. doi:10.1037/a0027184

Yeager, D. S., Hanselman, P., Walton, G. M., Murray, J. S., Cresnoe, R., Muller, C., Tipton, E., Schneider, B., Hulleman, C. S., Hinojosa, C. P., Paunesku, D., Romero, C., Flint, K., Roberts, A., Trott, J., Iachan, R., Buontempo, J., Yang, S. M., Carvalho, P., Hahn, P. R., Gopalan, M., Mhatre, P., Ferguson, R., Duckworth, A. L., & Dweck, C. (2019). A national experiment reveals where a growth mindset improves achievement. *Nature, 573*, 364–369. doi:10.1038/s41586-019-1466-y

Yeager, D. S., & Walton, G. M. (2011). Social-psychological interventions in education: They're not magic. *Review of Educational Research, 81*(2), 267–301. doi:10.3102/0034654311405999

Yosso, T. J. (2005). Whose culture has capital? A critical race theory discussion of community cultural wealth. *Race Ethnicity and Education, 8*, 69–91. doi:10.1080/1361332052000341006

Young, M. D., & Brooks, J. S. (2008). Supporting graduate students of color in educational administration preparation programs: Faculty perspectives on best practices, possibilities, and problems. *Educational Administration Quarterly, 44*(3), 391–423. doi:10.1177/0013161X08315270

Young, J. L. & Hines, D.E. (2018). Killing my spirit, renewing my soul: Black female professors' critical reflections on spirit killings while teaching. *Women, Gender, and Families of Color, 6*(1),18-25. DOI: 10.5406/womgenfamcol.6.1.0018

Acknowledgments

Curtis D. Byrd: Thank you first and foremost to the creator who blessed me with the opportunity to develop this book to support marginalized and underrepresented groups, who desire to pursue higher education. My life partner, best friend, and wife Dr. Stephanie Y. Evans has been my guiding light through writing my first book and have appreciated her support every step of the way. I would also like to thank my coauthor (Dr. Rihana S. Mason), who believed in me and invited me to present at the American Studies Association conference, where we met our publisher. Further, I am guided daily by my ancestors who preceded me and laid the foundation of love and structure to my life that I live by today: Palmer Byrd Sr. and Venella Byrd. Also, those who reinforced my life with their unyielding support, my spirited mother Michelle Byrd Williams; my uncles, Marc Byrd, Aaron Byrd, Reginald Byrd, and Palmer Byrd Jr (their wives and children); my cousins, Carlin Yarbrough, Carla Armstrong, Linda Faye Johnson, Micheal Byrd, Oberia Byrd, Rhamonia Byrd, Chris Byrd, and the talented Tony Brown; and all of my other family members. I have to acknowledge my mentors throughout my career, including Dr. Mary Clark (Wayne State University), Dr. George Jackson (master's thesis chair, Iowa State University), Dr. Ansley Abraham (SREB Doctoral Scholars Program), Dr. Orlando Taylor (vice president of strategic initiatives and research, Fielding Graduate University), Dr. Karen Watkins (dissertation advisor, University of Georgia [UGA]), and UGA dissertation committee members Dr. Laura Bierma and Dr. Louis Castenell. The following have been institutional partners throughout my career: Dr. Freeman A. Hrabowski III (president, University of Maryland, Baltimore County), Dr. Gordhan Patel and Dr. F. Douglas Boudinot (UGA Graduate School Initiatives), Dr. Michelle Garfield-Cook (vice provost for diversity and inclusion, UGA), Dr. Archie Ervin (vice president, Institute Diversity, Equity and Inclusion, Georgia Tech), and the Atlanta metro area chief diversity officers group who have all been dynamic leaders in the diversity, equity, and inclusion space within higher education. Finally, my dearest friends and colleagues who have supported me throughout my life: Cherryl Arnold, Dr. Shakiyla Smith, Dr. Peniel Joseph, Dr. Marla Bennett, Kamau Harris, Chris Afful, Cindy and Paul Adler, Kent Johnson and Keith Johnson, Dr. Jay Houston, Dr. Jerrod Bryson, Willow Woods, and my Smith's Olde Bar Steelers Crew!

Rihana S. Mason: I am eternally grateful for the support that I received from my husband, Derrick Mason, and my sons, Jelani and Amir. They were extremely instrumental in allowing me to dedicate my time and resources toward this writing project. Thank you to Curtis Byrd for partnering with me to write this book and for agreeing to share your years of experience with academic pipeline programs with the world in this way. Since my steps have been divinely ordered and prepared, there are so many people who opened doors, shared wisdom, or led by their example. I am extremely thankful for the support from my parents, Drs. Donald and Shirlene Davis and Dr. Freddy J. Williams (in spirit). I would not have been able to passionately advocate for the awareness of pipeline programs for others if it had not been for several key mentors: Dr. Pamela Scott Johnson (undergraduate mentor) and Drs. Robin K. Morris and Matthew Traxler (graduate faculty mentors) as well as my academic pipeline program directors/mentors, Drs. Karen Brakke and Margaret Weber-Levine (National Institutes of Health Careers and Opportunities in Research Program (NIMH-COR), Drs. Gary Allen and James Coleman (University of South Carolina Summer Research Institute REU), Dr. Allen Braun (National Institutes of Deafness and Communication Disorders (NIDCD), Christine Obrien (Ford Foundation Fellowship Programs), and Drs. Tamara Bertrand Jones and Anna Green (Sisters of the Academy). All of my former mentees from the TEVA Lab, the Ronald E. McNair Postbaccalaureate Achievement and the National Institute of General Medical Sciences Research Training Initiative for Student Enhancement Programs were also inspirational in making sure that more students are aware of the opportunities included in this book. They are also now successful examples of diversifying the academy. Several colleagues offered advice or encouraging words that allowed me to persevere with writing this publication. Thank you to Drs. Lori Bass, Gary Bingham, Monica Cox, Melanie Domenech Rodriguez, Stephanie Evans, Jon Grahe, Valerie Hunt, Linda Jones, Lakeisha Johnson, Nicole Patton Terry, and Keivan Stassun for leading with such great examples of how to get publications finished and modeling the importance of sharing information with others through various forms of media. I would also not have been able to complete this writing project without the prayers of my friends Keisha Cook, Shawnette Miller, Monika Robinson, and Lisa Zanders.

Finally, both of us would like to acknowledge the contributors of the Academic Pipeline Program's book for their content in the chapters based on THRIVE Index (listed by name in appendix C (p. 275). Additionally, we would like to recognize the unwavering support of Dr. Lycurgus L. Muldrow, director, Historically Black Colleges and Universities STEM Undergraduate Success (STEM-US)

Research Center and the newly funded National Science Foundation Historically Black Colleges and Universities Undergraduate Program (HBCU-UP) center at Morehouse College. We collaborated with him to use our lessons learned from programs included in this book and the THRIVE Index to create a national HBCU STEM database as a part of the HBCU STEM-US center's work. Also, we would like to acknowledge the opportunity that Georgia State University and provost Wendy Hensel gave us to showcase the THRIVE Index, in order to create the institution's first database of over one hundred and fifty diversity, equity, and inclusion programs. We are also grateful for Provost Hensel's communications manager, Jeremy Craig, who designed the actual DEI website based on our vision and content. We would like to thank the contributing academic pipeline programs that are in this publication and the numerous programs that will be added to our national database of programs that support underrepresented groups around the country. We would like to thank all of the research assistants who assisted with appendix and with reviewing earlier drafts of the book. Finally, we would also like to thank Hal Miller and Drip Coffee (Atlanta, Georgia), where much of this document was written.